America Under the Hammer

EARLY AMERICAN STUDIES

Series editors: Kathleen M. Brown, Roquinaldo Ferreira,
Emma Hart, and Daniel K. Richter

Exploring neglected aspects of our colonial, revolutionary, and early national
history and culture, Early American Studies reinterprets familiar themes
and events in fresh ways. Interdisciplinary in character, and with a special
emphasis on the period from about 1600 to 1850, the series is published
in partnership with the McNeil Center for Early American Studies.

A complete list of books in the series is available from the publisher.

America Under the Hammer

*Auctions and the Emergence
of Market Values*

Ellen Hartigan-O'Connor

PENN

UNIVERSITY OF PENNSYLVANIA PRESS

PHILADELPHIA

Published by
University of Pennsylvania Press
Philadelphia, Pennsylvania 19104-4112
www.pennpress.org

Printed in the United States of America on acid-free paper
10 9 8 7 6 5 4 3 2 1

Hardcover ISBN: 978-1-5128-2651-7
eBook ISBN: 978-1-5128-2652-4

A Cataloging-in-Publication record is
available from the Library of Congress.

CONTENTS

Introduction

In 1752 the wealthy South Carolinian Sarah Baker's husband, Richard, died, reportedly in a duel. By his will, she received money, a room in their house, and an enslaved woman named Phebe. To claim more of the material life they had shared (but her husband had legally owned), she had his estate inventoried by a group of men who put an estimated price on each item. Then came the auction. Joining the assembled participants, Sarah, too, bid on furniture, silverware, fabric, corks, chamber pots, and two more people, the "Negro Girls" Kate and Liddy.[1] This was her moment to reclaim as "hers" property that she had experienced ownership of until Richard died. As the day wore on, some items sold for more than the inventory takers had estimated, some for less. The profits from the sale went to pay the dead man's debts; the widow bought goods and enslaved women to support the next chapter of her life.

The Baker auction broke down a household by pricing each element of it, testing the prices, redistributing individual parts, collecting money in exchange, and paying off the creditors of the deceased patriarch. The public sale operated according to laws that organized social relations around property definitions. Kate and Liddy were people with kin networks and friends, personal histories and lives. Yet, because laws defined them as property that could be liquidated to pay the debts of the man who enslaved them, assessors could mark their starting price and sell them to Sarah at auction. Sarah Baker herself was a daughter, a neighbor, and a slaveholder with her own set of judgments and choices, but under another set of laws and legal practice, she was a wife. Her legal status meant that Richard, not she, owned the chair she sat in and the chamber pot she pulled from under the bed on a cold night.[2]

When the auctioneer presented each piece of the estate, he untethered it from the meanings it had accrued through human labor and human emotion to ask the assembled crowd for a number. Sarah Baker surely prized the silverware, and Phebe or Kate or Liddy had likely polished it. But it was the deceased Richard Baker who owned it, and his creditors had a claim to however much money someone would give for it. The crowd, asked for a number to affix to a spoon or a daughter, called out their own assessment of the item's value.

The history of North American auctions is the history of value in the development of capitalism. An auction brings people together to evaluate items, agree on a price, and exchange them for the equivalent value in some other form: typically cash but sometimes short-term credit. Through these exchanges, an auction creates a market. George Washington, speculating in 1785 on the worth of goods arriving from China soon to be put up for sale, called auctions "experiments" in valuing. He was referring, specifically, to the open-ended dynamics of bidding, where participants measured their own desire for an item against the signals they received from competitors' bids.[3] As with any experiment, the equipment, conditions, forms of measurement, and investigator all influence the outcome. With auctions, the participants, the goods, and the values carried by bidders all contribute to the form and function of these markets in microcosm.

An auction answers a set of questions—who gets what, and for how much?— that is frequently attributed to "markets" or "the economy" in general.[4] The specific details of an auction's experiment in valuing, however, resist such abstraction. Examining the dynamics of auctions allows us to slow down the transaction and open up a historical perspective on each constituent part of the market exchange.

In terms of market distribution (who gets what?), a history centered on auctions links the point of purchase to a longer life cycle of goods. Social experiences were bound up in every auction sale because auctions traded in goods with a history: used or damaged goods, land that had been seized, people with pasts. Auctioneers oversaw the kinds of recirculation and salvaging of value that constituted everyday economic life for the majority of people in early America. Yet, while these goods were isolated and priced at a moment of sale, they could not be easily disentangled from the social conditions that produced them. After all, value is created in human interaction; it is not intrinsic to an object.[5] The fundamentally social nature of value was evident in every early American transaction, where asymmetrical information about goods was common. The nascent money supply itself, made up of government- and eventually company-issued notes and IOUs, depended on social rituals in which people agreed to pretend that a piece of paper had a value because it was practical in the moment of exchange.[6]

As far as prices (the *for how much?* of market exchange), a history of auctions tracks a significant change from the early eighteenth century to the middle of the nineteenth century. Over the course of nearly a century and a half, individuals at all levels of American society created the belief that an object's price was the principal measure of its value. There had long been competing ideas about the nature of value: Was it an intrinsic quality established by God? a calculable measure of the labor needed to create something? a marker of familial investment in social or generational relationships? Increasingly, the idea took hold that value corresponded to an object's circulation through exchange, as communities began to embrace the concept of negotiation as a process linked to supply and demand. Value as something that could fluctuate in relationship to external forces, from availability to the amount of interest expressed by others, was new and contested.[7]

Moreover, through daily experiences with negotiation and purchasing, people came to believe that utility and invested labor as well as aesthetics, sentiment, and other components of value, could all resolve into a meaningful number that they could fruitfully compare to other numbers. And it was through this constant assessment and comparison that they increasingly came to make sense of their lives in economic terms. It was a fraught, halting process whose history is little understood due to its ultimate success. We talk easily about price and value today. We try to get our "money's worth" out of an object or experience we have paid for. When a purchase disappoints, most of us presume something went wrong in the details of the transaction, not in the underlying idea of prices themselves or in our ethical or moral beliefs.

Prices have a taken-for-granted quality in our stories about the American past, too, because the sources we use to tell that history present prices as facts. Merchants' account books list numbers next to descriptions and quantities in an orderly fashion, suggesting a straightforward connection between the two. Laws specify percentages of tax levies to be applied to the assessed value of land, implying a rational calculation to suit state needs. Even the personal letters of a slaveholder describe the sale of a teenager with a number and then go on to evaluate whether that number is low or high against expectation. Historians gather and document these numbers, noting averages and making comparisons across region and time. Yet these same numbers leave most historical questions unanswered: Why did a yard of crepe fabric correspond to one number in one ledger and another in a different ledger? How did assessors turn a prediction about a future land sale into a number for the tax collectors? What made a slaveholder like Sarah Barker think a number could capture the worth of an adolescent human she had long known? The so-called laws of supply and demand cannot account for the functioning of these sums.

A history of early American auctions reveals how value judgments became facts about value. Part of this process was rooted in the structure of public sales. Auctions were economic institutions, established by law, presided over by appointed auctioneers, and accessed by a wide range of participants. Sales were highly structured in format and yoked to a developing body of property law that governed familial and commercial relationships, such as those between Sarah and Richard Barker or between Richard Barker and his creditors. The assessors who sorted through the Barker estate were legally charged with estimating a price for each piece of property as best as they could, in anticipation of the sale to come. Yet, while auctions were highly structured by design, the social dynamics at their center made them unpredictable in outcome. Bidders made their own assessments as they reflected on their specific ideas and needs and reacted to the attitudes and behavior of others at the sale. The result of the sale had real meaning. It determined how much of the creditors' money would be repaid, if any. It set the boundaries of Sarah Barker's own estate and affirmed Kate and Liddy as valuable commodities. The dynamic of price exploration (bidding) followed by validation (payment) in the expanded credit system shored up the sense that the result of a sale was a solid economic fact.

Auctions were influential in North America because they were a versatile mode of selling that could be deployed in multiple contexts to handle every type of property, from real estate to used stockings to human beings to one-of-a-kind artwork. Sales took place on courthouse steps but also on wharves, in coffeehouses and taverns, in merchant warehouses, in homes, on city streets, and in dedicated stores. Court-ordered auctions were often presided over by sheriffs, retail auctions by those who established themselves as businessmen, charity auctions by reformers and volunteers. In all, auction transactions accounted for a substantial proportion of consumers' purchases and were a major part of the wholesale and retail landscape of eighteenth- and nineteenth-century North America. They shaped commercial experience and the economic imagination of residents at least as much as the shops and warehouses that dominate histories of buying and selling.

Explicitly and powerfully, auctions were also political tools. By auctioning off Indigenous lands, governments pushed Native people from their homelands and destroyed their means of subsistence. When slaveholders placed enslaved men, women, and children up for public sale, they subordinated Black personhood and kinship to white property rights. And when patriot neighbors gathered to bid on loyalist property, they punished political enemies and bound one another together as a new polity. Operating at the intersection of law, commerce, and politics, auctions enforced a powerful vision of public order and enlisted participants to endorse it through their bids.

At the same time, the open-ended elements of auctioning offered participants an opportunity to seize the levers of the market to make their own order. In the summer of 1815, for example, the white trustees of St. George's Methodist Church in Philadelphia thought they could use a forced sale to dominate the African American Bethel congregation, which to their minds had become too assertive. They seized the congregants' brick meeting house at Sixth and Lombard Streets and put it up for auction under a sheriff's sale—a public enactment of the court-supported power to price and redistribute property. But sheriff's auctions were public sales, which meant that the redistribution—and the price— were unpredictable. The Bethel congregation's founder and pastor Richard Allen attended the auction and outbid rivals by willingly paying the extremely high sum of $10,125 for the building, lot, and adjoining land.[8] With that purchase, he obtained security for the congregation, which one year later created the first independent African American African Methodist Episcopal denomination.

These dynamic and cross-cutting features make auctions the ideal focus for an integrated history of market values in the development of American capitalism. This book explores a web of relationships among auctions, auctioneers, bidders, and bystanders in order to connect the lived experiences of people in marketplaces to developing ideas about what markets should do. Following the shifting history of auctions reveals that social relations and moral judgments mattered just as much as supply and demand for the functioning of markets. And a far wider cast of historical characters make their way onto the stage in constructing those markets.

Some participants came to auctions eagerly, as they were a source of affordable goods and spectacle. Shopkeepers and country peddlers, for example, attended auctions to obtain smaller parcels of bulk imported goods at prices they could afford. These could then be passed on to their own customers as "cheap goods and auction bargains."[9] "Sale day" auctions conducted by sheriffs or the auctioneers they hired became predictable community events over the course of a century and a half. Auctioneers typically stood on a step or other elevated position to see and be seen by the bidding crowd, telling stories about their goods that entertained and informed. The theatrical and performative nature of many auctions offered a heightened emotional experience connected to economic exchange and the social possibilities opened up by expanding consumption.[10]

Many other participants, like Kate and Liddy, came to auctions unwillingly. Public sales channeled the redistribution of commodities at punctuation points in individual human lives, and most of those points were unhappy ones. They took place when a grandfather died, when an enslaved family was wrenched apart, when a business failed. They are a reminder that the circulation of material life signified grief and failure as much as optimistic acquisition. An auction could also be a punctuation mark in the history of a community, as in the notorious 1859 Butler auction of 436 enslaved people. These extended families—all dispersed by an auction held at a Georgia racetrack to pay for their enslaver's debts—later commemorated the two days of public bidding as "the weeping time."[11] Auctions marked and divided the history of larger political entities as well, as was the case with the auctions of seized property during the American Revolution, which both meted out and rewarded suffering through a long military struggle. Such sales offer an important way to understand the making and remaking of communities through economic life as participatory and contingent rather than planned from the top down.

*   *   *

Across regions and time, auctions are vivid examples of the ways that Americans used economic institutions in their social and cultural lives. The term "auction," from the Latin word for "increase," references a specific kind of public sale, sometimes called an "ascending-bid auction," in which each successive bidder offers a number higher than the prior bid. The sale closes, and the auctioneer's hammer comes down, when there is no bid beyond the highest price. This type of sale was the most common auction format in North America, with dynamics that mirror market culture more broadly: the price of any item is the result of negotiation, the interactions are competitive, and the line between who acts and who or what is acted on develops the illusion of being natural.

North American and West Indian colonies had another name for auctions: "vendues," from the Dutch *vendu*, which was itself a term derived from the French verb *vendre*, meaning "to sell."[12] If the word "auction" evokes increase, "vendue" underscores the fundamentally colonial origins of American auctions and market culture. Vendues were a regular practice of the government monopolies that established colonial ventures in the seventeenth century. The Dutch West India Company, a chartered monopoly, established fur trading posts and settlements along the Hudson River (in present-day New York). These settlements made up New Netherland until the English took control in 1664, spreading the vendue as a term and a practice in British colonies. Auctions of different types had existed for thousands of years, and their utility in the disposal of war booty and old ships became important features of the colonial economy, which fostered the ubiquity of auctions in North America. Further, British colonial conquest and expansion claimed Indigenous land and parceled it out in schemes that simultaneously compensated the people and polities that had claimed it, with auctions forging the link between property deed and debtor.[13]

Prior to the mid-eighteenth century, marketplaces in British America were mobile and dispersed, with no dedicated market towns or fair days and minimal official supervision of commerce. Local exchange took place at trading posts, on riverbanks, and in fields in an opportunistic fashion. Transatlantic trade was equally unpredictable, dependent on imports that could arrive at unexpected times and in varying qualities and quantities.[14] Because auctions could be quickly organized wherever someone wanted to make a sale, they came to handle a wide variety of colonial transactions that would have been parceled out to a pawnshop, a regulated fair, or a market stall in Europe.[15]

The colonial roots of auctions in North America are deep, and the stakes of their history are high for understanding the subsequent development of American capitalism. Enduring ideas about legal property, economic justice, and national morality were forged at auctions. Debates about auctions defined the very edges of economy and political belonging in the United States. Economic norms enacted at auctions dictated ultimately whom the economy worked for.

Research framed as the origins of American capitalism has often taken for granted the very end points it is trying to analyze. Scholarship focused on the nineteenth-century United States has presented value as an abstract concept that linked new institutions and instruments in a transformative financial logic. The proliferation of paper notes spread the idea that physical money had no intrinsic worth.[16] A growing financial services sector in insurance put a price on risk, which had previously been the province of God alone. The growth of securities priced products that existed only in a hypothetical future.[17] Bookkeeping innovations and standardized metrics also "put numbers to work," converting enslaved human labor into something abstract—but countable—called productivity.[18] Research into financial abstraction has placed particular focus on how enslaved people built a bedrock of capital accumulation in the United States even as they worked alongside, and provided raw materials for, a growing body of paid wage laborers.[19] Yet the now-familiar principles that price and value are connected, and that competition best reveals the number representing true value, were still coalescing in the eighteenth century. By understanding commodification as the enshrinement of abstract value, this influential scholarship has overlooked competing meanings of value that allowed some things to be fungible and others not. At auction, a human, a garden, a keepsake, a tool, or a piece of fabric transformed from having multiple meanings and registers of value to becoming, simply, legal property. To suggest that the fabric by its nature is inherently property takes for granted this important transformation.

Moreover, scholarly focus on institutions such as banks and insurers has reinforced the idea that those institutions and the men who controlled them constituted the economy, while poor men and women making shift in the shadows labored as the economy's "underside."[20] This approach has obscured the role of race and gender in establishing the rules of capitalism and has reinforced the marginalization of people who performed most labor and exchange. Gender and race were relations that organized the economy; at the same time, institutions—including auctions as well as banks—ratified which relationships counted economically.

Auctions integrated market, community, and household in explicit ways that put gender, race, and social bonds at the center of ideas about economic justice and worth. The jarring fact that human beings could come under the same hammer as material goods indicates the power of an auction to normalize new economic practices in North America. By the middle of the nineteenth century, slavery fueled the growth of integrated economies: the South, where human captives toiled to produce exports; the North, where industrialization turned commodities into finished goods; the West, where the state took Native land to facilitate commodity agriculture; and across the nation, as capital in human property underlay financial innovations in insurance and debt financing. The sale of human property at auction, a practice that linked the colonial days of the transatlantic trade to the national expansion across the southwest of the continent, had a profound effect on shaping the very terms of economy under capitalism. As the historian Stephanie Smallwood tells us, the reduction of human beings to numbers, whether those numbers were on a ship census or a price list, was an act of creating fictions—"false representations meant to make a stark political contest over the commodification of human life appear as a natural and forgone conclusion."[21]

Indeed, scholars of slavery have analyzed the way that the price of a human being was a mixture of projection, fantasy, and desperation on the part of buyers and sellers, adding up to a value that was at odds with the value enslaved people themselves gave their own lives and relationships.[22] Building on these insights, this book tracks the development of value regimes often treated as foregone conclusions in market interactions. Popular understanding of the American economy took shape in the routine—in the daily practice of witnessing and participating in auctions. Ideas about race and gender that were embedded in the sale of furniture, riverbanks, and mothers became the logic of American capitalism as they were enacted and reenacted through everyday market negotiations.

Both the structure of auction law and the dynamism of auction participation merged ethical values with commercial ones. Research on what has been called the "moral economy" of customary practice initially proposed that there was a conflict between markets organized around custom and fairness, on the one hand, and markets organized around supply and demand, on the other.[23] Over time, some scholars argued, the latter replaced the former. Recent research, however, highlights the fact that changing market meanings and practices were neither as sharp nor complete as this earlier formulation suggested. Regulated marketplaces designed to sustain a variously defined "common good" actually increased over the eighteenth century, demonstrating the enduring role of the state in economic practice. With oversight often applied in the form of licensing laws, these regulated marketplaces persisted well into the nineteenth century even as the idea of rational choice, prevalent in political economy models, gained adherents.[24]

At the same time, individuals were navigating material realities with their own sets of investments and priorities, which profoundly shaped commercial culture. The history of fraud and failure has demonstrated that variable pricing and profit maximization, both hallmarks of modern markets governed by supply and demand, emerged slowly and fitfully as cultural values.[25] From enslaved fathers to grieving widows, Americans had diverse understandings about what fair value in exchange relationships could be. Their conduct at auctions offers evidence of economic thinking that is otherwise hard to grasp.

Expanding print culture was an important site for the mediation of material and nonmaterial concepts of value. By the nineteenth century, authors had started to use the auction as a metaphor for commercial ethics, turning fraught conflicts over racial and class power into a unified language of value and values. In 1802, for example, literate Philadelphia parents looking for an appealing way to teach moral character to their middle-class children could purchase a new booklet, *The Lilliputian Auction*, and let the fictional child auctioneer Charley Chatter speak to their offspring.[26] *The Lilliputian Auction* was a "little Book of pretty Things." Only thirty-one pages, it covered the evils of violence, vanity, and conceitedness, along with the benefits of self-criticism, regular habits, and personal goodness as a way to identify the bounds of appropriate class behavior. As young Charley Chatter was dispersing the estate of his uncle Timothy Curious, Esq. to "little Masters and Misses," he brought together two long-standing cultural touchstones: the estate auction and the moral fable. In this way, a story about a familiar economic institution became the means to pass down a legacy of community values in a kind of commercialized catechism.

Meanwhile, auction notices and commentary joined more technical forms of print—paper money and price lists—in establishing norms of commodification. Together, they transformed the speculative fiction of objective value into an emerging genre of "economic facts."[27] Public sales generated public benefits when they published lists of quantities for sale, and those who subsequently attended auctions could keep account of goods sold and prices paid that, when taken together and compiled, became a set of data. These new facts encompassed more than any one individual's personal networks, and so came to represent purportedly universal value.

By focusing on a mode of exchange—the auction—this book illuminates the dynamic relationship between the material and symbolic dimensions of the early American economy. Scholars have used diverse methods to understand the culture of economic life. One rich set of studies chooses individual commodities—rice, sugar, pearls, mahogany, codfish—to elucidate the connections between producers and consumers.[28] This approach is particularly useful for understanding the geography of economies and how they changed over time. Another set of studies explores the human role in directing commerce by looking at groups of businessmen joined by a shared city, shared business networks, or family connections.[29] These histories highlight personal relationships and their contingent participation in failure and success. Marketplaces, too, have received attention, both as physical locations for exchange and the metaphorical joining of buyers and sellers.[30]

Auctions, however, show something more specific. Through their deliberate stagecraft, auctions relied on and also generated stories about exchange. These stories, which circulated widely in American cultures, showcase the symbolic resonance of auctions as sites of acquisition (for better or for worse) while also underscoring their material role in assessing and assigning value to the people and objects entering the marketplace as tradable commodities. In this book, I argue that auctions connected financial, social, and symbolic uses of exchange so that communities could sort out their ideas about value. In the history of auctions, we see that commercial practices developed within colonial power structures bore consequences a century later that established a taken-for-granted set of relations and social positions recognizable as nineteenth-century American capitalism.

*   *   *

America Under the Hammer uses auctions to track the development of market cultures in British North America and the United States from the early eighteenth century into the first half of the nineteenth century. The ubiquitous presence of auctions was a constant across the period, and, as each chapter demonstrates, critical debates concerning economic value coalesced around types of auctions and vendues at different moments in time.

As early as the 1670s, auctions offered a template for expanding colonial authority over the bodies of people living around the Atlantic. Chapter 1 illuminates how the British Empire used auctions to address the logistical dilemmas of colonialism in North America and, in so doing, fostered a legal and political economic culture around property. Royal governments created monopolies to spur the expansion of trade using public sales to justify the privilege granted and to ensure that transactions happened out in the open rather than in secret. Settlers in North America established legal forms of property that staked their claim over land and its productive outputs. Enslaved people were part of that property regime, and auctions, alongside other forms of sale, established conditions to normalize the commodification of people. Colonists lived in a cash-poor society dominated by credit relations, and the court-ordered auctions that arose from credit disputes functioned to convert one form of wealth into another. Colonial and metropolitan lawmakers crafted a body of property laws that deployed auctions to maintain imperial control over the definition and destiny of assets, making auctions not only the result of colonial conditions but also a tool of colonialism.[31]

But property law never worked in isolation. Thus, as the purview of auctions expanded, so did their role in establishing what exchangeable property was. Colonial agents used performances (walking the boundary lines) and tools (surveying equipment and maps) to convert hills and woods into real property. Auctions furthered the social process of property making—and the Indigenous dispossession it entailed—by publicly assigning a price to that property and drawing it into imperial politics.[32] Human beings, too, were enfolded in this process. The transatlantic slave trade turned people into racialized subjects and subsequently into commodities, a transformation publicly reinscribed at auction.[33] The effect of this repeated enactment of valuing linked to human difference was to turn social relations into economic calculations that bolstered power structures.

Auctions played a central role in the circulation of consumer goods by the middle of the eighteenth century. Chapter 2 reveals the ways people in British North America developed ideas about value through repeated use of auctions, which had regulated forms but not prices. At these events, they debated what goods—particularly the expanding world of imported textiles, ceramics, and housewares—were worth as well as how to distribute them in a socially and morally acceptable fashion. In this context, prices were established by developing and sharing knowledge, particularly about the past use and future potential of goods for sale. It was a social activity that drew on and reinforced relational ideas about gender and community obligations. It was also a process that engaged a tension within auctioning between participants' desire for a free, open sale in which bidders could collectively establish an item's price, and the efforts of auctioneers to limit and control bidding behavior to keep it in bounds of formalized consumer participation and consistent with community ideas about the moral functioning of exchange.

People who attended a local auction experienced pricing as a dynamic process that was only partially about supply and demand motivated by choice. When goods entered auctions, they often did so under pressure, such as during bankruptcy proceedings or the liquidation of a deceased person's estate. As such, auctions connected the functions of pricing and distribution to the context of local economies in which goods recirculated. Estate auctions, for example, publicly tested the link between value and price as goods cycled through the collective local process of valuing and revaluing neighbors' belongings. In this extended process, the value of goods and their rightful ownership were matters of contention and dispute. But as people collectively turned speculative value into economic "facts" in the form of concrete prices for specific items, they established the agreed-upon notions of market operations in their communities.

Chapter 3 reveals how the auctioning of loyalist property during the Revolutionary War (1775–1783) weaponized local group participation in pricing and distribution both to punish political enemies and also to bind together patriots through a shared sense of suffering that could be priced and literally accounted for. During the American Revolution, part of breaking away from the British Empire involved the emerging state governments seizing people, objects, and land claimed by loyalist opponents in order to price and redistribute them as property for patriots. Political commitments shaped value, which was then reflected in prices, a process that the patriot government hoped would also remedy the wartime fluctuations in currency and commodity pricing.

Reverend Stewart, writing after the American Revolution to the Loyalist Claims Commission in Britain in 1783, commented that the reported prices for loyalist property sold at auction during the war were hopelessly compromised.

"As it has generally been sold for four times the real value," he wrote, "we may conjecture that the purchasers have still an Idea of Paper Money . . . or they may have strange fanciful conceits of the extraordinary worth of everything among them since their Independence."[34] Another 1783 report to the same committee agreed that the wartime auction prices did not reflect the true value of the property but for the opposite reason: "Many of the Estates of the Loyalists were sold for less than one quarter of their real value and purchased for them by their friends and relations who remained in that country."[35] These postwar complaints expressed persistent belief in a "real value" that could be violated, rather than affirmed, by open bidding and community knowledge. Understanding auctions as sites of politically motivated distribution reveals how uneasy many were with the collective wisdom of market participants, particularly when they were political opponents. From their recent experiences, none of the correspondents trusted in a self-adjusting market.

The politics of distribution constantly challenged ideas about how, and whether, auctioneers and market exchanges more broadly should be managed. From the first official appointments of colonial vendue masters to oversee auctions through frequent revisions of auction laws, governments struggled to fit the exchanges these men presided over within a political context that controlled who received access to goods and under what terms. Chapter 4 illustrates how auctioneers' roles as commercial intermediaries who acted on behalf of someone else became increasingly suspect in the early republic. All auctioneers worked with and through an audience, representing community judgment, which added an active force beyond the buyer and seller in channeling the flow of goods and determining what was fair or at least acceptable. But the political auction wars of the early republic hardened long-standing suspicions that auctions were places of shady dealing and bad behavior, and these suspicions led to the public condemnation of auctioneers.

In locations across the United States, auctioneers in the early republic publicly enacted the new nation's economic and moral crises. Some auctioneers were agents of the state, which seized goods with the purpose of turning them into money to redeem financial and political debts. Other auctioneers were agents of private interest, using their persuasive skills and public authority to convince buyers of the worth and utility of the items they sold in order to help those who hired them turn property into cash. Meanwhile, auctioneers helped bind American markets to European creditors and producers, and at the same time they bolstered the United States as a nation committed to Indigenous dispossession and chattel slavery. In their behavior and their status as white men, they reinforced methods of assessment regarding the truth claims of exchanges. When their motives became suspect, consumers lost faith in their—or any commercial agent's—subjective authentication of value.

Chapter 5 demonstrates the ways that gender defined the economy by shaping what could and could not be priced. It uses the specific case of the Ladies' Auction Rooms to show how the so-called auction debate of the early nineteenth century was as much about naturalizing economic participation along racial and gendered lines as it was about democratic participation in the market. Arguing that female bids, bodies, and labor all became sites for reckoning value at a time when most measures seemed unstable and speculative, this chapter suggests that women at auctions—as commodities, as bidders, or as beneficiaries—became a focal point for gendering economic value itself.

A unified language of value and values, which became a feature of market abstraction, also challenged human and social hierarchies, especially in regard to the institutions of marriage and slavery. Auction stories proved useful, therefore, for shoring up the definitions of relationships rooted in gender and racial difference. Newspaper advertisements announcing the sale of "a Parcel of New Negroes, imported directly from the Coast of Africa" invited potential bidders to envision themselves as masters over a large, subordinate workforce. Printed tales of courtship as a bidding war deflected uneasiness about the intersection of economy and affection in the power struggles of daily life. Through the deployment of language that reified social relationships and hierarchies, auctions and the ubiquitous stories about them pushed Americans to associate a functional commercial system with exclusion and subordination.

Chapter 6 analyzes the symbolic uses of slave auctions in the abolitionist movements of the 1830s and 1840s to show how race and gender shaped an understanding of the economy as a realm operated by and for powerful white men. It also explores the way this totalizing view of human commodification was contested in the work of enslaved and free Black people who debated whether the market's mechanisms could be used for individual freedoms, even as it reinforced subordination. As abolitionists pointed out, auctions depended on racial violence to produce value. Auctioneers chained Black people up, physically pulled families apart, and were willing to make claims on their bodies all to push up the bidding price.[36] The public nature of auctions made the violence of the market visible and repeatedly enacted. Therefore, stories and images concerning the public sale of human beings were useful tools for reformers seeking a succinct encapsulation of the evils of treating humans as property. At the same time, by focusing on the raised hammer and the auction block, abolitionists and the generations that have followed have excluded vast swaths of the American public from responsibility for the country's economic direction. This chapter demonstrates that a critical understanding of how auctions functioned socially and financially—beyond the hammer and the table—reinstates the American public writ large into this foundational story of American capitalism.

By the middle of the nineteenth century, printed depictions of slave auctions had become a staple of antislavery publications, as abolitionists insisted that lines be drawn between what could and could not be priced. Mother and child on an auction block was a compelling image of the tragic result of negotiating human life through economic ideas and practices—and it was an image that abolitionists regularly used to challenge the inevitability of doing so. Earlier convictions that commerce encouraged enlightened behavior could not be sustained. One British critic sniffed that "the debauchery of the human heart is essentially the business of auctioneering." Auctions, he declared, promoted competition, hoarding, and monopoly at the expense of social connection and reasoned cooperation.[37] In auctions of enslaved people, critics thought less about whether open competitive bidding was fair and more about whether it was just.

The period crossing the eighteenth and nineteenth centuries is often presented as an era of economic rationalization, with new philosophies about the meaning of money and new methods of quantitative information gathering and risk assessment. Yet the very definition of what "the economy" was rested on social and cultural processes of exclusion that marked off parts of human experience into the realm of the noneconomic. Markets and exchanges served multiple purposes in human life.[38] When widows dissolved their husbands' estates and yet bid on their furniture and housewares, they were assembling new material lives and also integrating their past selves into present reality. When colonial governments partitioned Indigenous property to expose at public sale in a legal sham they were asserting imperial power over territory and people and also binding settlers to their property regimes. When enslavers put people under the hammer to monetize their personhood for profit, they were also violently reinscribing racial hierarchy. Understanding how people used auctions heightens our awareness of the economy as a field of social power in all its senses rather than a natural process of supply and demand or an abstraction.

Auctions exerted a major force on the character of the American economy. They were the tool by which American property law converted trees and earth into real estate and mothers with children into chattel with a price. Bidders determined the value of goods, land, and people, which they translated into a number—a price. The same piece of property could be revalued at auction many times during its existence, depending on the bidding audience's estimation. Taken together, auctions reveal what became one of the uncomfortable central truths of capitalism in the nineteenth century: material life had no fixed value. All Americans would have to reckon with the consequences.

CHAPTER I

Visible and Invisible Property

In 1727 the Virginia Assembly considered a petition from a group of white settlers in Spotsylvania County. These people and their families had "seated themselves" along the Rappahannock River in order to grow tobacco, which they
brought to the riverbank to transport "to other Parts of the Country," yet there
was no convenient place for traders to exchange goods for tobacco. There were
no buildings to store tobacco leaves or merchandise; there were no taverns to
host traders; there were no accommodations for horse- or oxen-drawn carriages.
The residents wanted a town, "whereby the Peopling that remote Part of the
Country will be encouraged, and Trade and Navigation may be increased."[1] The
petitioners expressed central dilemmas of British colonialism in North America. They wanted ownership of land that was contested by colonial governors,
the Haudenosaunee Confederacy, and numerous Indigenous groups living in
areas claimed by Virginia and Carolina.[2] They sought participation in a far-flung
imperial economy bound together by private ventures and distant governance, in
which information was hard to obtain and track. The petitioners were also in the
middle of a violent effort to turn African people into commodified labor with
the backing of laws that denied African kinship to favor white property rights.

　　Auctions were a solution to the Virginia colonizers' predicament. The
assembly chartered the town of Fredericksburg out of fifty acres of land border-
ing the river that belonged by royal colonial patent to John Royston and Robert
Buckner. The charter instructed a named group of directors and trustees to have
the land surveyed and laid out with roads, a church and churchyard, a marketplace, a public quay, and wharves for public use. Lawmakers directed the trustees
to sell the rest of the half-acre lots "at Public Sale or Auction, from Time to
Time, to the highest Bidder, so as no person shall have more than Two Lots."
Once the winning bidders paid, they owned the land outright, for themselves

and their heirs, free of all claims. The trustees paid Royston and Buckner, the former owners claiming the land, a flat per-acre fee out of the sale profits; the rest of the auction proceeds were for "Public Use, for the common Benefit of the Inhabitants of the said Town."[3] If any residents failed to follow the laws of developing those lots, trustees could seize and reauction them. Bid by bid, by settling on a price, the assembled people turned a riverbank into real estate and real estate into a settlers' trading town, all in the context of a political and legal system that used auctions to invest local power in property.

Auctions tied together multiple strands of colonialism by using economic negotiation and the legal system to establish a new property regime. Through regular public reenactment, they set the efforts of imperial agents and colonial lawmakers within the operations of daily exchange, weaving together a web of other efforts. Warfare and treaties pried land from Indigenous people. Mercantilist policies supported tight connections between colonial fields and metropolitan credit. Laws about marriage, inheritance, and enslavement bolstered hierarchies of gender and race that determined who would cultivate the land, who would "people" the colony, and who would accrue the value of that work.[4] Auctions, by determining who got the first chance at land and goods, who had to accept leftovers, and who was able to leverage leftovers into speculative profits, cemented economic and social security for some and profound vulnerability for others.

Auctions were often called "public sales," meaning both that they took place before the eyes of the community and also that sales ostensibly served that community. Colonial institutions from government monopolies to county courts used auctions to price and distribute goods, and by conducting business in the open and on behalf of the public, claimed the legitimacy of their power. Jury trials, elections, and public whippings were also sites for communities to consent to or reject government authority, and each incorporated different understandings of who "the public" was, whether it be adult men, voters, or free residents more generally. At auctions, a wide swath of people made up the public of participation, even as that same public used the sale to police the borders of belonging in the community.[5]

Broad participation in auctions, in turn, gave the assembled public the ability to shape economic culture. Bidding at an auction validated that the items put up for sale were in fact exchangeable, which opened the door to transformations in the way colonial settlers defined property. Bidders at the Fredericksburg sale, for example, were treating land as a liquid asset rather than inalienable inheritance or sacred homeland.[6] Their involvement in the sale marked a movement away from existing British property regimes, in which real estate was routinely sheltered from seizure and sale, to a North American property system that redefined vast acreage of Indigenous territory as private property owned by settlers and defended by the colonial state. On other days, at other public sales, bidders treated captive Africans as commodities to be exchanged. The routine, public enactment of putting a price on a child, sister, father, or friend reinforced the idea that some people could be excluded as subjects of the colonial economy and were instead objects to be exchanged in that economy. In this way, auctions exemplified the fact that property is a social phenomenon, established and maintained by people with varying backgrounds and relative power.[7]

The deployment of public sales in the British colonies created an "auction effect" that embedded ideas about race and gender in the definition and dispersal of property. Decade after decade, African and African-descended people were evaluated, priced, and sold along with Indigenous land and manufactured goods. As scholars such as Jennifer Morgan tell us, early modern ideas about value developed in tandem with concepts of difference in the rise of market economies.[8] Auctions rehearsed this connection, year after year, by exposing unique individuals and charging the crowd to compare and calculate. Social relations were thereby remade into economic rationality. Property in people made sense to Europeans because commodification was defined around human difference.

Within colonial economic culture, some forms of property were publicly exposed and other forms sheltered and protected, but "public" and "private" were not two dichotomous worlds. The career of eighteenth-century auctioning in fact reveals the lived connection between public and private, in contrast to the structural division of the two that has attracted scholarly attention.[9] Property—in the form of land, consumer goods, or enslaved human beings—moved between exposed public and concealed private contexts, as participants used property to shore up power by controlling access to individual transactions. Through public and private sales, intimate property relations were rehearsed and integrated into the developing market society.

A survey drawn up a decade after the founding of Fredericksburg reflects only a hint of the free petitioners' development dreams (see Figure 1). It is dominated by water and mountain ranges, with scattered plantation buildings sketched in along the banks of the Potomac and Rappahannock Rivers.[10] Infrastructure is scarce, settler populations dispersed. The map is a reminder that the legal structures of new social relations did not immediately result in a lived reality. Rather, it took daily practice, including regular public sales, to embed ideas about commodification and colonial power in Virginians' lives.[11]

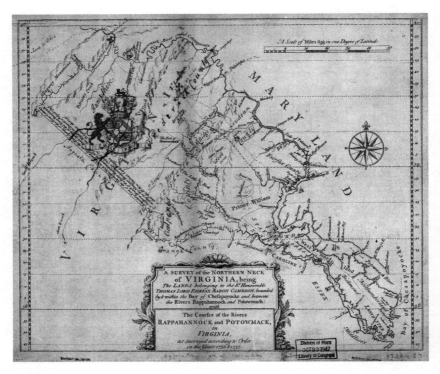

Figure 1. Surveys worked in tandem with auction sales to convert
land into real estate. John Warner and Thomas Fairfax, *A survey of the
northern neck of Virginia, being the lands belonging to the Rt. Honourable
Thomas Lord Fairfax Baron Cameron, bounded by & within the Bay of
Chesapoyocke and between the rivers Rappahannock and Potowmack: With
the courses of the rivers Rappahannock and Potowmack, in Virginia, as
surveyed according to order in the years 1736 & 1737.* Library of Congress.

Governments, Monopolies, and the Politics of Public Sales

In an Atlantic-spanning process, public sales of the seventeenth century played
a pivotal role in transforming the products of transatlantic commerce into the
working stock of London artisans and the labor force of American planters. Typically, this transformation took place at a sale by the candle, a form of auctioning
that started the bidding when an inch-high stub of candle was lit and continued as long as the flame burned. Royal governments wrote public sales into the
charters that established monopolies to scour Africa, Asia, and the Americas

for precious and valuable gold and silver, ivory, spices, and human captives. In granting charters, governments sought to harness individual ambitions to imperial political power. Yet their endeavors simultaneously raised questions of who should receive the benefits of the commercial world and whether consumers or the state would decide how to distribute the rewards of empire.[12]

The Royal African Company, chartered by the English Crown in 1672 to compete with Dutch slave traders, was one such monopoly. Its agents operated a system of forts and factories along the West Coast of the continent, where they traded goods for dyewood, gold, silver, and African captives. Some shipments returned directly to England, while others went to the Americas, where the company sold African people in exchange for sugar, tobacco, and other tropical goods, then returned with the cargo to England. When the fruits of trade gathered from around the Atlantic passed back through the metropole—one account explained—the gold was minted into coin, and then "the Elephants Teeth, and all other goods, which the Company received, either from Africa or the Plantations, in return for their Negros, are always sold publicly at a Candle."[13] In a regular cycle, the entire sprawling endeavor was set in motion to serve the English people whether they stood on wharves in Barbados to purchase human captives or in London, offering bids on ivory tusks until a candle sputtered out.

In practice, the selling of global commodities took many forms, raising questions of fairness. Company agents organized side transactions and arranged quick credit purchases for favored buyers to allow them access to the most desired goods. When less-favored consumers protested these schemes, the company responded by returning to auctions, confident in the reassuring openness of the method. In 1690 it instructed its West Indian agents to universally adopt sales by candle with ample advance notice to prevent the "clamours" of local planters and "give them satisfaction as much as in us lyes."[14] Selling by the candle, the company argued, meant that "no man can be imposed upon in the price."[15] There was time to consider what one was willing to spend and time to hear and react to other bidders' judgments, increasing the sense of openness and fairness in the transaction. There was not infinite time, however. The behavior of a candle flame was unpredictable enough to keep all potential buyers focused on the sale.

The sentiment that a public sale ensured proper distribution of the bounty of the empire circulated in the metropole as well as in the colonies. In 1694 a group of clothiers and dyers petitioned the House of Commons to lodge a complaint against another chartered monopoly, the East India Company. The petitioners alleged that, in spite of the company's charter, "for many Years last past, the said Company have sold their Red-wood, by private Contract, to Three or

Four particular Persons, who have ingrossed that Commodity, and sell it at Three times the Value for which it was formerly sold."[16] The English clothiers and dyers were unable to work their trades, they claimed, because they could not afford the overpriced dyewood. Petitioners deployed their words pointedly, using the contrast between "private Contract" and "public Sales" to support their argument about access and fairness. Auctions, open bidding, and small quantities would result in the fair valuing of the imports and also support craft industries without compelling them to work through middlemen. The House of Commons agreed: The East India Company must sell redwood "at public Sales, in small Lots."[17]

The larger implication was clear: if royal monopolies were to deserve their prerogatives, they needed to demonstrate that they did indeed serve the public good.[18] A 1698 "Act for Settling the Trade to the East Indies" specified a system for the East India Company and any other "Traders to the East Indies" that set boundaries around the commercial activities of traders on the one hand and local English merchants on the other.[19] Under this act, the company imported goods to Britain, sold them at public auctions held once per quarter "openly and publickly ... by inch of candle" in London to "private" merchants, and those merchants retailed goods or exported them for sale.[20] The flow of goods from Atlantic shores into the homes of English men and women connected the global and the local with auctions as the hinge.

Not everyone agreed that chartered monopolies best served the public, and the late seventeenth and early eighteenth centuries witnessed vigorous debate over the powers granted to corporations. Writing in 1685, the English author Carew Reynell argued that the East India trade, which brought to the metropole mainly goods for reexport, ultimately served individual merchants rather than the country as a whole.[21] Trade for the public, he argued, should involve importing raw materials that could be transformed through manufacturing that employed people and produced exports of greater value through the power of labor. Merchants, even those operating under government protections, were ultimately acting on private interests that were necessarily narrow. At best, these men who managed the chartered companies embodied a conflict between their quest for personal profit and their public responsibilities as colonizing and governing bodies abroad, a conflict that the economist Adam Smith later dismissed as a "strange absurdity."[22] At worst, importers who operated the international reexport trade worked "merely for money" not for the public.[23]

Governments mandated auctions for the goods acquired by chartered companies in an attempt to navigate the absurdity of conflicting motives by structuring monopolists' relationship to retailers as suppliers rather than as competitors.

A web of distribution, from the company to the merchant and from the merchant to the shopkeeper and consumer, spread the risk and the profits of commerce across the trading community. But when those commercial relationships ruptured, so did the political justification for awarding such power to a small group of individuals. In 1773 Britain's Tea Act permitted the East India Company to sell directly to North American consumers rather than going through the process of auctioning to merchants and retailers. Opponents of the act objected that the monopoly had been set up to profit directly at the expense of merchants' own "private Interest."[24] To their eyes, the new law confirmed a long-standing suspicion that state-supported monopolies were ultimately just another group of individuals pursuing wealth and their own interests, undeserving of special status and protected markets.[25]

In fact, long before the political explosion over the Tea Act, tensions between public sales and private interests were already thriving aboard the ships that transported Asian goods back to the imperial center. Many sailors shipping out with the East India Company jealously guarded the privilege of trading small amounts of goods on their own account. To a degree, company directors agreed that such trading ventures by sailors invested them in the success of the voyage and therefore should be permitted. Company factors, as well as maritime officers, routinely maintained separate commercial ties and pursued individual commercial ventures overseas.[26] But when sailors sought to expand their own profits beyond what was permitted by a limited quota and concealed items such as nutmegs and handkerchiefs in their clothing in order to sell them later on, those in power moved to stop them.[27] They labeled sailors' self-interested ventures as secretive exchanges of "surreptitious commerce" over the side of the ship that violated the expectations of the public auction. In the directors' eyes, a limited amount of "private" trading was motivating, but too much signaled the shadier connotations of secret deals, private in the sense that they were concealed and injurious to the greater good.[28]

For those in pursuit of business, company auctions also offered a solution to the problem of obtaining good information about global trade. Public sales generated public benefits in the form of pricing details that would otherwise be confined to the personal letters of merchants writing to their contacts in hopes of piecing together commercial news. By attending and paying attention to regular company auctions, scanning the lists of quantities on offer, keeping account of goods sold and prices paid at quarterly sales, businessmen created a set of economic facts that encompassed more than their own networks. Once collected, this information permitted traders to determine how much to purchase in the future and how much to pay their suppliers for the next shipment.[29] Regular, predictable public sales also helped merchants manage the long distances and uncertain conditions that their shipments faced. A steady rhythm of accumulation in a warehouse and dispersal through auction minimized price fluctuations and created consistency that reduced the risks of global trade.

The combination of publicity (announcing sale days, quantities for sale, and opening bids) and predictability (holding sales at regular intervals) created conditions by which auction prices could even be treated by the courts "as true universal measures of value," demonstrating the potential for specific public sales to create general market truths.[30] For traders, the list of prices generated by a sale was not just a measure of what customers were willing to pay but a confirmation, accumulated through repeated enactments, of what goods imported from around the world were worth. The features of public sales and the documentation they generated and circulated helped establish the idea that economies dealt in measurable, predictable facts.

Repeated public enactment of pricing and exchange reinforced the assumptions of what could be priced and what counted as a "fair" exchange, and this had calamitous implications for the African people captured and dragged in front of bidders. Through the work of chartered monopolies, the new economies, as Morgan writes, "were saturated with the commodification of human beings." Some captives even bore the branded scars of company initials on their skin, burned to mark them as claimed commodities.[31] The centrality of people with a price, and prices as commercial information that could be recorded, measured, compared, and used as rules for further transatlantic negotiations, warped the Atlantic economy around human commodification.

So powerful was this effect that even emerging developments in economic culture, such as the concept of commercial liberty, rested on the expanded trade in human captives. In 1692, two years after the Royal African Company insisted that West Indian agents sell captured Africans "by the candle," it faced complaints about the method's "tediousnesse." In response, the company agreed to allow their factors "liberty to sell in such manner and way as they shall judge most practicable & best for us."[32] They removed the auction requirement in order to expand human commodification in thousands of private transactions instead, and they called the change "liberty." The rhetorical link between Black enslavement and English commercial liberty spread as independent slave traders mounted a political campaign to protest the prerogatives of the Royal African Company. Demanding access to the lucrative trade in captive humans, they too cited "English liberty" as their economic and political rallying cry.[33]

On the western edge of the Atlantic Ocean, colonial lawmakers incorporated public sales into local power structures, not through monopoly rights but rather by appointing "vendue masters" to preside over local market exchanges. In both cases, the government's claims of authority over the manner of trade facilitated its legal property regime. Establishing the rules of public sales was a basic responsibility of local colonial government, and in 1729, Rhode Island passed a law that every town should select a vendue master at the annual election of town officers and require him to place a £1,000 bond. The vendue master, who was both an auctioneer and an overseer of public exchanges, was tasked to "sell all Goods of private Persons ... at any Vendue or Publick outcry" and before his "exposing of any Goods to Sale, shall publickly read the Conditions of such Sale."[34] He also had to limit himself to a 2½ percent fee, which he collected for his public service to the "private persons" of the community. In South Carolina, the governor appointed a master auctioneer to post notices, enforce rules, and in the minutes before the auction was to begin, ring a "Hand Bell through the most usual and frequented Streets in Charles-Town."[35]

In part, the embrace of public sales in British colonies suited the geography of settlement. In the early 1700s, the largest towns held a few thousand people, which limited commercial opportunities. Anyone looking to make a sale had to travel to meet customers where they lived, whether they were British American farmers interested in buying iron nails, Indigenous traders exchanging furs for brass kettles, or African Americans bartering vegetables for fabric.[36] As a mobile mode of selling, auctions fit this need well. Public sales often took place in taverns, but they could be stood up anywhere, and by setting a time for bidding, they gathered up dispersed customers ready to make a purchase. Low settlement density, therefore, was part of the reason for the widespread adoption of public sales.

With public oversight embodied in a vendue master came the opportunity for public benefit in the form of revenue. In 1713 New York's vendue law mandated duties to be paid for "Goods Merchandize, Houses, Lands, Ships, Sloops or Vessels, Slaves, & other things whatsoever, that shall be sold within this Colony at Public Auction Vendue or Out-Cry" (excepting sheriff's sales, estate auctions, and the excise). For every hundred pounds of current money sold, the auctioneer had to pay "Ten Ounces of [silver] Plate" to the colonial treasurer "to be applyed to such use or uses as the Governour Council and General Assembly shall think fit."[37] Subsequent revisions changed the goods protected from duties and the percentage of the duty, as lawmakers experimented with this tool for public revenue.[38] Other colonies followed suit. A 1751 South Carolina act required auctioneers to pay a 2½ percent tax on the sale of "all Goods, Wares and Merchandize" to the public treasurer (excluding sales of lands, houses, "Negroes," wrecked goods, or estate or court-ordered auction sales).[39]

The political use of public sales was clear in these laws. The people described as "slaves" or "Negroes" were explicitly not part of the public to be served by them. Instead, they were repeatedly listed as "things" that "shall be sold." Colonial authorities mobilized the auction effect of public sales to reinforce their own power and define the community they served.

Colonial governments also attempted to use public sales to wrest control over the Indigenous fur trade from individual traders and thus establish the primacy of the state's jurisdiction.[40] To manage that trade "for the sole use, benefit, and behoof of the Publick," South Carolina authorized commissioners to seize "skins, furs, slaves, or other goods or merchandizes" traded illegally as well as to oversee the public sale of such goods by Charleston shopkeepers.[41] John Davenport announced a June 1759 public vendue under the Philadelphia courthouse by order of the commissioners of Indian Affairs of "a large Parcel of Provincial Skins and Furrs, consisting of Full Deer-skins and Indian dressed Skins."[42] Urban auctions of skins and pelts, part of an effort to forestall economic and diplomatic disputes between Indigenous communities and colonial ones—oversaw only a fraction of the circulation of these goods. Most often, transactions took place in the woods and at trading posts between Indigenous and European people who had developed personal relationships. In establishing auctions, therefore, governments sought to manage competing economic activities of white residents within a larger political framework of imperial and colonial authority.

Courts and the Power to Punish

Colonial courts held auctions that rooted public property making in the expanding practice of using legal tools to resolve social dilemmas. Sheriffs or the auctioneers they hired conducted court-ordered auctions for civil debt case enforcement, seizures from violations of regulatory laws, and settling of probate for the estates of the deceased. Auctions enabled the courts to address both matters of public law, which concerned the allocation of shared resources, and private law, which covered individual disputes over property such as debt cases.[43] By channeling familial grief, neighborly squabbles, and Black and Native people's assertions of autonomy through a ritual of pricing and sale, court-ordered auctions supported a specific economic culture. That culture endorsed patriarchal property rights, the power of creditors over debtors, and the ability of the state to treat humans as property.

In the realm of public law, sheriff's auctions routinely liquidated property for government purposes. In Connecticut, a 1712 law decreed that the colony treasurer was to "demand and receive" any property left unclaimed by a deceased person's heirs as well as all land taken in judgment for money due to the colony and sell it at auction. Such a sale, according to the law, was to "make and confirm, in the Name and behalf and for the Use and best advantage of this Colony."[44] New Jersey established a similar process for compelling residents to contribute to such community projects as building jails and courthouses: anyone who refused to pay their share would face a warrant for their property to be seized and auctioned. After the sale proceeds covered the mandated rates and fees, the constable would "Return the Over-plus, if any be, to the Owner."[45] The promise of a carefully calculated over-plus refund was surely little comfort to the family whose housewares had been forcibly converted into value for the state, no matter how methodically the process was conducted or what purported public would benefit.

People who disrupted public order and broke laws intended to secure it became targets of punitive auctions that likewise funneled proceeds into the public purse. Colonies established a broad range of laws that triggered the seizure of items proximate to an infraction. They took boats found oystering out of season, cattle permitted to stray onto someone else's property between November and April, and steel traps set out at the wrong time unless to capture "beasts of prey."[46] All could be put up to public auction, a form of punishment that turned a piece of property employed in breaking the law into money by taking it from its original owner and selling it to someone else. The guilty party lost the item to a bidding neighbor and the government collected the auction-derived value as a form of revenue.

This method of securing payment was well-suited to communities that lacked cash and for whom material goods were the most fungible forms of wealth.[47] Ordered to pay a fine for breaking the law, few colonists could quickly gather up gold and silver coins, or even the limited forms of paper money that circulated. Instead, they needed to convert some material property into a form of payment whose value could be accounted for.[48] A constellation of lending, pawning, and selling activities sustained the majority of cash-poor people attempting to manage their financial lives in a context where legal tender was scarce. In holding an auction, the sheriff did not wait for such community exchanges to yield a form of payment that the government would accept. He stepped in to turn a set of bedsheets into money to cover the fine, drawing on his authority to select the goods to be exposed and converted.

The power of exposure and conversion mobilized in a sheriff's auction aided in the collection of import duties and local taxes as well. In 1716 South Carolina created property and poll taxes to raise funds to help pay for warfare against the Yamasees, a conflict ignited by clashes between colonial traders and settlers on one side and allied Indigenous groups on the other. To enforce the tax, the law named a set of inquisitors to gather information on the property owned by each resident and pass this information to a group of assessors who calculated each person's share. Anyone who refused to pay was reported to the colony's chief justice who issued an execution ordering the marshal to seize and auction off the goods of delinquent debtors to cover the amount they owed.[49] In a similar move in 1721, the colony placed a duty on imports, and again, if a shipmaster or importing merchant did not arrange payment, the law authorized the treasurer to seize from any ship and sell at auction "such negroes, liquors, goods, wares or merchandize" sufficient to pay the duties due on the shipment.[50]

Unlike a fine or a fee, which could be paid directly behind closed doors, sheriff's sales exposed the desperate actions and mundane disappointments of free residents on courthouse steps and invited the public to participate in punishment through purchase. As the bodily humiliations of public whipping and the pillory in criminal cases became less common for white residents, economic public exposure at the hands of court officials was increasing.[51] The exposure of a sale inflicted a different kind of damage, not to the body but to credit and reputation, which were the social and financial underpinnings of colonial societies.[52] Credit and the ability to delay payments depended on trust built of social standing. Family and community ties strengthened one's credit, and individuals who wanted to access financial forms of credit were at pains to defend their reputations. Being caught up in a sheriff's auction widened the exposure to community scrutiny, as whispers about unfulfilled promises and rumors of unpaid debts entered the structures of the courts and were broadcast in an open sale that drew on community witnesses and participation.

Bidding audiences were never fully controlled by the authorities who hoped to harness the power of public witnessing to enforce colonial power. Community members had their own agendas, desires, and ideas about local leaders, all of which shaped their participation. By the end of the century, disrupting a sheriff's auction became a form of protest against the government. In refusing to bid, audiences sought to deny the state its power to punish those who did not pay their taxes through seizure and sale of their livestock. They acted collectively, constituting a public authority to counter that of the courts.[53] Massachusetts men who sympathized with indebted farmers after the Revolution attended sheriff's auctions to intimidate, and they directed their threats at both the assembled community, to prevent them from bidding, and the legal agents who conducted the sale.[54]

Court-ordered auctions also played an important role in defining race as they established the rules of the economy. Tax assessments put prices on enslaved people that court-ordered auctions then tested, reinforcing the link between price and ideas about racial difference and value. The 1716 South Carolina tax provision, for example, gave extensive directions for assessing the value of "negro and Indian slaves, mustees and mulattoes . . . whether the same be men, women, or children, without any manner of difference or distinction of age or sex." Once the tax law established the category of "slave," it began to parse out ideas about value that were founded in distinctions among people. Referencing the purported public opinion that "an Indian slave [was] . . . reputed [to be] of much less value than a negro," the law directed assessors to precisely account for this relative value. It stated, "All and every person and persons possest of Indian slaves shall only pay for each Indian in proportion to half the value of what shall be rated and imposed for each negro . . . all and every such slave who is not entirely Indian, shall be accounted and deemed as negro."[55] Ideas about the value of "negros" and "mustees," and even who would be included in these categories, were thereby proposed in the tax assessment. These ideas were then ratified in the hands of the auctioneer, who drew on local beliefs about value to transform physical objects and humans alike into legal property.

References to common knowledge about relative value in human property found in the text of laws obscured the devastating violence that produced such knowledge. By the early eighteenth century, colonial governments had for decades used auctions to punish and profit from military campaigns by expanding enslavement. In New England, the end of King Philip's War (1675–76) opened a round of auctions of captive Native Americans. In some cases, these public sales distributed Indigenous people as unfree laborers in New England households; in others, postwar auctions brought Native people into intercolonial slave-trading ventures. The Massachusetts Bay's treasurer John Hull held two auctions of more than 190 Native people who had surrendered in September and August of 1676 and put the profit toward the cost of the conflict.[56] One purchaser, Samuel Shrimpton, sent six of the people he had bid on to further sale in Jamaica.[57] Judicial enslavement created both a legal framework for slavery and a process of valuation—through an auction—to fix a price on people. The government, in turn, benefited financially from transactions that then paid for further colonial expansion.

The auction's role in expanding the terrifying conversion of human beings into priceable goods stretched its shadow over free people as well. In 1740 Virginia, the General Assembly crafted a law to support a military expedition against the Spanish that treated free deserters as if they were seized goods, "to be sold by the Sheriff, at the Court-house Door, immediately after the Adjourning of the Court, to the highest Bidder, for ready Money, as a Servant, for the space of Five Years."[58] The assembly explicitly linked the aims of public punishment (of the deserters) on the one hand and a form of human commodification on the other, in the act of the sheriff's sale. Under the law's provisions, the sheriff selling a deserter's freedom for five years would collect "the same Fee as for selling Goods taken and sold by Execution." In similar fashion, the people who turned in the deserter were paid a reward, and any remaining profits from the sale went to the treasurer for public use. The sheriff's auction, with its predictable rituals, schedule of fees, and generation of public revenue, offered a template for expanding colonial authority over the bodies of residents in multiple situations.

The punishing power of the auction to turn humans into commodities likewise extended to police the boundaries of slavery. A 1741 North Carolina law stated that any "negro, mulatto, or Indian" slave who was freed for any reason had to leave the colony. If they had not left within six months, parish churchwardens were instructed to capture the person and sell them at public vendue, "the Monies arising thereby, to be applied, by the Vestry, to the Use of the Parish."[59] Once again, the proceeds of the sale went to support the free people of the parish and to reinforce the contention that a human could be priced and sold in the same manner as an inanimate object or animal that had escaped its pen. The auction effect, seen in the shipside sales of captured Africans, unspooled its consequences by redefining free people of color as a potential form of property and simultaneously excluding them from the parish public.

Private law, like public law, employed auctions to adjudicate power in personal relationships by converting those relationships into financial transactions. Civil litigation over unpaid debts surged in the eighteenth century as new financial instruments, such as bills of exchange and promissory notes, enabled people to forge contracts with those outside of their regular communities of exchange. When these new contracts proved unreliable, the legal reach of court officers extended farther than that of community pressure; where shaming was impossible, suing filled the gap. Bills and notes were also more rigid in their terms than the formerly ubiquitous long-running credit accounts, making them more likely to be resolved with technical legal actions than with shared arbitration.[60]

Each individual lawsuit originated in the details of promises violated, but the forms of litigation and the sessions of the court turned all such messy personal details into a routine part of the economy. Printers took advantage of frequent debt litigation to expand their businesses. They sold blank forms of "Writs, Summonds, Executions, Recognizances . . . Sheriff's Bonds, Constable's Bonds, Complaints to the Superior Court" that, once purchased and filled in, circulated along with the seizure and sale of property.[61] The presence of such forms, in turn, reinforced expectations about the court's role in financial matters. Because they were standardized, they also shaped and even limited the ways that users could articulate the connections among personal relationships, material life, and the rules of fair exchange.

The large volume of debt cases meant that the threat of a court-ordered auction spread deep into the community. The serving of writs was a common, visible event that involved a wide circle of women as well as men, servants as well as masters, in negotiating property relations, from the moment a sheriff appeared at the doorway to demand security (typically in the form of goods) to guarantee court appearance. Where possible, those targeted in such actions, whether insolvent debtors or struggling widows, tried to broker property to hedge against losses. Some temporarily "sold" their property to neighbors to protect it from creditors' claims; others tried face-to-face negotiation with authorities, pleading with the sheriff, for example, to take a table in the corner rather than a kettle over the hearth.[62]

Lawsuits frequently ended with an auction and another chance for the public to intervene in property relations, thus testing the rules of expanding colonial authority over residents, in this case free debtors. When a judge or justice of the peace issued a writ of execution, a court officer took the named goods, waited a prescribed number of days to allow the owner to redeem them, and then, failing that, sold the goods at public vendue to pay the debt and fees, with the "overplus" returned to the owner.[63] The pressure of the public sale was meant to force the indebted party to comply with the court order. A 1747 South Carolina law stated that "if the Defendant before the Day appointed for the Sale shall pay the Money ordered to be levied, the Goods may be re-delivered to him, but upon his further Delay or Refusal, the Constable shall expose the Goods to Sale at public Auction, and shall apply the Monies arising by such Sale to the Discharge of the Judgment and Execution."[64] In 1748 a Virginia law followed a similar five-day procedure for the public auction, specifying that the sheriff sell the goods "for the best price that can be got."[65] And although the courthouse steps were a potent symbolic location for disposing of goods taken in a legal action, court officers could venture widely to hold sales wherever they thought a bidding audience might convene. John Taylor, sheriff of Chester County Pennsylvania, used the Rose and Crown tavern to conduct a sale of a house and 225 acres of land, taken in execution of a lawsuit against Joseph Cloud. The sale, announced for between twelve o'clock and two o'clock on an August afternoon in 1727, was to determine the best price the sheriff could obtain for the impatient creditor Edward Horne.[66]

Predictable court-ordered auctions reinforced norms of exchange by turning court day into sale day and setting the terms of payment—typically cash or short credit.[67] Those with access to the courts resorted to framing their disputes as legal matters because it was a way to restore credit—in its mixed eighteenth-century sense covering social virtue and financial stability—in front of the larger community, even as that community was becoming more transient, crowded, and diverse. The courts became a place to probe community rules under pressure. Sheriff's auctions, with their own exchange of visible signs in the form of bids made and bids refused in a context of public exposure and loss, enforced the material consequences of this expanding docket of lawsuits.

Exposing and Concealing Property

Was anything safe from the ruthless sheriff's auction? For the first decades of colonial settlement, land—defined as "immovable" property in the English legal tradition—was often protected from circulation while personal goods, recognized as "movables," were fair game to the claims of creditors in debt litigation. Land could not be seized to pay unsecured debts and was protected for heirs and widows at the death of a landowner because it was a form of property that had been seen as a static bulwark of privilege, to be preserved from generation to generation. Laws that coded some forms of property as movable and others as immovable established a system that initially protected landed wealth from the estate auctions that executors held to settle the debts of the deceased.[68]

The ability of legal coding to shield some forms of property from the auctioneer spurred creative redefinitions of wealth in colonial settings. Unlike elites in Britain, many in the American colonies held a substantial portion of their property in the form of imported African and African-descended people, and they looked for ways to adapt the legal system to shore up this wealth and their power. Given the demands of the emerging plantation economies in the southern colonies and Caribbean, land itself had little value without human labor power to cultivate it, and enslavers wanted to bind the two forms of property together to preserve their investment in both. Human property was in every commonsense way mobile, whether enslaved people were trudging from row to row in a field or fleeing into the swamps to escape captivity. Yet South Carolina lawmakers, following practices in Barbados, attempted in a 1690 law to classify enslaved people as immovables. In defiance of—or because of—everyday experience with highly mobile Black people, white lawmakers sought to render them still and therefore protected from seizure or attachment under the principles of land ownership.[69]

When the South Carolina law was disallowed by the English Privy Council, colonial enslavers looked for other ways to embed their economic interests in the legal definitions of property. In Virginia, lawmakers in 1705 successfully passed a law "declaring the Negro, Mulatto, and Indian slaves within this dominion, to be real estate."[70] The law ensured that these racially coded humans were inherited within families of enslavers and not subject to seizure for unsecured debts. The seemingly impossible designation of a human being as real estate served to keep those same human beings out of sight of the exposing necessity of sheriffs' auctions. The legal designation did nothing to protect enslaved people from exploitation. Rather, it made their exploitation and alienation from kin central to the early development of capitalism in this colonial context.

Routine auctions converted colonial laws concerning debt into expected facets of the economy. Multiple colonies in the late seventeenth century moved to treat land, formerly understood as static and perpetual, as movable property, a legal fiction designed to suit the financial calculations of powerful creditors. Laws opening land to exposure, pricing, and sale looked in two directions—toward dispossession of Indigenous people on one side and toward cultivating metropolitan credit on the other. English settlement depended on colonists' expansive use of credit to purchase imports, and they traded these same imports, such as cloth and metal tools, to Indigenous people. Merchants pursued these trading relationships even when their Native counterparts did not provide furs or other goods in return; rather, merchants offered their wares on credit, secured by a mortgage on Native land. A 1675 law in Massachusetts that permitted creditors to seize a debtor's freehold land revealed how merchants' creation of debt in trading relationships with Indigenous people supported a larger design on Native landholding.[71] If the merchant creditor called in his or her debt and the Indigenous person could not pay, the creditor foreclosed with the aid of courts and sheriff's auctions, dispossessing Indian communities of their homelands. This form of foreclosure, initially targeting Native customers specifically, in time applied regardless of race or nation, as laws created to support colonial conquest became widely adopted rules regarding debt.[72]

Auctions were likewise central to the process of creating new mobile, fungible forms of money because an auction, initiated to circulate property, stopped that circulation momentarily and held it up to spectators for the purpose of revaluation. Over time, more forms of property—people, land, furniture, imported goods—were swept into the auction process, challenging older English practices that held some property back from circulation in order to preserve specific social relations. The rights of heirs to a portion of their parent's estate is one example of a principle that was dismantled as colonies bolstered the power of creditors to access property. In Pennsylvania, for example, the protections that had reserved two-thirds of a person's land for his or her child were stripped away by a 1700 act that made all of a deceased debtor's land liable to be taken and sold at auction to satisfy creditors holding unsecured debts, with nothing set aside for heirs.[73] Evidently, it was too radical a change, and five years later, the legislature modified the law to allow for situations in which the earnings on a debtor's property could be deployed to repay debts, with the debtor retaining title to the land itself. The specter of the public sale loomed over each of these colonial modifications to English laws about inheritance and landed property.

British merchants were not satisfied with local colonial experiments, and they demanded the legal exposure of all forms of property so that they could recover the debts that colonial buyers accumulated. In 1732 Parliament responded with a sweeping law that applied only to its North American and West Indian colonies. The "Act for the More Easy Recovery of Debts in His Majesty's Plantations and Colonies in America" declared that real estate, houses, and enslaved people were all to be treated as chattel for the purpose of repaying unsecured debts. In other words, no mortgage was required to expose an estate to the risk of seizure and forced auction sale. Debts incurred through all the commonly used tools in credit-dominated British colonies—including book debt, promissory notes, and bills of exchange—could be targeted in a court's execution order, whether those debts had been initiated to purchase imported goods or imported people. The law sought to deny colonial debtors the traditional protections of real estate as a special form of property that could be shielded from seizure—protections that landholders in Britain itself retained.[74] While some colonists were able to secure land through specific legal instruments (such as the entail), for the majority, the new law mandated a market in land, houses, and enslaved people and treated them all as chattels whose value could be found through bidding.

Thus, auctions turned legal code into lived experience. As conventions of judicial sales mapped onto the evolving understanding of property, auctions fused the intertwined power of the state and market over individual lives, with particularly damaging consequences for the growing number of enslaved people in British North America. The day of an estate auction became a day of reckoning. Anne Dupont, administrating Dr. Alexander Dupont's estate in 1751, announced that she was putting up for sale to the highest bidder "all the effects of the said Dupont consisting of negroes, horses, cattle, household goods, medicines, &c." on June 25. The date was also the deadline for his debtors to pay up and his creditors to file their accounts so "that proper measures may be taken to discharge them."[75] Dupont's judicially supervised auction pulled enslaved Africans and African-descended people from families and homes and into public exposure for pricing, a practice that increased after the passage of the 1732 "Act for the More Easy Recovery of Debts." Land sales increased in tandem, as new plantation owners sought out people to purchase and put to work.[76] Social relations of the plantation shaped developing economic logic.

The auction effect operated in the other direction as well. By repeatedly exposing colonial communities to the idea that people could be priced and thus confirmed as movable property, auctions supported a notion that economic logic determined social relations rather than the other way around. Decades of colonial lawmaking had come together to create slavery as an inherited status that rested in the bodies of women of African descent. Early on, tax laws separated English and African women for different treatment.[77] Marriage laws in multiple colonies punished unions between "white" women and "Negro or other Slaves."[78] The legal concept of *partus sequitur ventrem* deemed that offspring followed the condition of the mother, making slavery an inherited condition of being born of a woman held in bondage. All of these legal measures had profound effects on the intimate lives of women and men in slaveholding societies. The public sale of a human being at auction made the argument that an individual mother belonged on a property list of "negroes, horses, cattle, household goods, medicines, &c." and that all of those diverse entities—whether made of flesh and blood, linen, or brass—had a value that could be uncovered when taken away from their social context of family and daily life.

Print and the Auction Effect

Colonial newspapers, which were hybrids of political and commercial communication, were a key platform for the cultural work of shaping the everyday economic vocabulary and norms that grew from public sales. From the first publications, auctions appeared alongside other forms of commercial activity. In July 1717, the *Boston News-Letter*, the sole North American newspaper in publication that year, included a small section titled "Advertisements." These few inches of text, tucked on the final page of the newspaper, listed only a handful of items, a mixture of what would later be understood separately as political and commercial matters:

> An announcement of the political appointment of two notaries
> Three notices for houses to be sold or rented
> One advertisement of "several servants" from England for sale
> Two auction advertisements, one for imported Madeira and one
>   selling two ships and their equipment
> A notice demanding payment from participants in last week's book
>   auction

Early auction advertisements sat next to general notices and, like them, educated readers in how to navigate the spatial geography of urban commerce. Customers interested in Ambross Vincent's Madeira were directed to sample the fortified wine at tastings held in the cellars of Captain Keeling and Mr. Winste in the days leading up to the auction, which would be at the Crown Coffee House.[79] Categorized as an "announcement," the notice gave specific directions for potential buyers to act—first to sample, then to bid.[80]

As they expanded into every colony, eighteenth-century newspapers became part of a dense and varied culture of advertising that included handbills, shop signs, and strolling vendors' cries, all of which created a context for individual transactions.[81] Newspaper advertisements themselves focused on the origins and abundance of goods, indicating even to a casual glance the significance of variety, both in the types of goods for sale and of the multiple options within each type. Columns of type on the page permitted, and perhaps even encouraged, a marketplace of comparison on the basis of abundance measured in length of type. For the literate, key words and typographic techniques, such as placing the word "CHEAP" in all capitals at the top of an advertisement, informed potential customers of another element of comparison shopping—relative cost. Some promised to sell goods at "low" or "reasonable" prices as well as offering discounts for cash purchases.

Auctioneers promised the opposite—that the highest price would prevail when goods were sold "to the highest bidder." Auction advertisements developed to highlight the context of a sale price and the details of the transaction itself. They used "exposure," a term borrowed from colonial market regulations, to affirm that goods or land would be "exposed to sale" rather than merely "sold."[82] With this language, auction notices promised that there were no private deals taking place behind the scenes to manipulate the outcome of the sale. Each witness to an auction could verify the identity of the highest bidder and thereby validate the transaction. Additional promises that the sale would take place "without reserve"—in other words, without a minimum starting price—confirmed that buyers, not sellers, should ultimately determine the price of an item for sale.

In the middle of the eighteenth century, auctioneers began to use a new term in their newspaper notices—the "private sale"—to signal terms and conditions of their expanding businesses. In 1746 the auctioneer Benjamin Church announced his Boston auction of recently imported European goods, including various types of fabric, fashionable buttons, "choice Green tea," furniture, and wearing apparel. At the same time, he announced that he would sell "by private Sale sundry Sorts of European Goods, Green and Bohea Tea, Chocolate, &c."[83] Regular retailers did not describe their routine business as "private sales," but when auctioneers began to experiment in different ways of selling, they used the term "private" to mark a departure in their practice.

A private sale was an invention, marked as a distinct alternative to an auctioneer's regular business in public selling. The word "private" in eighteenth-century North America had a wide range of meanings that focused on either the quality of being hidden from view or the quality of having no formal connection to the government or church.[84] Unlike "public," a term that was extensively used and approvingly linked to political institutions or people with responsibilities for governance, "private" could be seen as a positive or negative condition: the sailors who established "private" ventures while simultaneously operating a trading mission for a government-chartered monopoly walked a fine line between appropriate personal ambition and selfish, secretive dealings. Colonial clergy warned their congregations against economic behavior motivated by narrow, "private" interests.[85] Yet the moral and cultural resonance of private matters was not set in stone. Only in the late eighteenth century did "private" take on meaning as the gendered feminine side of a public-private dichotomy.

By picking up the phrase "private sale," newspaper advertisements demonstrated that public and private sales were not opposites but rather one supported the another in establishing patterns of commercial access. Men like Gabriel Winter, selling his house "by way of vendue," hedged his bets by announcing that he was willing to sell the house "by private sale by any time before" the auction.[86]

In his presentation of public and private sales joined in a sequence, he indicated that a public sale, in this case required by law, was a sale of last resort. In January 1760, Adam Hold of Oxford, Pennsylvania, proposed an even longer chain of potential types of transactions. He planned to sell a farmhouse and land, plus another lot. Interested buyers could first apply to him to buy the property outright. If the lots were not all sold by early February, he would hold a public auction at the home of Daniel Mackinet in Germantown. And he had a final backup plan: if the vendue also failed to finalize a sale, the current owner would rent out his lots.[87] By placing announcements of public sales in the pages of the newspapers, sellers were frequently opening up the possibility of a series of transactions with a shifting locus of control over price and distribution.

Private sales labeled as such in the newspapers acknowledged that goods moved through a cycle of desirability as they were evaluated by purchasers. In 1748 one Charleston merchant advertised that his goods, a mixture of striped and checked linens, beaver and felt hats as well as shoes, tobacco, and firearms would be sold "at very low Prices" in his store until February 9. Then, "what remains on Hand, will be sold on that Day at PUBLICK VENDUE, at the same Place."[88] In this way, after discerning customers were given the chance to make selections, leftover goods would be opened up for public bidding and inevitable bargains. The following day, again at the same store, a different merchant began selling newly imported versions of the same types of goods, at retail, beginning the cycle again. The sequence could be flexible. In seventeenth-century London, the shift went in the opposite direction, when leftovers from publicized book auctions ended up in local shops for individual (private) sale.[89] Alternating venues and modes of sale kept goods in circulation, in search of a buyer.

Human commodities also cycled through different types of sales, some involving large groups of people and others focused on individuals. As slaveholders tried every means to wrest financial value from those they owned, the routine valuation of people torn from kin and community established human commodification as a form of economic logic linked to difference defined by race. For example, public pricing rituals, including both the auction and the set-price sale, manipulated knowledge about people into commercial facts about property. Johann Bolzius, a minister living in Georgia, explained the difference between these two types of sale by linking them to racial ideas about enslaved people. He first remarked that "the best way to buy acclimatized Negroes is at public auction, if a planter has to sell his slaves because of debts." Bolzius's comment underscores the effect of the 1732 Act for Recovery of Debts, which exposed human property to litigated debt collection. By the 1750s when he wrote, court sale days were a predictable venue for a potential buyer to bid on another human who was already living in the colony. Bolzius called these enslaved people "acclimatized," implying that the health and behavior of Black men and women could be assessed in terms of value, and then priced individually—after all, they were being sold as part of local court action. For "new negroes" recently arrived, Bolzius continued, "one agrees on a price with the buyer of the shipload, enters the ship and picks out which and how many one wants to have."[90]

This second method he referred to—sometimes called a "scramble" in the West Indies—suited sellers and buyers who viewed imported Africans as only loosely differentiated commodities rather than as familiar individuals (see Figure 2). In a North American scramble, importers like the Charlestonian Henry Laurens coldly separated newly imported men and women into categories, fixed a price per head for each person in a category, and then permitted buyers onto the ship or into the "yard" to select an individual representative of that category to purchase. It was a terrifying, chaotic experience for the enslaved people as they were grabbed by buyers with unnerving "eagerness" on their faces.[91] Eager buyers had little information about the people they purchased, who might have traveled thousands of miles from the West Coast of Africa to the West Indies and finally up the coast of North America. The sorting, categorizing, and confining of this group of people were critical to obscuring personal information and ultimately denying the humanity of the enslaved. Such measures reinforced buyers' beliefs that the human beings before them were indeed property, fixed with a price. Dislocated and suffering from weeks of violence and illness, the enslaved had few ways to convey who they were. As a factor in Kingston, Jamaica, or Charleston, South Carolina, divided them into groups of "prime," "puny and ill-assorted," and "emaciated, sickly, or refuse Slaves," he calculated ways to increase his own profit by controlling the "prime" category and to further his business connections by holding back some of the healthiest people for private sale to his friends and associates.[92]

The market problem of insufficient information triggered cycles of public and private sales as North American sellers attempted to eliminate the association of African people imported from the Caribbean with used goods. In 1772 James Burnett sent a group of enslaved people from Jamaica to South Carolina for his agent to sell, but the effort went badly, from his perspective. The agent tried to "barter" them for produce or sell them to individual buyers, but ultimately had to accomplish their "disposal" through a bargain auction that yielded

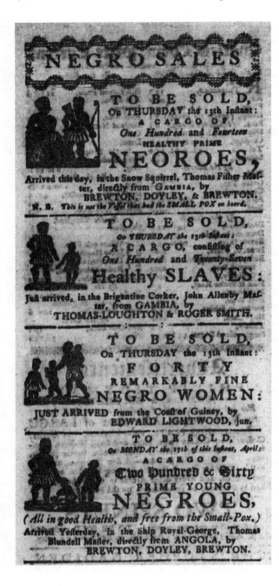

Figure 2. Sales of large numbers of newly arrived African people as part of a "cargo" were typically conducted via a scramble. The humans for sale were not individually differentiated but rather were described with grading terms such as "prime" or "fine" in addition to information about their origins and attestations of health. The woodcut figures, in contrast, suggested individuality, age differences, and even family groupings. Coherent Digital, 623 S. Fairfax Street, Alexandria, VA 22314, *South-Carolina Gazette*, selected page, South Carolina Newspapers online database, April 13, 1769 issue ©.

low prices and small compensation for Burnett.[93] In Burnett's eyes, he was forced to submit to the price-setting wisdom of the bidding public, a loss of control (and imagined profit) he resented. It was a pattern that continued into the nineteenth century as enslavers and slave traders tried first to sell directly to buyers from homes or showroom pens and only resorted to a public auction for the so-called inferior human property or most desperate situations.[94] The human cost of this cycle was high as enslaved people found themselves displayed, priced, and relocated multiple times across a lifetime.

Newspaper and handbill advertisements for public sales deployed the factors' vocabulary of value with terms such as "choice" and "likely," and in so doing, trained the public how to "read" descriptions of human beings as commercial information.[95] Stock phrases in newspaper advertisements formalized and publicized notions of how to turn a human into a commodity.[96] An auction in 1760 Boston exposed to sale wholesale fabrics with names describing their weaves and finishes ("Parcel of Calamancoes, Shalloons, Buckrams"), furniture described with positive adjectives ("A handsome Book-Case, new"), a human described by color and gender ("a Negro Man"), and the notation "&c."[97] The designation "&c." was a common final insertion in multiple eighteenth-century advertisements, from retailers' lists to estate auction announcements.[98] Frequent recirculation of goods and people for the purpose of revaluing and redistribution expanded alongside this shared commercial vocabulary.

Enslaved people sought to escape the cycles of commodification, but newspapers bound them back in with practices that solidified race as the marker of difference that made some people enslavable. Papers routinely printed runaway notices alongside auction advertisements, and the conventions of both types of notices translated individual characteristics into commercial information. Runaway notices in colonial newspapers went into great detail about the clothing, facial expressions, skills, and personalities of the people who had escaped in ways that focused on their financial value.[99] In fact, advertisements seeking the return of human property were far more detailed than advertisements seeking sale to a new buyer. Papers presented captives for sale as collections of brief descriptors onto which prospective buyers could attach their fantasy of a valuable laborer. Runaways appeared as distinct individuals described to be apprehended because of their value. A study of colonial American runaway advertisements discovered that while slaveholders tended to give specific ages for white runaway servants, they employed approximations or general terms such as "young" in describing enslaved people. The difference did not come from a lack of specific knowledge about enslaved laborers but rather reflected what mattered in terms of "externally commodified value."[100] A white servant's specific age mattered to the remaining length of the indenture that bound him. An enslaved person's status as "young" emphasized the long future of profitable labor and reproduction that her or his body was expected to produce without end until death. Words about age category were in fact statements about a person's capacity for labor, and in the case of enslaved people, their potential labor value paired with their status as "Negro" gave them a market value.

The representation of enslaved people on the pages of North American newspapers participated in the political shift within colonial societies from one in which enslaved people were a public concern to one in which they were defined by their status as private property. In the seventeenth century, the matter of runaway slaves was treated as a problem of public order and punishment: residents who failed to help pursue people seeking freedom faced fines; those who located fugitives were rewarded for their efforts by government authorities.[101] In these early decades, property claims rested within public obligations. Eighteenth-century papers, in contrast, "encouraged the privatization of a once-public practice."[102] Enslavers publishing runaway notices offered monetary rewards that they would personally pay to anyone who assisted in restoring their human property.

Auctions forged a bridge between the public and the private through this transition that transported human property in two directions. In Maryland, for example, a 1727 law addressed the situation of runaway servants and enslaved people who had been turned over to the local sheriff in keeping with the older practice of treating runaways as a public problem. If enslavers failed to redeem their human property, the law stipulated, the sheriff was to announce an auction, sell the servant or enslaved person "to the highest Bidder," and collect his fees from the proceeds.[103] In this as in dozens of other situations, colonial governments used auctions to convert an array of disruptions—crime, neglect, disorder, escape—into a transaction around price. Finding the price through a public event defined property and government authority.

*   *   *

In the nineteenth century, the sale and circulation of land would be praised as an "American" bedrock of equal opportunity and the chance for individuals and families to rise economically and politically.[104] Yet such opening up of opportunity was premised on closing off key sources of support grounded in kin ties in the form of dismantling enslaved families, foreclosing on Native families, and dispersing white heirs. The legal expansion of property that could be liquidated and sold underwrote the credit economy of American colonies, which generated economic opportunities. But that liquidation and circulation created its own hierarchies, of creditors over debtors and the politically powerful over the politically dependent, in keeping with the goals of the colonialism that auctions served. And while people at auctions renegotiated the value of the property circulating from one owner to another, some factors, including race, were becoming nonnegotiable as markers of value. The routine auctions of human beings, supported by court processes and extended in print, ensured that human commodification forged economic knowledge.

Public sales were an essential part of this process of property making because they were broadly and fundamentally social in the way they operated. The wide and varied use of auctions in British colonial settings in the late seventeenth and early eighteenth centuries developed in tandem with the creation of bodies of property law and legal practice. Their sales revealed the social and material consequences of the developing systems of law, and as experiments in valuing, they held those consequences up to the public for their judgment.

The public exposure of an auction thus forced colonial power struggles out into the open and demanded that local residents participate, whether through active bidding or active witnessing. Both were powerful acts. To be a witness in the early eighteenth century was to stand at the heart of knowledge production, given the value that courts, evangelical congregations, and enlightened scientists and philosophers placed on firsthand observation and testimony.[105] Each public sale assembled a group of witnesses by virtue of its rules and forms as a commercial mode of distribution, and witnesses could be from all ranks of colonial society, including those who could never dream of bidding on the property set up for sale. In this way, the legal experiments of Parliament and colonial legislatures themselves were worked into knowledge about economic value. Auctions served as a template for expanding colonial authority, but they also became a key device for community reflection on the link between power and price.

CHAPTER 2

Neighbors, Bidders, and Economies of Knowledge

Benjamin Franklin, writing as Father Abraham in a 1760 pamphlet, went to an auction and did not like what he saw. He admonished the "great number of People, at a Vendue of Merchant-Goods" to be wary of what they were bidding on: "You call them *Goods*, but if you do not take care, they will prove *Evils* to some of you." He despaired of the way they judged value based on lower-than-expected prices, fashion, and the opinions of their neighbors. The structured public valuations created by courts and colonial governments in the preceding decades invited participation, and to Franklin's alter ego, the scolding Father Abraham, participation was the problem. The notional bidders lacked the moral fortitude to judge true value; as a man of erudition, he knew that tea and printed cloth were mere "knickknacks," not worth the money spent on them.[1] The price was a false signal, enticing people to purchase what they did not need.

Mary Coates, an actual Philadelphian who attended auctions in 1760, had other ideas about imported fabrics and the opinions of neighbors. Coates, a widow who ran a city shop with the help of her daughters, came regularly to the auctions overseen by vendue master Thomas Lawrence in a stall by the courthouse, as she had for over a decade. She purchased fabrics and other items for her own business and those of her neighbors who bought "in partnership" with her by pooling their funds.[2] Coates and her associates viewed imported cloth as business stock. They wanted bargains, but purchase price was only one part of creating a bargain, which rested on carefully evaluating an item's specific purposes and calculating how to extract the value in a collaborative community. In their bidding and redistribution of goods, they helped create a body of knowledge about prices that shaped a wider sphere of economic practice and commodification.

By the middle of the eighteenth century, public sales were playing a central role in the circulation of consumer goods, and the dynamics of these sales reveal two intertwined features that shaped the social meaning of prices in British North America. On the one hand, public sales were open and collaborative, as bidders collectively discovered a price and, consequently, the value of goods put up for sale. No one—not the bidders, the sellers, the observers, or the local officials— had complete information about the objects' past or their potential for the future when they came together, and everyone had a stake in the answer. On the other hand, public sales operated under rules and structures that formalized consumer participation in order to shape an outcome that was consistent with community ideas about the moral functioning of exchange. The business of an auctioneer was to control when, where, and how a community of bidders came together, and his efforts were informed by local understandings about material life.

Distinct features of auctions made this double function of economic knowledge particularly visible. Goods entered auctions under duress, whether via bankruptcy proceedings, as overstock, or as the contents of a deceased person's estate.[3] These qualities connected the functions of pricing and distribution to a specific local context. Goods then exited auctions to be recirculated in local economies. Auctions provided raw materials at affordable rates for petty retailers who otherwise struggled to secure the connections and credit that structured much of the eighteenth-century economy. In colonial North American cities, which had limited numbers of licensed middlemen and intermediary dealers between the importers and small shopkeepers, the vendue distributed goods across the economy.[4] In this way, vendues overlapped in function with the often illicit second-hand trade in clothing and other used goods that was a common occupation of the poorer sort in urban centers. Tavern keepers, hucksters, enslaved men and women, and unlicensed residents and transients sold used goods in what some scholars have called an "informal economy."[5] But as auctions demonstrated, such exchanges constantly intersected with, and supported, commerce blessed by the approval of local magistrates; the same goods could move through multiple circuits. Public sales operated within a broader economy of knowledge in which information about particular goods was dispersed across the social contexts that the goods traveled on their way to and from the block.[6]

Information about prices within this broader economy was dispersed and idiosyncratic. The widening availability of imported items coincided with the erosion of price controls, leaving many to wonder how much they should pay for tools, teapots, or thread if the prices fluctuated with market availability. Comparative price information, which could provide a context for judging bargains, was not always easy to come by. Customary prices, such as those set for bread, were limited to a few necessities.[7] Colonial assemblies set prices for specific agricultural goods to be used as commodity money, but these varied from colony to colony and often differed from the prices attached to those same goods in private transactions. A business press centered around London, which had begun to emerge in the seventeenth century, gathered and publicized price information to allow merchants to make decisions about imported goods.[8] But while bread might have a customary price and rice an international commodity price, what was the price of handkerchiefs? Of handsaws? What if these were slightly used? Customary or "just prices" could only go so far when dealing with goods of ambiguous origins or classifications, and such goods dominated everyday exchanges.

Auctions supplied an answer. Unlike a transaction in a retail shop, in which criteria such as quality and quantity ostensibly determined the price charged by the seller, at an auction the price determined the value. It was only at the end, when the hammer strike closed the bidding at a final price, that the assembled community learned what they really considered the worth of an object, piece of land, or human being to be.[9] At that moment, the various components of value—aesthetics, sentiment, utility, invested labor—resolved into a number that consumers could compare to other sale prices.

That number was embedded in a social context that Father Abraham and Mary Coates both understood, though Coates considered it for good and Abraham for ill. For both, economy and society were tightly knit. The goods may have come from English workshops or Barbadian sugarcane fields, but the value was negotiated locally, and each seller, bidder, auctioneer, witness, and lawmaker had a stake in the outcome. Neighborhood auctions embodied an interactive model of economic life in which distant suppliers, local tragedies, busybody neighbors, and the constant movement of goods converged to link price, value, and material life. Through their contributions, they embedded ideas about race and gender in judgments about monetary value and appropriate market behavior.

Servants, wives, hucksters, sailors, and farmers had ideas about the connection between value and price, nurtured in their participation at auctions, that were not captured by the era's well-studied debates over the money supply. By midcentury, most local transactions in British colonies depended on long-running credit arrangements that intersected with a mixture of coin and paper money issued by colonial governments and land banks. As the paper bills changed hands up and down the social ladder, fluctuated in value, and competed with bills issued by neighboring colonies, they challenged ideas about intrinsic order in society and governance.[10] Auctions generated a different set of open debates about whether prices were fair or appropriate in how they dispersed goods through a community. A colonial marketplace, the historian Barbara Clark Smith argues, was a place of "collective public consent" to transactions and prices, guided by a shared sense of fairness.[11] Local auctions focused public consent on price, in the form of numbers bid. Price was a signal, but people had to know how to read the signs because price was a social relation, too.

Pricing and Placing Goods

Franklin's fictional bidders and Coates's real-life associates both confronted the complexities of valuing material culture in the eighteenth century. As ceramics, textiles, and other manufactured goods became more widely available, Americans and Europeans shifted their household labor arrangements to earn money or credit to acquire them.[12] As a result, people owned more goods of greater variety at the end of the eighteenth century than at the beginning, and owning these goods yielded social and economic benefits.[13] Family members and friends used regular exchanges of goods to forge and cement social ties.[14] Urban shoppers pursued specific wants through eager comparison shopping.[15] Poor men and women bought, pawned, and used clothing, raw materials, and other goods to supplement meager incomes.[16] At all social levels, material culture became a significant tool for navigating the economy and society because it was mobile, accessible, and could be converted into an emotional or financial investment.

To deploy material culture in these ways, people had to understand something about prices, which were the access points to goods beyond local bartering relationships. In this endeavor, they contended with multiple ways of valuing, as information about what prices were, what they should be, and where they came from was partial and conflicting. As long as the Atlantic trade remained centered around London, the frame of reference for commodity prices of imports into the British colonies was imperial as much as local. Long considered a trade secret, commodity price information first became public business knowledge through the practices of merchants engaged in international trade. Dutch merchants in the mid-sixteenth century began to publish business newspapers listing information about prices current or the market prices accepted widely during the current season. By the seventeenth century, Amsterdam prices of commodities became the point of reference for sales around Europe. Though goods might sell for more or less, they tended to concentrate around a benchmark price that literate Europeans could access in print.[17] Eighteenth-century London merchants printed their own prices current, which in turn became benchmark figures for British colonies. Readers in North America and the West Indies could purchase copies of these English business papers, and merchants and planters used London price information to make business decisions about buying and selling commodities.[18]

Colonial newspapers published their own "price current" lists as well. In 1720 Philadelphia's *American Weekly Mercury* printed price currents for flour, bread, salt, tobacco, muscovado sugar, pork, beef, rum, molasses, wheat, Indian corn, naval stores, and several other items. Most were priced per measurement, such as rum, listed at 3s. 6d. per gallon. Some had a range, such as Madeira, listed at £16 to £20 per pipe. The paper's editors thought comparative price information would boost local commerce, and because "the Design of this Paper, being to Promote Trade," they asked merchants to participate by "Acquainting Us with the true price Current of the Several Good's inserted in it," including corrections and expansions.[19] By 1725 the Philadelphia paper printed price currents for New York as well as Philadelphia, along with news of ships arriving at and departing from the northerly city.[20] Circulation of goods through one port or another and prices of those same goods were closely linked in print.

European prices for commodities shaped colonial trading relationships, but they did not define them. Merchant exporters had to balance the prices they paid to rural suppliers against those they charged for imports. Information from newspapers and business correspondence helped merchants respond to surplus harvests and lean years in Europe and the Caribbean, which came with rising and falling prices for commodities such as sugar and grain.[21] At the same time, merchants had to respond to the developing expertise and savvy of fur traders and farmers who supplied them and set their own prices. Different kinds of trading relationships shaped different assumptions about what needs prices had to meet. Rural suppliers frequently charged local customers less than they charged merchant exporters, believing that while prices attached to local transactions needed to serve social cohesion, prices for "outsiders" were limited only by what an individual buyer would accept in a transaction.[22]

For wide swaths of British colonists who were not engaged in long-distance trade, the frame of reference for prices was the Bible, with its directives against usury, and an understanding of the "public good" that embraced social, political, and economic interdependence.[23] Guided by these references, seventeenth-century lawmakers in Massachusetts, for example, set price limits, admissible markups, and other controls at times of high migration and imports and repealed them during depressions, when the supply of goods dried up.[24] Belief that exchange had to be guided by ethics was widespread beyond Puritan New England, which meant that price controls focused on goods and services that ensured "safety, security, and sufficiency" and whose abundance promoted social order.[25] Port towns in the seventeenth and eighteenth centuries set, variously, prices of flour, grain, bread, bricks, leather, sawing wood, and grinding corn.[26]

Colonial debt litigation reinforced a community's shared understanding of commercial fairness in ways that went beyond the limited practice of government-mandated prices. In court, litigants referred to the concept of "settled" and "customary prices," which were embedded in ideas about the value of goods and services to the community. In a 1765 Massachusetts case over debt, for example, lawyers for the plaintiff argued that "the Price for Boarding and Schooling is as much settled in the Country, as it is in the Town for a Yard of Cloth, or a Day's Work by a Carpenter."[27] As their statement suggested, the rising importance of contracts to secure economic agreements favored a straightforward interpretation of settled prices—a price was fair if both parties had signed off on it. But if two parties agreed to a price that was too high above the "reasonable" or "customary" one, was the agreement fair or enforceable? Modern-day economists describe prices as signals about the value of a particular good or commodity; and for eighteenth-century Americans, value had economic and moral dimensions that were not sharply distinguished from one another. [28] Father Abraham deemed the prices of auction goods to be wrong not because they were calculated in error but because they reflected and also encouraged the bad values of envy, covetousness, and laziness. While his view of consumer motivation was narrow and judgmental, his perception that prices had a fundamentally social origin and social significance was widely shared.

If prices were linked to local ideas about worth, why would they change? Authors on both sides of the Atlantic discussed the implications of variable prices—for flour, thread, or for money itself. In his pamphlet on the currency supply, the Boston merchant Hugh Vans called the price of an item its "comparative value," which was, he said, "understood by every Body." Because it was rooted in comparison, that price came "either from the Plenty or Scarcity of the Commodity to be sold, or from the greater or smaller Number of Buyers"—in other words, from supply and demand.[29] But the underlying value of an exchange had different dimensions, he contended, depending on whether the object in question was a necessity or a luxury. Whereas some articles—such as air, water, and food—had intrinsic value because they were necessary to life, other articles had "accidental" value based on human choices, "guided either by Reason, or meer Humour & Fancy."[30] Daniel Defoe wrote similarly of the potential disconnect between price and value in *The Compleat English Tradesman*: "Goods may be high-priced, and not dear, low-priced, and not cheap; the Rates of all Goods are to be measur'd by their Goodness or Badness."[31] He went on to note that the moment of exchange might involve a price but it could not truly capture value because with many objects value was revealed only over time in their durability and longtime use. By implication, if value had so many socially embedded components so did prices.

Few residents of British North America read early political economists, but many listened to sermons, and ideas that value was variable, rather than intrinsic, circulated from the pulpit as well as from the pages of newspapers and pamphlets. As early as 1704 Bostonians heard their minister Samuel Willard inform them that "the Word of God indeed hath not fixed the stated Value of things, because these things are to vary according to Circumstances."[32] Prices, too, could change, and that change was not necessarily a sign of lawbreaking or unchristian behavior. To say that demand led to changing prices did not mean that there was an undifferentiated force called "demand" that shaped the flow and cost of goods. A buyer's need for bread and her need for tea were not part of the same calculation or understanding of the marketplace.[33] The former came from the enduring drive for basic survival; the latter from a more fashionable, and therefore changeable, desire to participate in a type of social life centered around the brewing and sipping of stimulating hot beverages in cups designed for the purpose.

Debates about prices were therefore also debates about distribution. Who got tea and who got bread were questions about who should, socially and morally, have either item. It was not at all a widely shared idea that price, and a person's ability to pay the cost, should be the mechanism for sorting out issues of distribution. Franklin's Father Abraham used a moral lens to differentiate between necessary goods and luxuries, warning that luxuries were the product of imperial trade that colonies would do better without. It was an idea Franklin pressed in 1766, when he testified in Parliament that imports from Britain were "either necessaries, mere conveniences, or superfluities." Cloth was necessary, and currently "cheaper" when obtained from Britain, but not for long, as it was the colonies' "interest to make every thing," which would lower the price of locally produced goods and circulate them, to the benefit of colonists.[34]

Auctions were a public exploration of the link between value and prices, and they created regular opportunities to debate what prices meant. As Father Abraham noted, bidders expected that prices at a public sale of goods would be low, carrying in their minds an implicit comparison with some other price achieved under different conditions of sale. Moral judgment and politics stepped into the gap between those two numbers. Benjamin Booth of New York advertised his list of imported dry goods for sale with a pointed explanation as to why he would only accept cash, not credit: he was in competition with auction prices. He stated that "public vendues, subject to no regulation, are very detrimental to the community, by giving room to the most unfair practices in trade, and that there is no legal way of suppressing them, but by underselling them." He resolved to do just that and to provide "better and cheaper commodities, than can generally be had at vendue."[35]

Lawmakers in South Carolina likewise targeted "under-Rate" auction prices as the source of social and commercial ills. A 1750 law warned that "it has become a Practice to vend all sorts of Goods, Wares, and Merchandize by Retail, at Public Auction in the said Town, to the great Prejudice of the Shop-keepers and others who deal in the Retail Way" who could not compete.[36] The following year, the South Carolina Assembly claimed that auction prices injured not only shopkeepers but also Charlestonians up and down the economic structure. The first victims were the poor "Inhabitants of the said Town who have no other Means of supporting themselves and Families, than by selling out Goods in small Parcels," which auctions could do more cheaply.[37] Second were the "Merchants and others abroad" who would be discouraged from sending goods to the port if it meant being undersold by auctions. Third was the harm to local merchants, who paid rent and taxes and therefore "cannot afford to dispose of their Goods at so low a Price" as those without a fixed place of business. Defending the local economic order with a series of new regulations, the law blamed "transient Persons, who are chiefly the Occasion of such public Auctions or Outcries."[38] It was to no avail. Nine years later, the effects of low auction prices had purportedly quashed the productive will of free craftsmen "who neglecting their respective Occupations, idle and loiter away their Time in Expectation of gaining Bargains at such Auctions or Outcries." Lawmakers attempted once more to limit the scope of auction bargains by banning the public sale of any set of goods "at a less Sum than *Five Pounds* current money" and restricting the sales to Tuesdays and Thursdays.[39]

In the opening years of the American Revolution, sales at Charleston's auctions became so competitive that a new generation of bidders drove prices high, seemingly "without regard to their value." According to a 1777 law, purchasers at these public sales then turned around and sold "the same to such as are in want of them." The scheme, the law alleged, raised the prices of "almost every necessary article to a most exorbitant and expensive height," made it "extremely difficult for the poor and industrious to procure the common conveniences of life, and "depreciate[d] the currency of the continent and of this State."[40] Prices of "goods, wares, or merchandizes" that appeared to lawmakers to be divorced from their value were a commercial and a political problem. The wartime resolution was to ban auctions outright—except those conducted under governmental authority and explicit approval.

Whether they were attacked for being so low as to undercut the businesses of local retailers or too high for those "in want" of goods, eighteenth-century auction prices functioned at least as much as cultural signals as economic facts, with implications for the social function of prices overall. Lawmakers interpreted local pricing to be a product of social relations that needed to be managed: the behavior of sellers was a problem for the way they enticed and manipulated customers; the behavior of buyers reflected their inability to act in morally justifiable ways in the eyes of lawmakers. The numbers determined at public sales were firmly and openly tied to a constellation of local relationships that held both collective knowledge and conflicting visions of the future. Unlike the more abstract prices of transatlantic commodities, prices forged at vendue forced British colonists to confront conflicting ways of valuing as they tried to resolve the dilemmas of distributing goods.

Goods with a Past and a Future

The price of an item on an auction block was a product of its past and a projection of its future use. Dependent on the mobility of goods and people, auctions participated in a widespread commercial culture made up of property with a history. Circulation of used goods frequently began at home, when a servant was outfitted in used clothing, a brother inherited an older sibling's tools, or an enslaved woman bundled up textiles before running away. Furniture, tools, utensils, and blankets passed from one generation to the next. A variety of types of auctions—including estate auctions, sheriffs' sales, and regulated vendues at which residents sold their belongings for cash—moved the practice of circulating goods from such gift or illicit economies into local market economies by setting a price and, at the same time, locating a new owner. Although not all the items sold at such auctions had been used, they were all objects whose biographies had been interrupted, whether through the death of a previous owner, damage sustained in transit to a new location, or seizure by the courts.

A local body of knowledge about those biographies created the context for auction sales and brought nuance to the process of acquiring goods. While many commentators who wrote about consumer behavior focused on the emotions of desire and greed, the exposure of an auction was just as likely to reflect regret and woe. Bad financial decisions shadowed a debtor's property as it was priced and sold by a sheriff on the courthouse steps. In March 1756, personal and financial desperation drove Daniel Richards to the auction block. His wife Anne had "eloped," and he announced that he would pay no further debts of hers. But he felt the burden of his own debts, too, and prepared for the liquidation of his estate with an auction announcement that revealed a household undone. A public sale of dwellings, land, fields, livestock, and household goods would convert it all to money for the disappointed husband.[41] Scholars have tended to focus on the ways that consumption enabled new identities in a positive, self-making fashion, but the unmaking of selves in the dispersal of personal property and real estate was routine.

While a quick sale of parts of material life could help a seller like Richards survive, sales under duress exploited while they rescued, revealing the underside of auction bargains and the prices they established. Putting up pieces of one's material life for sale gave average people access to ready money they hoped to use to sustain their families. Designed for quick liquidation, auction sales used cash and short credit, in contrast to transactions in shops and merchant warehouses, where long-term credit and forgiveness of debts prevailed. By turning goods into money, auctions supplied funds to people with little more than the clothes on their backs and only tenuous, low-quality credit. Poor people "in great want of cash" in Europe might take clothes to a pawnshop; in the American colonies, they auctioned them.[42]

Yet the bargains that bidders engineered at a sale meant that impoverished sellers typically had to accept small sums for goods they might have valued highly. Late in the century, lawmakers in Pennsylvania understood that many people had few choices when it came to selling their worldly goods to make ends meet and were driven to auctions in desperation. Arguing against a proposed tax on used goods sold at vendue, Assemblyman Robinson of Pennsylvania pointed out that "it is the necessity of the poor people; it is their inability to obtain money for necessary purposes, that fills these places with the goods and merchandize, we see daily selling." Robinson argued that low prices were a signal not of the low quality of the goods themselves but rather the desperation of the sellers: "You hear it said, that vendues will sell goods fifty percent cheaper than the shopkeepers. Does not this clearly prove it is dire necessity, that obliges such sacrifice?"[43]

Boston's Society for Encouraging Industry and Employing the Poor hoped that they could harness the expectations of low prices at auctions to achieve social and community goals.[44] Between 1751 and 1759, the subscriber-sponsored society launched a linen manufactory to put economically struggling residents of Boston to the work of spinning and weaving for a regular wage and thus prevent them from falling on the charitable support of the town. Ministers applauded the effort, believing that "the lower sort may be happily formed to a habit of industry."[45] Sponsors also hoped that by hiring this group and encouraging flax-growing farmers, they would create an industry "to such Advantage as that Linen of all sorts may be made cheaper among ourselves" and lessen the need to import it.[46] In 1752 they tested that idea by holding a public auction to sell eighty pieces of linen produced by the venture. The *Boston Evening Post* announcement promised "each Piece to be put up at a low Price, marked upon the Linen."[47] Potential buyers were invited to come the day before the sale to examine the pieces of work. But the bargains were not good enough. The Linen Manufactory, a partnership of public and private efforts at poor relief, could not produce linen cloth that was cheap enough and of sufficient quality to compete with linen imported from Ireland.[48]

Auction bargains were more successful in sparking economic energy by breaking up the bulk of larger lots sold at vendue so that small sellers could serve their customers, thereby recirculating value in the economy.[49] Mary Coates was part of a network of Philadelphia petty retailers who bid on the auctioned lots and then divided the goods among themselves, reimbursing one another sometimes weeks after the sale. She made regular appearances at vendues herself, typically buying groups of goods costing £10 to £20 for each sale she attended, and likely subsequently delivered shares of her purchase to others. Others in her network did the same, as evidenced in the pocket-size receipt books she carried to record her payments to those who "Bot in pardnership" with her (see Figure 3).[50] Her small reimbursements to them of a few shillings or pounds at a time, spread over five hundred pages of handwritten notations and signatures, looked nothing like the imagined extravagance of Father Abraham's heedless vendue attendees. Instead, she used her bidding network to obtain basic elements of eighteenth-century clothing construction. She paid Jonathan Carnals £2.1.4 for sixteen yards of cotton linsey that he had purchased as part of a larger bundle on December 1, 1766. She reimbursed her sister-in-law Elizabeth Paschall, a frequent copurchaser, £1.10.10 for tapes in the summer of 1762. For Coates, Carnals, and Paschall, vendues were workplaces as much as they were showcases of the latest fashion.

Coates's working networks cultivated a body of local economic knowledge that deepened over time. From the start, she drew heavily on family connections, as in the case of her extensive commercial ties with her sister-in-law. She also sometimes arrived at a household with reimbursement in hand to find only a child or spouse present to collect the money on behalf of the purchaser. Buying

Figure 3. The shopkeeper Mary Coates reconciled her collaborative
vendue purchases with other small sellers in Philadelphia.
Mary Coates receipts, 1748–1759. Coates and Reynell Family
Papers (0140). Historical Society of Pennsylvania.

in partnership at vendue was part of a local redistribution that turned past failures into future profits, depending on local connections of trust and forbear-
ance. In early September 1750, she reimbursed Mary Jacob (for her husband
Samuel Jacob) £1.9.9 for goods that Jacob had bought in partnership with her at
two separate August vendues. By the 1760s Coates's networks had become more
elaborate, and her reimbursements referred to "goods bott. at Sun[dr]y Times at
vendue," indicating that she was operating within a form of running local credit
rather than just a discrete set of shared purchases.[51] In bidding on goods she and
her associates planned to sell in their Philadelphia shops, Mary Coates gleaned
information from her fellow bidders about how much her customers might pay
for small packets of the goods. She contended not only with her own profes-
sional judgment about style and quality but also the opinions of others at the
vendue, who might include future customers and future competitors.

The burgeoning debt cases of the eighteenth century created a wide field
for the local economy of knowledge, as Coates and others cultivated new life for
their businesses by turning a neighbor's loss into salable stock. Many of the Philadelphia vendues that Coates attended were court-ordered sales, presided over
by a sheriff- or colony-appointed vendue master who facilitated the recirculation
of goods while collecting the proceeds for creditors. She made selections from
the auctioned shop goods and household furniture of Thomas Williams, a hat-
ter, which included "hats, furrs, trimmings for hatters use, dye stuffs; and a large

assortment of shop goods, fit for the season" for the sum of 3 pounds, 5 shillings, and 7 pence.[52] On August 20, 1750, Sheriff Richard Sewell organized a vendue of "shop-goods, a choice parcel of household goods, wrought plate, and sundry other wares" starting at ten o'clock in the morning in Isaac Foulke's house.[53] Foulke, a shopkeeper, had assigned over his accounts to a group of administrators tasked with settling his debts.[54] This sale generated strong interest among Coates and her partners—she reimbursed three different men who had bid at this auction. The four people who bought Foulke's goods in partnership also shared the information that "2 flasks of Oyl" had sold for 5 shillings and 2 pence.

Merchant death joined merchant debt as an instigator of auctions that redistributed goods to pay off creditors and seed smaller local businesses. When the New York merchant John Keteltas died in 1768, his widowed mother and brother-in-law hired an auctioneer to liquidate the business and bring in cash to settle the estate's accounts. The "Handsome assortment" of goods that Keteltas had earlier advertised "to be Sold cheaply"—"men, women, and children's worsted hose, worsted and cotton caps," calicoes, flannel, and camblets—were sold off at a series of auctions and some subsequent sales; the purchasers' names and patterns suggest that many who attended were small shopkeepers looking to stock their own businesses.[55] Mrs. Elvendorp, for example, spent more than £90 at the Keteltas auctions between May and December 1768 on fabric, handkerchiefs, cravats, and thread mitts. Keteltas must have received a large shipment of hose before his death because, on August 6, the vendue master sold 775 pairs from his stock to the assembled bidders. Elizabeth Hale bought twenty-four pairs of hose—too many for one pair of legs, not enough to supply a major retailer. The hose she chose were the cheapest sold that day, only 7 pence per pair. The rest were knocked down by the auctioneer for as high as 6 shillings 9 pence, though most were more in the range of 3 to 5 shillings a pair. It is possible that some of the hosiery was not even new imported stock but rather used items.[56]

What all of this meant was that when Mary Coates paid William Harrison 48 shillings and 9 pence on November 10, 1750, for an assortment of stockings that the two had bought in partnership at a Philadelphia vendue, her sense of the stockings' value was shaped by experiences of pricing them in multiple contexts. Imported stockings and hose were everywhere in the formal and informal economies of British North American cities. Poor men were hauled into court for theft of them; enslaved people ran away with them; substantial merchants and transient peddlers alike sold them. Available in multiple colors, plain and decorated, stockings and hose enabled many consumers to take part in fashionable imported culture. They were easy to conceal or hide in plain sight, worn down the street. All of these qualities made them suitable to stand in for money in legal or illicit exchanges.[57]

As stockings circulated from this larger economy of knowledge through an auction, they gained a price determined by the assembled crowds. Scholars of early American marketplaces have focused on the ways that explicit market regulation sought to control the behavior of sellers so as to offer straightforward comparison shopping to consumers, usually in cases of foodstuffs, groceries, and other basic items. Laws against forestalling, engrossing, and regrating, for example, controlled the timing and flow of goods into urban markets so that no individual seller or buyer could gain special advantage in terms of pricing or access. But the price of stockings was derived collectively in a group of people who not only compared one pair with another but also thought about where those stockings had come from (unwanted overstock, fresh imports unexpectedly put up for quick sale) and where they were going (small retailers' shelves, peddlers' sacks, sisters' wardrobes). Consumers' economic knowledge was wide and distinct from the preoccupations of supply, demand, and taste-making that dominated merchant calculations. Judging a price to be a "bargain" could only take place in this wider frame.

Estate Auctions and a Test of Value

We do not know what Mary Coates said to the men and women who stood beside her as she bid on fabrics in response to vendue master Thomas Lawrence's descriptions of lots. What words did she use to evaluate the quality, and how did she decide which numbers to call out as she acquired stock for her shop? Did shopkeepers from the countryside follow the city-dwellers' leads, or did they bring their own ideas about reasonable prices with them to the vendue stall? Their successive bids and terms of negotiation are very hard to see hundreds of years after the fact because they drew on unwritten rules of commerce and personal relationships that were negotiated face-to-face, with little footprint in the historical record.

Estate auctions, in contrast, followed a formal, court-overseen process that recorded the valuations, classifications, and negotiations over goods, and in so doing, they made visible the invisible rules of material life and lived political economy. They embodied the ways that society and economy were intertwined. And they produced a series of linked documents, with lists of numbers meant to represent the value of a deceased person's property. Free white men typically penned the lists, but their speculation and judgment were tested and revised repeatedly within the broader community at an auction. The resulting sale price, noted on yet another list, became the object of further judgment and reflection by those in attendance.[58] These lists map the interaction between prices and broad community participation. While estate auctions had numerous distinct features—for example, they were often held at the deceased person's former home—the central function of publicly testing the value of goods against available knowledge about them was shared across different types of public sales.

When a person with assets to be settled died, a probate judge appointed three men, usually neighbors, to go through his or her house, describe personal property, and put a price on it. Appraisals reflected what the committee of three thought the items were "worth," and from the start, that meant what price they would fetch at a public sale.[59] The inventory appraisal was a speculative document, created in the home of the deceased or close by, as neighbors took into consideration what they knew about the goods and what the local community would pay for them and wrote a number, representing that possible price, next to each item. A code of unwritten rules shaped what the men recorded. When they walked into the bedchamber of a man whose death had left a widow behind, they of course saw her clothing and the marital bed, but they might leave both off the inventory of items the deceased owned, reserving them for her.[60] His clothes might also escape official notice, set aside for his sons as they grew.

The appraisal began the process of commodification by fixing a brief description and a number representing a speculative price on a deceased person's property. The men who appraised South Carolinian Littleton Hill's estate, for example, described objects in ways that were based on where they had been found in the house (see Figure 4). One set was "In a Trunk," another "In a Box." Rummaging through "the box," appraisers pulled out nine groupings of goods to fix a price on, including "2 Remnants Cambrick in a Paper a Bundle Rags a Bundle of new Linen 10 Ruffled Caps 16 Plain do [caps] 1 Pair of Riding Stockings" for £15. Another heterogeneous group from that same box was described as "19 Towells and Napkins 16 Linnen Pocket Hand 3 Silk Hand a Paper thread a Paper Mens Gloves," valued at £7.

Next came the auction, which tested the appraisers' judgment against the public economy of knowledge. The items put up for sale to cover the deceased person's debts were still associated with their social context and history, but this stage of commodification required consideration of potential buyers. Bearing their needs in mind, the auctioneer re-sorted estate goods and enslaved people into lots organized around commercial categories. At the Hill estate sale, there were five lots devoted to linen that sold at different prices, a £5.10 lot of rags, and

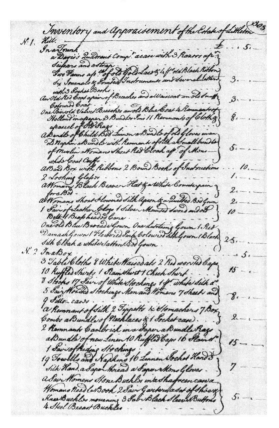

Figure 4. An estate inventory presented one view of the deceased person's material life, organized into groupings, to which assessors attached speculative prices. Littleton Hill, February 20, 1752, Secretary of State, Recorded Instruments, Inventories of Estates, S213032, South Carolina Department of Archives and History.

a £13 lot of handkerchiefs (see Figure 5).[61] The inventory appraisal had been organized room by room, whereas the auction was framed around the possible interests of potential customers. The auctioneer, by regrouping with an eye to what would appeal to bidders, removed goods from one social context and placed them in front of another—that of a community of consumers.

An auction required a different kind of strategizing than a walk through a dead man's house, and this shaped the order in which bidders encountered items for sale as well as the groupings of goods and human property. The recorded inventory for Richard Baker's estate, for example, listed two boats and fourteen enslaved people first, next to the highest appraised values. By contrast, the Baker auction began strategically with small items instead, such as decanters, hinges, and other tools. Bidders then were guided to the more expensive items, starting with firearms and silver, then enslaved people and boats. The auctioneer finished the sale with furniture, housewares, and dry goods, many of them purchased by

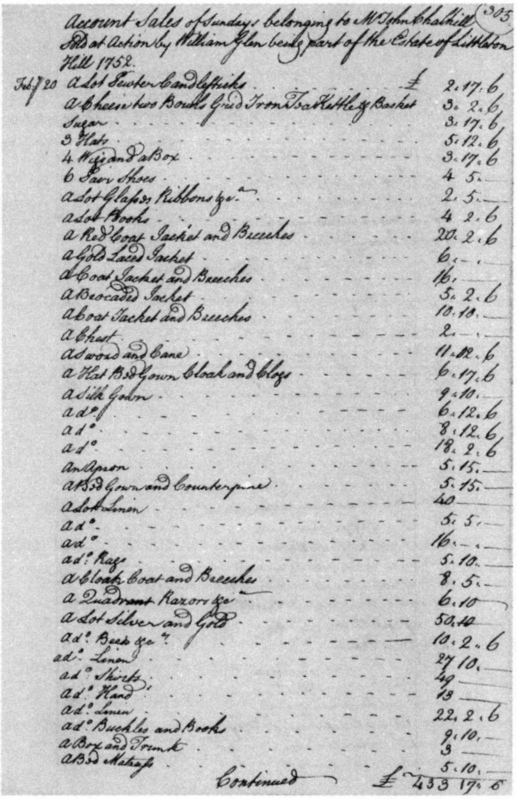

Account Sales of Sundays belonging to Mr John Chalhill (305)
Sold at Action by William Glen being part of the Estate of Littleton
Hill 1752.

Feb 20	a Lot Pewter Candlesticks	£ 2.17.6
	a Cheese two Bowls Grid Iron Tea Kettle & Basket	3.2.6
	Sugar	3.17.6
	3 Hats	5.12.6
	4 Wigs and a Box	3.17.6
	6 Pair Shoes	4.5.—
	a Lot Glasses Ribbons &ca.	2.5.—
	a Lot Books	4.2.6
	a Red Coat Jacket and Breeches	20.2.6
	a Gold Laced Jacket	6.—.—
	a Coat Jacket and Breeches	16.—
	a Brocaded Jacket	5.2.6
	a Coat Jacket and Breeches	10.10.—
	a Chest	2.—.—
	a Sword and Cane	11.12.6
	a Hat Bed Gown Cloak and Clogs	6.17.6
	a Silk Gown	9.10.—
	a do.	6.12.6
	a do.	8.12.6
	a do.	18.2.6
	an Apron	5.15.—
	a Bed Gown and Counterpane	5.15.—
	a Lot Linen	40
	a do.	5.5.—
	a do.	16.—.—
	a do. Rags	5.10.—
	a Cloak Coat and Breeches	8.5.—
	a Quadrant Razors &ca.	6.10
	a Lot Silver and Gold	50.10
	a do. Books &ca.	10.2.6
	a do. Linen	27.10.—
	a do. Shirts	49
	a do. Hand	13
	a do. Linen	22.2.6
	a do. Buckles and Books	9.10.—
	a Box and Trunk	3
	a Bed Matrass	5.10.—
	Continued	£ 433.17.6

Figure 5. An auction sale presented another view of the deceased person's property, organized to sell to a particular audience. The account records bidders' prices. Littleton Hill, February 20, 1752, Records of the Secretary of State, Recorded Instruments, Inventories of Estates, S213032, South Carolina Department of Archives and History.

the widow Sarah Baker. Her bedding, furniture, and housewares were scattered across several rooms in the inventory, but they sold one after the other at the auction, inviting head-to-head comparisons of "old chairs" and dry goods.[62] The auctioneer thus strategized his displays to anticipate the flow of the sale and also the appropriate destination for particular items. The idea that it could be appropriate to parcel and sell daughters, uncles, and grandparents was central to the logic of the entire process.

The test of the three appraisers' judgments took place in an engaged community with opinions about who should have what and at what price. Charleston County inventories during the 1750s and 1760s suggest that the auction value of estate goods was about equally likely to be above as below the appraisal price. Of those auctions that earned less money than the appraised value of the estate property, total sales were as much as 20 percent below the appraised prices as a whole. Auctions that brought in higher-priced bids than the appraised value saw much bigger discrepancies between the two, reaching as high as double the appraised value.[63] This difference does not necessarily mean that frenzied bidding drove prices above their "reasonable" level. Appraisers carried their own sense of what an enslaved person or a household object was worth, based on their familiarity or unfamiliarity, which might not line up with the collective knowledge of the bidding audience.

A failed auction test had consequences for the wider web of debtors and creditors when the bottom-line number of the estate appraisal did not align with that of the subsequent auction. Virginia lawmakers fretted about the cascade of errors that could follow when, "through the Ignorance or Partiality of Appraisers," goods were "valued at much less than the true worth."[64] Because administrators and executors had to post a bond as security to cover the sale, they had an incentive to underestimate the value of the estate in order to hedge their bets on what the bidding community would determine to be the proper price. The incentive worked against the interests of those for whom the sale was held. A "too low" appraisal allowed an executor or administrator to successfully discharge her duties by meeting expectations, but it was "to the great Injury of Creditors and Orphans" if the maximum possible total was not realized in the sale.[65]

Although appraisers had the estate auction in mind when they listed a price next to each item they evaluated, the sale followed its own dynamics, ultimately making visible the invisible rules of colonial material life. At the auction of Sarah Saxby's estate, bidders included two of the three men who appraised her goods before the sale as well as the vendue master himself.[66] When he appraised Saxby's silver toothpick case, Samuel Hurst and the other appraisers wrote down £1.10; when he purchased the case, Hurst paid £3.2.6. In the audience at Richard Baker's estate auction, one of his appraisers bid on goods, another conducted the auction, and his widow bid on and bought the bulk of the household furnishings. The same people, in different roles, participated in the economy of knowledge that moved goods from the ownership of one person to another, through the mechanism of proposing and revising prices.

The value test of an estate auction was compromised when the tight connection between appraisal and sale loosened. Though an estate auction was organized to dispose of the goods of a single person, auctioneers accepted additions from outside the family. The resulting porous boundaries of an auctioneer's stock provided chances for any number of neighbors to turn goods into cash without committing to a capital-intensive business venture. Such commingling created headaches for estate reckoning. The sale documents for David Villaret's estate in September 1742 had to be corrected after the fact, when another man's goods, sold on the same auction day, became mingled with this deceased man's accounts. The auctioneer noted that the final sale tally had to "Deduct the first Seven articles being the Goods of Mr. Adams the Saddler."[67] An additional adjustment the following July noted goods bought by one of the administrators "for which he never Accounted."[68] Heterogeneous groupings from multiple sources threatened to confuse the prior social context of an object's value, misleading bidders seeking to make the correct link between value and price. At the same time, mixed lots prioritized the community of consumers as the context for establishing price, challenging long-standing assumptions about authenticity.

Getting the story behind the goods straight was part of judging the intent of the sale, which was a factor in determining the items' worth. Death itself granted an owner's estate a certain legitimacy, one legal treatise in the early nineteenth century later claimed: "property, belonging to persons that are dead, are not so likely to be faulty, as those which are parted with by persons in their life time."[69] Laws governing auctions made a distinction between sales that had to take place and those that were put up by choice. New York's early auction tax, for example, did not apply to the property of people who had died or to goods taken by sheriffs in execution of a sentence. In 1751 South Carolina lawmakers passed a new round of restrictions on auctions, but they decided that sales of goods that had languished on shop shelves for more than one year or were damaged, wrecked, or condemned need not be regulated. Auctions of deceased colonists' estates, residents moving out of the colony, debtors, and people going out of business were frequently exempted from regulation and taxes.[70] As they debated which auctions to encourage and which to control through additional taxation, legislators settled on the distinction between people who were "obliged to sell" at auction because of legal procedures or business failure, and those who chose auctions.[71]

Building on the tenets of property law, estate auctions explicitly called out racial and gender hierarchies and linked them to prices. Estate inventories named enslaved people, and then classified them by age and sex, preparing them for sale at auction and mirroring the auctioneer's commodifying advertisements for "sundry likely Negro Men and Boys."[72] After the death of South Carolina's John Ninian in 1743, appraisers listed four people as part of his estate: "A Mustee girl Flora," "Negro Woman Nanney," "Negro Boy Monday" and "Negro Wench Nanney," each with a speculative price attached. The account of the subsequent sale grouped the women, now described as "A girl Flora," "Old Naney & Daughter," and sold to the same buyer for £220, well below the £400 that the individual appraisal prices had suggested. The "Boy Called Monday" was sold separately at very close to his appraised price. None of the enslaved people, representing at least one family, remained with Ninian's widow, which meant that their ties to family and place were torn apart for the purpose of the sale.[73] Nanny, Flora, and Monday faced frequent rounds of valuation in their lives; this sale was only one such experience. A deposition, a tax assessment, lawsuit execution, new will, or a medical examination could all trigger the process of one human being looking at another and recording a numerical value. Each context shaped the looking and the number.[74]

The fact that an estate auction put property into circulation for no fault other than the bad luck of death had particular influence on the pricing of human property. Illness, disability, and injury in the bodies of the people themselves were all forms of "fault" that could influence an enslaver's decision to sell, as were personality traits or a history of escaping in search of freedom. Knowing this to be true, buyers were intent on understanding the motivation for a sale of human property.[75] In the specific case of an estate sale, the seller's motivation, most buyers believed, was straightforward and not influenced by the humanity of the people put under the hammer. By the nineteenth century, court officials elaborated on that belief to make affirmative claims about the people they were selling in order to appeal to bidders. They promised that they were selling trustworthy people—"family negroes"—who had been turned into valuable assets by their enslaver's death, as opposed to unknown and untested human property that no one could vouch for.[76]

Venus, a woman enslaved by John Bruce in South Carolina, resisted his power to profit from her as an asset. She fled captivity multiple times in the 1750s and 1760s, even living under the assumed names of "free Hannah" and "free Mary" as she worked as a washerwoman in Charleston to support herself and her children.[77] When Bruce died in 1765, his executors went looking for her, offering a reward of 50 pounds for anyone who could return Venus and her children to the workhouse, presumably so the family could be inventoried and sold on behalf of the estate.[78] The executors Stephen Miller and Isaac Legare published their notice after the initial estate auction had taken place, "consisting of household goods and slaves, with sundry other articles."[79] They sought Venus to continue the process of settling the estate, balancing the demands of creditors against the value she and her children represented to them. Contrary to the beliefs of white bidders who favored estate sales, her inclusion in such a sale would reflect only her status as valuable property; it revealed nothing about her desires or behavior as a woman and mother.

Estate auctions highlighted intrafamily struggles over money, property, and power. Widows were central actors in estate auctions, hiring auctioneers, setting reserve prices, and meeting with potential buyers. When American lawyers published treatises in the early nineteenth century, they acknowledged this fact, commonly using women's names and female pronouns to discuss cases of estate auctions.[80] Some women felt their marginal status confirmed by estate auctions. Others gleefully embraced the freedom offered by cash sales. One widow, Johannah Baker, stubbornly refused to give her adult daughter a portion of her dead father's estate, claiming she would "sell at Public Vendue every thing that belongs to the said Estate and will Convert the money from thence arising to her own use," rendering no account to anyone.[81] The proceeds from her husband's vendue turned a past life as a wife into a future of new possibilities.

The phenomenon of widows bidding at their husbands' estate auctions reveals one way that price setting and the distribution of property embedded an understanding of gender. Under South Carolina law, a widow had dower rights in real estate, which meant that a portion would be secured to her first, before her husband's estate was settled with his creditors. But these protections did not extend to personal property, including the furniture she sat on every day, the dishes she ate from, or the tools she used in her garden. All of those were appraised and liquidated for the benefit of creditors. Sarah Baker used the mechanism of the estate sale to secure her own title to her goods.[82] The fix was in and the neighbors approved because they did not interpret these practices as fraud and deceit but rather as a part of the community passing judgment on the value of the Bakers' material life.

Perhaps Sarah Baker hoped that her neighbors would take the further step of ensuring that she receive a price break as she bid against them to reconstruct her household. It appears that was not to be, as her recorded bid prices closely matched the appraisal prices of the items from the estate, likely because price remained a social relation tied to a functional role. She did manage to restore to herself all the beds and most of the household furniture, wearing apparel, and plain dishware. She also bid on a number of lots that may have become inventory in a new business: six-and-a-half-dozen chamber pots, forty bottles of oil of turpentine, and seventeen pounds of cocoa. She did not get most of the high-value items: slaves, firearms, boats, or the bulk fabric and trimmings, and she may never have bid on them.[83] The property she secured, at prices near the assessed value, closely aligned with expectations about free women and property.[84] It was not unusual for neighbors and the law in the eighteenth century to pass judgment on the appropriate ownership of household goods. Published elopement notices in the newspapers and the common-law "doctrine of necessaries" both demonstrate that the community took part in judging which purchases were "reasonable and prudent" for a wife of a particular rank to make and allowed her the latitude to acquire them.[85]

Estate auctions were an important piece of a larger legal and economic culture that determined who could buy what and at which prices. Each document produced in settling an estate—will, inventory, account, report of sale profits—linked pieces of property to prices and, in so doing, probed the value of a deceased person's material life. The participation of the same individuals as appraisers and bidders, as well as the appearance of the same bidders at multiple sales, ensured a kind of community feedback loop concerning price and value in all its meanings.

And still the work was not done. After the appraisal, after the bidding, came collection. Estate auctions were designed to have the benefit of quick liquidation, but sellers could end up re-creating the debt relationships they were trying to resolve through the sale. As always, the social context of debt emerged in the work that prices did to maintain hierarchies. Grey Elliott was clearly frustrated in June 1768 when, ten months after the estate auction of John Perkins's human and household property, so many purchasers had not paid. The conditions of this sale had allowed those purchasing goods for over £8 to tender a bond, to be discharged after six months; the smaller purchasers had paid in cash.[86] Yet "little if any notice" had been taken of his previous newspaper announcements requiring these individuals to make their payments, and he was compelled "to sue every person whose debt shall be unpaid" in order to settle with all of Perkins's creditors, bringing the prices resolved at the initial auction back under the oversight of the courts.[87]

Because they drew on the collective judgment of buyers, sellers, and spectators within the same community, local auctions frequently revealed unpleasant truths about the relationship between value and price. Nowhere was this more evident than in estate auctions, where the emotional value of goods had the greatest potential to cause a rift between buyers and sellers.[88] Sellers, usually related to the deceased, came to an auction with ideas about the value of goods that were based on past experience and emotional attachments as well as concrete plans for the money to be earned. Buyers were in the market for bargains, though they might be swayed by a good story or the reflected glory of the collection as a whole. Neither saw emotional value as illegitimate to determining price, but each factored that connection differently. In Charleston, South Carolina, Margaret Manigault's friend stopped by in late November 1792 to see if she

"wanted anything at the sale of Mrs. Blake's furniture." Their circle of acquaintances was deeply interested in Blake's estate auction, which they believed would
sell off large quantities of silver plate owing to a mistake in her will, and so they
tracked the quantities and markings on the spoons, baskets, and other elegant
tableware. Mrs. Blake's four dozen "beautiful" English teaspoons were an especially poignant collection in the sale. Purchased only the year before and barely
enjoyed, they were engraved "EB" and, her friends lamented that they would not
fetch the price they deserved.[89] The women had a shared sense that used spoons
sold cheaply would fail what they took to be the social and economic goals of the
sale—cementing their friend's legacy and bolstering the family's funds.

Disciplining Prices

On their own, prices could not accomplish all the conflicting social and cultural goals that some hoped they would. Prices alone did not make some items
accessible and keep some out of reach. "Fair" prices could not keep a family from
needing charitable support. "Bargain" prices did not level social distinctions
through shared material culture. Some thought prices were the natural result
of competition, but the auctioneer business revealed the many ways that prices,
their moral meanings, and their function in distribution could be controlled. In
this way auctioneers departed from other retailers, who rarely discussed specific
prices in their advertisements and instead developed a commercial vocabulary
to engage potential customers in the art of valuing goods through the lens of
consumer choice.

   Auction advertisements trained consumers with specific directions for how
to participate in a sale. For thirty years starting in 1741, John Gerrish advertised
his services as an auctioneer in Boston, and his business reflected the ways that
auctioneers disciplined consumption. He started out with an evening vendue
sale of imported fabrics, used clothing, and furniture in the home of a Boston
tobacconist. By 1758 he was ready "to fix himself down (or set himself up) in
the known Character of Auctioneer, or Vendue Master, so long as he shall be
able with Spirit to do such Business."[90] Over the next two decades, he expanded,
rented new spaces for an "auction room," took on partners, and engaged in targeted advertising to British clients, country traders, and anyone with goods "to
dispose of."[91] His increasing specialization in the types of goods he sold and his
elaboration of services paralleled similar advertisements placed by auctioneers
in other cities. Auctioneers frequently added brokerage or commission agent

services to their work, selling goods for others in public or private sales. None, however, reached the level of specialization or renown of the premier London auction houses Sotheby's, founded in 1744, and Christie's, founded in 1766, which specialized in books and art, respectively.[92]

Gerrish drew attention to what he called the "Character of Auctioneer," and in one sense, this was the character of a collector, selecting and grouping consumer goods, livestock, and human beings. Scholars recognize auctions as "social processes for resolving definitional ambiguities" about the price, ownership, and distribution of goods.[93] Yet auctions and auctioneers also played a key role in establishing those definitions, analogous to that of specimen collectors in the early modern period. Collecting was an essential practice to the development of modern science. The "cabinet of curiosities," an extensive collection of objects from the natural world placed in a room or closet, came to define scientific categories of classification and analysis. Auction lots served a similar function, by creating categories of goods and legitimizing the auctioneer as an expert by virtue of collection. Both early modern science and business benefited from record-keeping strategies that deployed empirical observation, evaluation, and categorization.[94] These practices further shaped what would be included in and what would be excluded from authoritative scientific and economic knowledge.

Collecting culture and successful sales both relied on strategies of display, including physical arrangement of items and mediated access to those arrangements.[95] Early modern collectors led colleagues and guests to their cabinets of curiosities to look and learn. Some created traveling exhibits and charged a small fee.[96] Auctioneers used the practice of preview, in which they directed potential customers to view goods at one location before bidding on them at another. Anyone eager to purchase calicoes or earthenware from the Boston merchant Nicholas Roberts's auction needed to mind the clock, as they could only inspect them "from the hours of 8 in the Morning, till Twelve; and from One till Four in the Afternoon" prior to the sale.[97] They also needed to know their city because, although the sale was scheduled for the Sign of the Star tavern, to inspect the goods they had to locate Roberts's warehouse on King Street. The practice of preview placed time and distance between looking at goods, considering the purchase, and calling out a price in a commitment to buy at a time when most sellers lacked the luxury of space or time in presenting their wares to customers. Instead, door-to-door peddling, shops squeezed into residences, and wharves and warehouses dominated retailing in towns; trading posts, factors' stores, and riverbanks were sites of exchange outside of town centers. Any kind of display was frequently mobile, individual, and highly variable, as even shopkeepers with dedicated rooms for their goods typically pulled items out from shelves crowded with an assortment of disparate objects to show to customers and then had to pack them away again.[98]

Early modern collectors imbued objects with meaning by classifying and grouping them in ways designed to tell a story about foreign cultures, civilization, or human worth. The inventory of a collection could list an "African charm," a rhinoceros horn, an "Indian canoe." The collector then connected these items through stories and guided movement from one object to another, exhibiting an intellectual and social power over participants and the knowledge that could be abstracted from the collection and used to make sense of other information.[99] A collector's classifications, over time, fed connoisseurship and scientific knowledge. An auctioneer, in contrast, collected and distributed items in quick succession; holding the collection together for too long signified a business failure (see Figure 6).

Auctioneers told implicit stories on behalf of their employers, creating a temporary order so as to recover the value of diverse goods. Confronted with a commission of bulk goods, auctioneers created smaller groupings for bidders interested in smaller quantities. These lots, defined by the auctioneer, were supposed to consist of goods similar in type or quality. Sarah Kemble Knight went to an auction in early eighteenth-century New York to buy fine Dutch paper. She noted in her diary that she "bought about 100 Rheem of paper wch was retaken in a fly-boat from Holland and sold very reasonably here—some ten, some Eight shillings per Rheem by the Lot wch was ten Rheem in a Lott."[100] John Gerrish, the long-standing Boston auctioneer, had more variable goods to sell, so he created lots by his own sense of their appeal. At the auction on November 29, 1763, Lot Number One contained "Silver and other curious watches," all warranted by a third-party business partnership. Lot Number Five was all kinds of hair—human and horse, grizzled and brown—along with silk cawls to dress wigs. Lot Four was men's hats; Lot Seven was women's shoes.[101]

Gerrish's lots responded to and reinforced nascent specialization among traders in Boston. Knowing many of his customers were the small business-people who depended on auctions for their stock, he subdivided his goods to target, and thereby draw boundaries around, specific kinds of businesses: the wigmaker, the dealer in women's shoes. Other auctioneers engaged in the same kind of market segmentation by dedicating specific days of the week to sales of particular types of goods. People who frequented the New Auction-Room on Royal Exchange Lane, Boston, knew that on Mondays and Fridays they could

Figure 6. This satirical English engraving pokes fun at the group of wealthy bidders at an art auction, who do not seem to notice that the picture (a windmill, referencing Dutch art) is held upside down. The sale takes precedence over the cultivation of expertise on the part of buyers. "The Auction; or Modern Conoisseurs" (graphic). England: s.n. ca. 1770. Library of Congress.

bid on English imports in the context of other English imports. On Wednesdays only those with an interest in books, paper, and cutlery need attend.[102] This method of dedicated days did not rule out opportunities to attend multiple days of the week, but it permitted and rewarded customer focus and self-selection.

The Charleston educator Hugh Anderson complained that selling in lots made no sense when it came to books. He wrote to the *South Carolina Gazette* in 1748 that "the present Method of disposing of Libraries of deceased Persons, or of those departing this Province, or others, by exposing them to Sale at public Vendue, in Lots or Parcels not sorted or entered in Catalogue, is liable to many Losses and Inconveniencies both to Buyer and Seller (since any Person who may incline to purchase a single or few Books, must take the whole Parcel of different Languages, Subjects, and perhaps odd Volumes for which he has no Occasion)."[103] He proposed instead to collect and store libraries, selling off individual books at private sales but waiting until "a sufficient Number is lodged in the Subscriber's Hands" before auctioning them in a "proper House in Charles-Town separately, by the Rules of *Auction* practiced at *London* (the Time, Place, and Quality of books being previously advertised in the *Gazette*)." Anderson called for better recordkeeping but also informed judgment on the part of auctioneers rather than a desire to group and sell quickly through lots.

Anderson was correct that the size of a lot mattered. Philadelphia's Mary Coates depended on lots that broke up a large volume of imports into smaller sets. But lots that were too small competed head-to-head with small retailers. South Carolina's 1750 law "for the Security, Health, and Convenience" of Charles Town insisted that auctioning small lots created unfair competition for local retailers. Lawmakers therefore required all auctions to sell in larger quantities—no cloth in smaller quantities than "by the Piece," no beer or liquor in quantities less than a barrel."[104] In the middle of the Revolutionary War, the opposite logic prevailed. Legislators deemed it a "great evil" that the prevailing practice was "of setting up to sale large quantities of goods, wares and merchandizes . . . and persons who are desirous of buying merely for the use of their families, are thereby prevented."[105] They decreed that it was now unlawful for anyone to create a single lot with "more than one piece of any sort of woollen, cotton or linen cloth, or more than one dozen of such other kinds of goods . . . as are usually put up or sold by the dozen."[106]

As a social venture, an auction in eighteenth-century British North America needed consumers from local communities for legitimacy as well as for sales. After dividing up items into lots, auctioneers advanced norms of commercial behavior in creating a market by instructing bidders where and when to gather. Buyers planning to attend the sale at Nathaniel Wheelwright's wharf, for instance, were told to "be at the Place of Sale a little before 10 o'Clock, so that the Sale may begin exactly at TEN."[107] Even Giles Alexander, forced to discharge his debts from within his cell at the Boston jail, patiently explained to those interested in bidding on his "7000 acres of Land in two Townships" that the auction would begin, in jail, at 9 o'clock in the morning and "to continue till all is sold for the most it will fetch."[108] Bringing together bidders at a single time and place sometimes required multiple tries. A scheduled sale of the cargo seized from the ship *Escarboucle* in 1757 was postponed when the auctioneer decided that a week's advance notice was "too short for those Gentlemen that live at any Distance to give their Attendance."[109] A Boston vendue master held most sales in the evening but promised to "oblige all Customers that cannot attend public Sales of Evenings. . . . When there is a large Assortment of Goods sent in for PUBLIC SALE, it will be held in the Day Time."[110] John Chaloner in

Philadelphia promised that a stage wagon stood at the ready to transport people out to his auction at Elijah Weed's ferry, for 6 pence a person.[111]

Assembled as a market, spectators played their part as referees of a sale. In the eyes of the law, the presence of even nonbidding audience members at an auction was understood to be a measure of the community's tacit agreement to the economic transactions on the stage. Lawyers defending a sale against charges of fraud pointed to spectators—who might not bid but did not object to a given sale—as witnesses, proof that a sale was congruent with the community's understanding of the law and economy.[112] The spectators had, by this reasoning, made a price acceptable by assembling at the sale. Such "witnessing" was a key form of public participation in the eighteenth century. In a courtroom, for example, spectators gave legitimacy to decisions made by juries; by recognizing the jury, those who watched but did not speak conveyed power. In the same way, witnessing the execution of a court judgment, which would include public sales by law, was a significant source of the public's collective authority.[113]

Public authority was only as reliable as public judgment, however, and the legitimacy of auctions and their prices was challenged when a sale was linked to immoral actors or spectators. The Presbyterian minister Archibald Simpson, attending the South Carolina auction of a murdered man's clothing, books, and horse, despaired when one of the alleged killers himself appeared among the bidders. The murderer took hold of the auctioned property, "held up the clothes pierced in many places with bullets & other shot," and poking his fingers through the holes, declared "see what the Rats had done"![114] The assembled bidders, grumbled Simpson, "were a set of the greatest ragamuffins," drinking and cursing, and so evidently not shocked by this winking nod to crime in the evaluation of mutilated clothing. To ensure a more serious public, another auctioneer required potential bidders under the age of twenty-one to purchase tickets, to be credited against future sale. Gentlemen's sons were exempted from the rule, because he believed they were serious or at least had fathers who would cover their children's bids.[115] In other situations, ticket systems determined who had the right to constitute the public at a public sale.

Catalogs and other forms of print culture extended the experience of attending an auction, creating norms of commercial behavior and spreading the idea that value and price were linked in particular ways. Like estate inventories, auction catalogs contained terse descriptions that reduced a wide range of factors that might influence the meaning or value of a piece of property to a few words.[116] Sharing a commercial vocabulary, these documents reinforced a specific commodified view of the objects they listed. As preview catalogs circulated around cities and into the countryside to entice out-of-town buyers, they disseminated an increasingly abstract view of property and commercial goods.

Over the course of the eighteenth century, American colonists, like their British counterparts, used forms of print to separate economic culture into "fact" (represented in shipping lists, estate accounts, and paper money) and "fiction" (represented in novels) in representing value. As prices themselves became facts, reducing the many ways of valuing an object to a single number, money became naturalized, "like an instrument instead of something that was made to be used, in some ways and not in others, as part of institutional practices."[117] A sum of money—a price—increasingly became the self-evident way to talk about value.

Retailers' account books, which record a terse description and a price for each transaction, appear to reinforce the idea that prices operated as facts in North American port cities by the eighteenth century. In May 1743 Mordecai Dunbar sold Abigail Pinnegar a pair of shoe buckles for ten shillings in his Newport shop. Two years later, he sold her a pair for twelve shillings. There is no description in his accounts explaining either number or how those particular sums became attached to those particular buckles.[118] Why would Pinnegar accept the difference in price? Part of the answer could be in the details of the buckles themselves, their materials, or their decoration; another could be the broader market, as perhaps shoe buckles were scarcer in 1745 Newport than they had been two years before.

Such reasoning about prices resulted from a historical process informed by auctions. Auctions, which were fundamentally social, ultimately helped construct an understanding of prices as testable against fixed principles. The price at the end of the bidding determined, in that moment at least, the value of the object. In the middle of the eighteenth century, that development in thinking about prices was partial and incomplete, as people discussed "auction bargains" that were relational rather than absolute. Seemingly factual genres, like inventories or catalogs, included lists of numbers that were speculative and subject to manipulation by the auctioneer's tactics on the one hand and local judgments on the other. Any effort to discipline prices was liable to crumble.

*   *   *

The idea that community norms define proper market rules and practices was the heart of the early modern moral economy. Regulated marketplaces drew on customary legal expectations by policing weights and measures, limiting acceptable profits, and restricting exchange to particular days and times.[119] The expansion of auctions in the eighteenth century in part reflected the enduring appeal of a regulated economy, where the state set the rules of exchange to better serve the public good.[120] Auctioneers had to obtain licenses, keep careful records and report sales, and mark their transactions publicly. Fixed auction sale days were set apart from private sale times. John Lawrence in Providence, Rhode Island, even hung a flag out in front of his building when an auction was taking place.[121]

While auction processes were regulated, its prices were not. The goal of the auction was to find the price and therefore determine the value, resolving ambiguities about ownership, proper allocation of property, utility, and desirability in a way that was acceptable to the wider community that attended this singular event. As the regulations, the critics, and the disappointed spectators testified, auctions were a dynamic process, not a static ritual performed under customary rules. Over the course of the eighteenth century, more goods entered people's lives and buyers and sellers became more mobile, making the value of goods and their rightful ownership matters of contention and dispute. Auctions took on a prominent role in local economies by providing a forum for bidders to weigh relative values in the context of their experiences, expectations, and beliefs and then tie that accumulation of knowledge to a number.[122]

Every discussion of auction bargains, whether chastising or celebratory, took for granted the idea that potential buyers had a sense of what prices *should* be. But such a sense first had to become seen as a worthwhile skill and then had to be cultivated. Buyers could identify bargains only by comparing prices to what they imagined, had seen before, or expected. They patched information together through conversations and experiences; misinformation circulated easily. Local exchanges still involved barter, in which people determined the equivalent value of thimbles or wheat or midwifery services in moments between individuals and did not use the mechanism of price to mark the equivalence.[123] Local eighteenth-century auctions, by repeatedly and publicly determining value, helped push participants to expect a deal, in the form of a price.

Complaints about auctions often tagged them as schemes of outsiders who had no knowledge of or stake in the local community and who aimed to swindle the neighbors. But the truth was that complaints about eighteenth-century auctions were also complaints about neighbors. It was their poor judgment that led to unduly low prices. It was their greed and laziness that allowed auctions to undersell the local merchants and shopkeepers. The economist Nancy Folbre notes: "Markets require not merely the rule of law and regulation of the state, but also the economic infrastructure of families and communities."[124] Auctions were explicitly designed to draw a community together to act on shared value judgment, and the markets that arose had such judgments embedded within them.[125] When communities fractured over political conflict, those judgments splintered. The role of price as a signal of relationships took on a new patriotic urgency.

CHAPTER 3

Loyalist Property and the Price of Suffering

William Nichols was a prosperous merchant in Watertown, Connecticut, in the early 1770s. But as the conflict between Britain and its thirteen North American colonies escalated, he refused to sign a nonimportation pledge enforced by the Patriot Association, and in that act, his whole family became a target of rebel neighbors. According to a missionary's sympathetic testimony at the end of the war, he was "frequently insulted and abused by the mob," beaten with clubs, "thrust into the Stocks," and had his house broken up because he refused to reject British imports flowing into warehouses and vendue stalls.[1] In fear, he fled to British-occupied New York, followed by his wife, Sarah, and their children. In 1779 the County Court determined that as a man who joined the "enemies of the United States of America," his estate was forfeited and to be auctioned off.[2] William Nichols died at the end of the war, but Sarah and the young children went in exile to Nova Scotia, where they lived in poverty, hoping that the British government would repay them for the losses and suffering their loyalism had brought them.

How to value that suffering? Although testimony about Nichols's mistreatment at the hands of the rebels was certainly compelling, the Loyalist Claims Commission—created in London in 1783 to evaluate and compensate the losses of loyalists—was most interested in the value of his land and personal property. The British government's approach to loyalist suffering required evidence of a particular kind: lists of property linked to prices. Sarah Nichols therefore submitted several appraisals of her property when she made her claim to the commission. The first inventory and appraisal took place on December 11, 1776, before the Justices of the Peace in Connecticut, for £654.17.11 sterling. Another, compiled by memory in Nova Scotia in January 1784 and sworn to by Thomas Osborn and Ezekiel Welton, fellow exiles living in Nova Scotia, was for £1,673.4.5

New York money. Additional appraisals and a copy of the probate court's 1779 judgment forfeiting Nichols's real estate, valued at £481 Lawful Money, soon followed. Sarah also had a deed for the homestead—110 acres with a house and barn—that indicated the purchase price of £650, although, she noted, "her late Husband made very Considerable Improvements."[3]

Prices on inventory lists needed contextualization, and for this, participants called on familiar colonial economies of knowledge. To supplement the diverse written records, Sarah marshaled the testimony of former neighbors now living in Nova Scotia.[4] Welton, who had grown up a quarter of a mile away, asserted that "for many years [he] was almost daily in the House of the said William Nichols; and consequently, had almost a perfect knowledge of his personal Estate." He commented that several items on the list had been undervalued, noting that because Nichols had been a merchant, he "consequently had an opportunity of procuring those articles cheaper and of a better Quality than his neighbors." In Welton's judgment, the sale price on the land deed had also been undervalued. The original owner had owed Nichols money on book account, and Nichols deducted this from the price; in addition, he had paid off some of the seller's other creditors. The land, in other words, had circulated in the local economies of long-standing credit chains. For a comparison, Welton noted, lots adjacent to this property had sold, prior to the war, for $6–$7 per acre.[5] Welton was not an impartial party—he had married the widow Sarah and lived with her in Nova Scotia—but the measures he described of valuing property lost to the vagaries of war and politics were common among exiled loyalists as they struggled to fit the chaotic experience of war and plunder into the legal frameworks of diplomacy and property law.

Joseph Munn, the "negro man" priced at £60 in Sarah Nichols's assessments, likewise challenged the account of value lost and suffering endured. Although Sarah Nichols claimed that he had been "taken by the Rebels and put into the American Service,"[6] Munn told a different tale: that William Nichols, "with intent to elude the Law," just before escaping to New York, sold Munn to Timothy Hickox as a slave, even though Munn had already joined the American forces and continued to serve in the Continental Army during the war.[7] Sarah Nichols tried to quantify her suffering, but the dispersal of human, landed, and personal property as well as the fluctuations in money systems made this calculation extremely difficult.

Every one of the rebelling states during the American Revolution passed laws to confiscate and then sell at public auction the property of some group of loyalists; scholars have debated the mix of motivations—revenge, revenue, social ambition—that drove them to take these measures.[8] In 1776—in his first install-ment of *The American Crisis*—Thomas Paine wagered that "America could carry on a two years' war by the confiscation of the property of disaffected persons, and be made happy by their expulsion. Say not that this is revenge, call it rather the soft resentment of a suffering people."[9] Part of Paine's proposal was prag-matic—that seizure and auction of loyalist property was a potential solution to the problem of funding a revolutionary war. But Paine also offered a broader context that suggests another way that auctions of loyalist property functioned in revolutionary politics. Paine envisioned the American public as a body linked across social classes in the shared emotional expressions of "soft resentment" and "suffering." By disavowing an older and cruder motivation of revenge, Paine cast property seizure as a cathartic experience for a beleaguered population.[10]

A powerful tool of political rhetoric, suffering was also a daily experience for the men and women caught in a long military conflict, whether due to their political alliances, like the Nichols family; their unfree status, like Munn; or their misfortune in bearing the hunger, violence, and exile of war. North Amer-icans' suffering was physical, cultural, and economic. Recognizing this, Paine highlighted the double nature of seizure and sale, in that they served both the financial and emotional needs of rebelling Americans; in fact, the auction linked those needs. Wartime measures weaponized the open participation that embed-ded public sales in local community economic knowledge.

In this way, auctions of loyalist property inflicted and also rewarded suf-fering, translating loss into recompense. They were a public exercise in alchemy, transforming the wealth of traitors into an investment in the United States. For this alchemy to take place, property had to be stripped of its previous social and cultural meanings and rendered a priceable good. Auctions had long been a tool for this kind of work, clearing title and engaging in price discovery, as communities determined fair rules of exchange and property distribution. Colo-nial governments had used them to punish people who failed to pay taxes, keep their livestock in order, attend militia musters, or confine oystering to the proper season.[11] Patriots depended on these features of publicity and collective partic-ipation to reinforce their claims to legitimate government worthy of patriot sacrifices. They also depended on the social and emotional experience of an indi-vidual farmer bidding on a loyalist neighbor's sheep to redeem some of his suf-fering as the war dragged on.[12]

If emotion stirred patriots' words, consumption focused their actions, from the sacrificing renunciation of import boycotts to the theatrical dumping of tea and spinning of homespun.[13] In these well-studied protests, imports that had bound together the British Empire took on new political meanings as it broke apart. Crowds destroyed or refused goods that were products of British imperial trade. Auctions, however, were consumer acts that dealt in goods that already had owners, meanings, and histories. Sarah Nichols's eight pewter plates and large brass kettle were not fashionable imports but sturdy implements of every-day life, likely passed through several generations.[14] The crowd did not destroy the kettle or refuse to use the plates; rather a committee put one price on them, and a bidding crowd confirmed or revised that value in the process of redistrib-uting them. The auction's reconfiguration of meaning around goods, humans, and land that people already owned engaged the deeper structures of consumer culture in a revolutionary age, including the legal supports of ownership, the meanings of prices, and the emotional qualities of material culture. They were a haltingly national exercise in the politics linking value and values.

The Logics of Seized Property

The public sale of loyalist property existed in a larger wartime context of all kinds of appropriation, evaluation, and redistribution of goods. Armies pur-chased supplies from home-front farms. Officers wrote out thousands of "certifi-cates of indebtedness" in receipts for goods taken to support the army, including food, lumber, and livestock. By linking objects and prices, each receipt expressed a judgment about the value of the item taken as well as, potentially, the relative power of the individual who gave and the army that took.

Existing economic culture and legal structures around property provided ways to make those judgments. Connecticut used the familiar tool of estate administration—a committee of three impartial men—to assess the value of citi-zens' contributions to the war effort. In 1780 Comptroller A. C. P. Moses Seymour of Connecticut employed Thomas Catlin, Hebor Stone, and Jacob Baker to travel the state appraising cattle for the use of the fighting force. Based on these men's assessments of individual animals, David Norton received £26.8.0 for contributing two "fat cattle" weighing 1,100 pounds each to the war effort, and Ephraim Baites received £38.8 for 3 fat cattle weighing 1,600 pounds each.[15] The owners received receipts, the army got the animals, and Seymour recorded the transactions for when Norton and Baites came to the comptroller to claim their due.

Prizes taken at sea also outfitted the war effort, and captains and crew on privateers had their own procedures for converting an enemy ship into sets of salable items. Francis Lewis, a New York delegate to the Continental Congress, had to explain to his peers that these seizures followed a different logic of valuing and ownership than the negotiations between a farmer and a militia officer over cattle. He could not do as Congress directed and appraise and purchase woolens and linens captured as prizes by the armed sloop *Montgomery* to clothe George Washington's army. First, the *Montgomery*'s captain and crew "insisted upon having their property disposed of in the customary manner, at a public vendue."[16] Second, the four New Yorkers appointed to appraise the goods "declared themselves inadequate to the appointment, being totally unacquainted with the value of those goods." Instead, the appraisers and the crew arrived at a shared agreement "that all should be sold at auction, except the woolens and course linens, which the Congress were to take at the rate of a dollar currency." The auctioned goods, Lewis noted, sold at "about one thousand per cent" what they had cost, all to the benefit of those who had taken the risk of serving as privateers.[17]

Into this familiar set of wartime transactions came a new species of property: the farms and household goods of loyalists, which patriot militias saw as the spoils of war. As early as February 1777, Brigadier-General George Clinton's militia had begun taking "sundry effects" from "disaffected persons."[18] New York's Committee of Safety had to decide what to do with these effects—were these in fact spoils, belonging to those who captured them, or were they supplies to be managed by the political entities funding the war? While troops desperately needed supplies, in principle, armies should not plunder. Wartime violence theoretically followed certain rules, and legal and customary restraints provided a framework for revolutionary acts.[19] The North Carolina Presbyterian minister Samuel McCorkle preached that food could be taken from enemies as legitimate military supplies, but the seizure of furniture or enslaved people was a crime, signaling the breakdown of military discipline.[20] Following a parallel logic that made distinctions among types of goods, New York's Committee of Safety divided the "sundry effects" seized by Clinton into categories. They ordered the medicines appraised and stored, the steel and old guns appraised and sent to the armory, the grain and livestock sold to the Continental Army commissary, the backgammon table destroyed, and most of the other goods sold at public auction, with the proceeds sent to the treasurer.[21] Appraisals and auctions were the tools used to mark cultural differences among seized goods.

Early ad hoc militia seizures set a pattern for more systematic action to follow. In February 1777, New York's provincial convention passed a resolution formalizing the confiscation and auction (after ten days' notice) of personal property of all persons "gone over to the enemy."[22] Committees of safety in other states passed similar resolutions, empowering commissioners to seize and sell the personal property of anyone who aided or joined the British, in some states without a trial.[23] Confiscation was a legal process; wartime plunder was not, yet an auction proved a flexible tool that bridged the two.

Colonial property law had evolved to treat real estate as a particular species of property and so, too, did Revolution-era polities, beginning with the sequestering of real estate. Both patriot and British occupying forces used the tactic of seizing and holding on to the real estate of political enemies, following an English tradition of land seizures that punished Jacobite rebels who had challenged the English throne earlier in the eighteenth century.[24] In April 1777, when the Continental Congress received a report about loyalist activity in Delaware and Maryland, John Hancock urged Congress to direct lawmakers in these states to arrest and isolate "all persons of influence, or of desperate characters" who have acted against the "American cause" and appoint county commissioners to inventory and take charge of their estates, using rents on their land to pay for the imprisoned loyalists' upkeep.[25] States passed series of laws to seize and sequester the property of "absentees" who had left the colony in the face of intense political pressure or "enemies," including loyalist government and military officials actively conducting the war against the rebelling states.

During the war, state legislatures went beyond sequestration and ordered the confiscation and sale at auction of estates, through laws that defined the previous owners as belonging to political categories deserving of property loss. Some laws singled out individuals by name for trial. Others named specific "traitors" and placed their estates under attainder, for seizure without trial. Some targeted groups of "absentee" landowners for taxation, followed by forfeiture and seizure if the taxes were not paid. The combination of tactics in a single state could be extensive: after the war, when a New York loyalist reprinted the multiple statutes from his home state in *Laws Against the Loyalists*, his publication ran over 150 pages.[26]

The legal approaches to identifying enemies and their property employed terms both legal and cultural to mark political boundaries: targets were "absentees," "non-resident proprietors," "traitors," "conspirators."[27] Massachusetts first froze the property titles of "refugees," then sequestered vacant lots of "absconders."[28] Each term had legal meanings that justified dispossession of property. The state's first confiscation act targeted "notorious conspirators" by name, the "notorious" providing legal cover for seizures without due process.[29] But these were also cultural terms. Legally "absentees" resided elsewhere in the empire, deriving wealth from their colonial property. South Carolina's confiscation act, passed in 1782, named 232 loyalists for property confiscation and banishment, a quarter of whom were British merchants and landowners who did not live in South Carolina.[30] Culturally, those deemed "absentees" were cast out for failing to affiliate with local communities and prorevolutionary political sentiments. The act specified that out of the money collected, "eight hundred soldiers are to be raised, to fill our continental line," explicitly tying the sale of property to future public purchases.[31]

As patriot communities consolidated over the processes of seizing and selling, some tried to manipulate the connection between the cultural value of political loyalty and the monetary value of personal goods, bringing the state in to ratify personal animosities that played out over property during the war. Thomas Rowlee Jr. of Bennington, Vermont, reported that Austin Selye "was a Tory & when he Stole my Gun, Coat & Hankerchief I immediately Seized his Cattle and Drove them to one of the Commissioners of Sequestration for this State, which have Been Sold for the Use of the Same." Rowlee billed the commission for the value of his lost goods, brandy, breakfast for nine men (who helped with the cattle), and pasturage.[32] By placing the property he lost and the property he took in the context of a righteous war, he claimed a value for his gun, coat, and handkerchief as down payments on political loyalty.

Austin Selye lost his cattle suddenly, when his neighbor accused him of being a Tory, but other personal animosities burned slowly and methodically. Grace Growden Galloway, whose husband Joseph had left for British lines with their daughter, received updates from visiting neighbors on the capture of Philadelphia loyalist property and sought out legal advice on her own account. When agents finally came to take an inventory of her household goods "even to broken China & empty bottles," she met them with defiance, stating that "they may do as they pleased but till it was decided by a Court I wou'd not go out Unless by ye force of a bayonet."[33] The council told her that as long as her husband was alive, her real estate could be seized under his attainder, though "support for the wife and children shall be awarded by the Judges of the Supreme Court."[34] That news was little comfort, and soon another group of men came to complete the appraisal, followed by an official who bashed in her kitchen door with a scrubbing brush and forcibly escorted her out with only two bonnets and her workbag.[35] It would be decades before the courts acknowledged that the property Galloway had inherited from her father could in fact not be seized for her husband's actions—too late for her. When the final decision came down, Galloway was dead.[36]

Officious or apologetic in the face of outraged loyalists, commissioners had leeway in deciding which property to take and sell. They used judgments about wealth and gender to aid their valuation and swing the local balance of power.

Ebenezer Hoisington went to Watts Hubbard's house in July 1777 and took "a quantity of" salt, sugar, barley, rye, and boards as well as other grain and some animals but did not record taking furniture or housewares, which he presumably left for the use of Hubbard family members, who were among the original town deedholders.[37] Sometimes multiple commissioners took several days and several trips to confiscate the property: a pair of oxen one month, a horse and saddle two months later.

Loyalists, in turn, tried to stay a step ahead of the commissioners and sold or loaned their property out to friends who were less politically suspect and who could be counted on to challenge confiscation. Just as colonists had developed ways to dodge the sheriff's auction, loyalists used the manipulations of property law and possession to maintain their capital. In Vermont, Captain Leonard Spaulding spent more than a year tracking down the estate and goods of Timothy Lovels, who had disbursed his sheep and blacksmithing tools to others as well as leasing some of his lands before fleeing to the British. Some of the recipients of Lovels's scheme paid Spaulding off immediately in order to keep the leases, some denied that the goods belonged to Lovels, some demanded a court order before they complied with the commission.[38] As a former New York judge Duncan Ludlow commented after the war, "Such was the irregularity during the first periods of the War on taking possession of a Loyalist's Estate," that any individual loyalist's postwar inventory could not "be taken for evidence of the whole stock and furniture."[39]

Sometimes, the commissioners arrived too late to control the chain of seizure, identification, transport, and storage that they used to link material value to political power. Susannah Martin, whose loyalist husband was on the run, auctioned off her own property to raise the money to join her husband in exile rather than allow it to be seized and auctioned off by the new patriot government.[40] In the fall of 1778, John Lacey Jr. and George Walls Jr. came to Bucks County under the Pennsylvania Council's orders to inventory and appraise the goods and chattel of Joseph Galloway, only to discover that "after Mrs. Galloway was moved to Philadelphia last Winter, the people from Bristol & Burlington, came and took away what was left—which we are told, they Sold at public sale— and divided the money."[41] In other words, local communities could hold their own auctions to redistribute goods, to punish loyalists, and to reward patriots.

The crowd in Bucks County deployed seizure and auction in a way that echoed the revolutionary food rioters who seized rum, sugar, molasses, salt, and tea from storekeepers and sold them for what they deemed "reasonable" prices, in defiance of merchants who hoped to charge more for scarce goods in wartime.[42] Both types of crowds used ideas about ethical economic transactions to frame their politics. The food rioters drew on long-standing community ideas about fair exchange. The Galloway neighbors linked what they saw as treasonous politics to forfeiture and orderly redistribution among a law-abiding public. While looting and destruction could be condemned as illegal violence, the neighbors' auction of Galloway property linked the crowd action to state-sanctioned patriot politics. The public nature of auction sales as well as their tradition of dividing and redistributing collections of goods lent a degree of political legitimacy to what the Galloways saw as blatant theft.

The public auction ran parallel to other revolutionary crowd traditions, including the looting of wealthy, politically powerful men's homes. The Stamp Act protests of 1765 had encompassed both the public theater of broad daylight and the late-night destruction of houses, including that of Lieutenant Governor Thomas Hutchinson of Massachusetts. Outraged political opponents in Boston had blamed the "Frenzy of Anarchy" unleashed by mobs that were easily manipulated into destruction, an interpretation echoed in the report from the Galloways' Pennsylvania country house thirteen years later.[43] Yes, there had been an auction, on terms set by the neighbors. But as the foiled patriot appraisers reported: "The Mantion House they have—Wickedly abused—broke Window-Sashes, and Glasses—striped the Inside of everything that was loose."[44] An auction preserved some structures of private property and therefore political legitimacy, in that seized goods were sold, but abuse of property was considered senseless.

As commissioners soon discovered, most property owned by accused loyalists was itself tangled up in webs of community indebtedness that greatly complicated the translation of enemy property into patriot reimbursement. When Mary Adams of Pittsburg, Pennsylvania heard that Alexander Ross had been declared a traitor and his property was subject to confiscation, she promptly delivered a cache of Ross's accounts and papers, stored by her late husband, to the commissioners. Expecting a payment for her participation, she heard nothing. In 1784, once again, she petitioned the Supreme Executive Council of Pennsylvania: "This business has been conducted in a dark mysterious and confused manner in passing through the Hands of several agents."[45] Seven years later, she was still keeping watch over the final settlements of confiscated estates in her neighborhood, which were delayed, she suggested, because "some of the Commissrs. Appointed were indebted" to one of the estates "and therefore I apprehend were careless about bringing it to a close."[46] Part of the evolving law around loyalist seizures concerned property on which creditors had a claim that could not be easily detached from those webs.

For patriot governments to secure the cultural and political loyalty of the public, they needed to support common ideas about property ownership, even as they hoped to quickly liquidate enemy land and goods. This obligation meant honoring the claims of patriotic creditors but also requiring past debts to loyalist estates be made good. Legal structures established over decades provided the cover of legitimacy. Pennsylvania's 1779 attainder act named thirteen "divers traitors" whose property would be seized and sold for the commonwealth. Americans who owed money or rent to the accused traitors were instructed to report their debts (and pay a discounted amount of them) within three months, and those with "lawful debts and claims thereon" needed to submit their claims, with evidence signed by witnesses, within six months. The Supreme Court heard and determined each claim, with sale proceeds flowing through the state as public moneys.[47]

For many states, involvement of real estate called for the structures of probate law. In Massachusetts, county probate judges were tasked with administering sequestered estates, following procedures that approximated those for people who had died without a will.[48] Probate courts were institutions familiar with collecting rent and paying debts from an estate. They understood arranging support for dependents. The minister William White explained the gendered legal logic of the revolutionary governments to Elizabeth Fergusson, a loyalist wife: "ye supreme Court had adopted ye rule prescribed by law in ye case of those who die intestate—wc allows to ye Widow one third & in the case of no children, one half."[49]

By applying the context of probate law to loyalist women and children, patriot governments viewed these individuals' suffering as growing from their familial and social positions rather than from a free political choice. Appraisers in Massachusetts were instructed to carefully observe gender conventions when they entered the house of an absentee: "If the said absent person left a wife behind him or family you are to apprize the bedding utensils and implements of household furniture every article separately by itself" because those items would be allowed for the "use of the wife and family."[50] Appraisers were trained to identify the suffering of certain women and children connected to loyalists and mitigate it, in spite of the imperative to use loyalist men's belongings to reward patriot suffering. In rural Vermont, the commissions worried about sustenance, permitting wives to keep corn, milk, salt, and pork.[51] Judges could also decide to mark off one-third of the real estate for the use of a wife in her loyalist husband's absence. Some states, like Virginia, preserved dower property from confiscation; others, like South Carolina, did not.

Well-connected widows used several strategies to claim property that the state intended to seize in the period between the confiscation decree, the inventory taking, and the auction. The day that her household goods were advertised in the *Pennsylvania Packet* for a future auction sale in October 1778, Elizabeth Fergusson successfully petitioned the Pennsylvania Supreme Court to pause first before seizing the goods, identified as parlor, bedroom, and kitchen furniture and accessories "for her Accommodation," including "twelve Pictures of Birds, 3 of them broken by Accident at the Time of Inventorying."[52] Her petition corrected the work of the men performing the inventory, offering a "memo" that "the three Stands were inventoried under the Appellation of Tables but are only 16 Inches square—The Plate Warmer also was inventoried under the Appellation of an Oven."[53] The committee establishing the inventory lacked either the taste or time to understand that the small table-shaped pieces of furniture were actually tools for elegant life, as they supported a harpsichord, a loom for weaving fringe trim, and a washbowl. Two years later, these items, along with dozens of bushels of grain, were all confirmed to be "her own Property for her Maintenance" and removed from the list of potentially auctionable goods. Fergusson herself attended the eventual auction, where she purchased a small set of bedroom goods and a few pigs, totaling just over £55.[54] Those who attended the auction to bid against her were likely disappointed to see so many of the originally advertised items missing, though some of them purchased the wagons, carts, and "a Negro man."

As the story of Fergusson suggests, emerging patriot governments distinguished "household goods and wearing apparel" as specially coded goods. These items, whose particulars varied according to the class and race of the owner, were a species of property that belonged with wives and not with the polity. Patriots' belief that this type of property should be preserved against public taking was further reflected in the Continental Congress's discussion of how much money to demand of each state in the funding of the war. In October 1777 representatives considered (and then rejected) a proposition that would have calculated the relative "value of all property except household goods and wearing apparel within each state" as the basis for its contribution to the war effort.[55] In other words, these items could not be included in the public accounting available for raising money. Auctions of loyalist property helped in the process of sorting out the relationship between material and political life.

Distinctions among types of goods were always political, but ideas about rightful ownership did not map neatly onto lines dividing patriot from loyalist. When Cornelius Clopper, a former provincial congressman, "went to the enemy" in early 1777, his wife and daughter were allowed to join him but take only their clothing and furniture "necessary for their accommodation" as well as provisions and liquor "necessary for their comfortable subsistence," which were not to include the silver plate, bonds, deeds, or cash over £50.[56] His daughter Catharine quickly submitted an appeal to stop the auctioning off of the rest of the family goods, insisting that Will and Sook (two young enslaved people) along with several items of furniture were in fact hers, not her father's.[57] By the end of the week, the committee tasked with investigating the claim had decided that, although they had unearthed "no full and direct evidence" confirming property ownership, they had concluded that the two enslaved people were "absolutely necessary for the comfortable subsistence and accommodation of the said Catharine Clopper and her mother, the wife of Cornelius Clopper, according to their rank and situation in life."[58] Sook's physical presence and labor value to Catharine's comfort served a cultural purpose that outweighed the sale value that her body placed at auction would bring to the patriot cause. The ideals of male revolutionaries included firm understandings about the proper relationship between Black and white women, and they were willing to overlook political disloyalty and financial gain to invest in that relationship. South Carolina's confiscation act, unlike those of other states, harshly denied loyalist women dower rights to confiscated property, but the law was soon modified to preserve loyalist women's ownership of "household furniture, plate, linen, apparel, carriages, and carriage-horses, with such negroes as are generally attendant upon the families."[59] The people called "such negroes" did not go under the hammer for the patriot state, although this provision did not prevent "the families" from selling off their human property—perhaps at another type of public sale—when they determined that their immediate financial value was worth more than their value as attendants.

That calculation, concerning the financial value of enslaved people, drove some of the largest transfers of wealth during the wartime process of confiscation and redistribution. Property in people was movable for the purposes of slaveholders fleeing neighbors and militias, plentiful when compared with dwindling stores of commodities, and generally understood as more valuable than paper forms of money.[60] Prerevolutionary legal developments had encouraged the practice of selling people held in slavery to resolve the financial dilemmas of enslavers, a practice taken up by individuals and state governments confronting the costs of war.

Patriot rhetoric called out traitors and, in some cases, government-issued bills of attainder treated loyalist men as criminals, subject to the seizure and sale of property by sheriffs. Much of the process of auctioning loyalist property, though, more closely followed the rules established for the dead and indebted.[61] Auction sales were not simply punishment nor merely an efficient method of redistribution. Rather, they drew from established laws and norms, along with ideas about different kinds of property and ownership. Linking the auctioning of loyalist estates to creditors' claims normalized the revolutionary proceedings. As in intestate sales, widows bid on family property held in the husband's name.[62] And as always, talking about property and value was simultaneously talk about cultural and political value. Such links among the different registers of value shaped acceptable patriotic behavior as seizure of property progressed to sale.

Sale Day and Public Judgment

In keeping with the rules of public sales, a newspaper notice announced the day of a loyalist auction, details about the location, a preview of the land or goods to be sold, and affirmation of the fact that the property was sold as confiscated goods. These legal notices helped clear the title to the property and also publicly alerted the communities of the action.[63] Accused loyalists reacted with alarm when they saw these notices: "I have perused a Publication in Mr. Holts paper Dated Dec 14 mentioning that My Brewing Utensils and sundry other articles too tedious to mention, are to be sold at my own house. . . . Specifying also that I am with the Enemy" wrote a desperate Thomas Lewis from the Poughkeepsie jail in which he was being held on parole to Henry Livingston, one of the local commissioners for sequestration.[64] He was right to worry; people had already been asking about the potential sale of his brew house, and a petition from his near neighbor testifying to his patriotic change of heart was the only weapon he had to attempt to stop the sale.

Loyalist auctions took place at taverns, at the homes of departed loyalists, and at courthouses, drawing crowds of neighbors who traveled from sale to sale to bid. Commissioners served alcohol, adding to the festive feel of the event.[65] Of the seventy people who purchased items at the auction of John Biddle's Reading, Pennsylvania, estate on February 18, 1778, one-third appeared three days later to buy goods at the smaller auction of Reynold Keen's estate. Joseph Collier spent £1.3.6 on a tablecloth and hand towel at the first auction and £9 on a musket at the second. Mrs. Barre spent more extensively, over £40 on silver spoons and the best bedstead at Biddle's auction and more than £55 on books, pictures, a copper kettle, and a coverlet at Keen's auction. Henry Haller, who served in multiple roles regarding the confiscated estates, was also an active bidder himself at both auctions, purchasing housewares, Windsor chairs, and a two-year-old colt.[66] Some Pennsylvania neighbors may have planned to sell their purchases later, but many individual selections were likely for private use.

Some loyalist auctions were small affairs. At the vendue in Rutland, Vermont, on July 8, 1778, Commissioner Joseph Bowker auctioned off small household items for a few shillings each: iron kettles, a dyeing tub, a cradle, looms.[67] Michael Dunning, another Vermont commissioner, described the auction at Nathanel Selye's house in the fall of 1778 in notes that emphasized the transfer of goods from one person to another: "Taken from Adam deal one Pair of briches and sold to John downer for 1-8-0. . . . Taken from Joseph Andrewson one looking glass and sold to doct Johnson for 9-6-0."[68] The language was personal, transforming a consumer act of acquiring goods into an intimate transfer of property from one neighbor to another. The fledgling apparatus of a revolutionary state put its energies into selling one man the used britches of another.

Other loyalist auctions were extensive sales of hundreds of acres, enabling purchasers who had lost their own property in the course of the war to achieve new gains in the form of prime real estate.[69] At an August 15, 1782, auction in Jacksonborough, South Carolina, John Bailey's extensive property was divided among seventeen bidders in tracts typically around three hundred acres at a total recorded price of £110,926.5.[70] Large sales combining the estates of half a dozen loyalists drew big crowds, creating new dynamics of buying and selling. Commissioners took advantage of having a crowd of bidders to consolidate sales—new goods could be added to an existing planned sale as they were seized.[71]

In war as in peace, the community context of economic life shaped auction sales. Auctioneers interacted with bidders who knew well the possibilities of the goods that their neighbors owned. When authorities began to auction the estate of William Brown of Lyme, Connecticut, the crowd asked the agent "if he intended to sell the Negros," meaning the people Brown held in slavery. The agent said no, so "the Negroes were left and they took various ways & means for a living," some laboring on farms and some apprenticed to craftsmen.[72] Decades later, several of the formerly enslaved people became paupers. Their town selectmen looked to the state, hoping that some proceeds of wartime auctions might remain to fund the support of these individuals set free by an auctioneer.

Auction days became patriotic displays that affirmed the community of rebels by reconstituting the material worlds of political opponents. They functioned as a kind of inverse of the nonimportation and nonconsumption movements that historians have identified as the earliest "rituals of consumer protest."[73]

Signing one's name to forego East India tea or spinning wool on the town square made a material commitment to deprivation in the name of a political cause. Attending the auction of a loyalist's seized property, in contrast, was a material act of acquiring more, through a group exercise in price setting and distribution of goods. Spoon by spoon, one family's property moved out across the county into new households.

Sale prices accomplished that redistribution in a manner that was highly individualized. Consider the fate of Henry Moll's seized goods. When the appointed appraisers walked through Moll's house in Windsor, Pennsylvania, in August 1778, they grouped like items together and valued each set as a whole: 3 spinning wheels and 1 reel were valued at £2.10; 14 beehives were valued at £14, with the notation that each one was worth £1.[74] A month later, a new group of community members assembled to bid on Moll's goods. This group treated them as unique items deserving individual judgment, not as categories with standard prices. John Foust bought spinning wheels, seemingly one by one, because while two of them sold for £1.3, the last one went for £0.15. Adam Claist did not take away any spinning wheels from the lot, but he did buy the reel separately, for £0.2. Foust also bought 3 beehives, at the comparative bargain of £2.12, but three other men also bid on and won hives, paying between £1.1 and £1.16 apiece. The specifics of the item mattered, as did the desires of the bidders. In August, appraisers considered Moll's clock, one of the most valuable items in the estate, to be worth only £25. In September, Foust paid more than double that amount at the auction. The other most valuable property, the horses, likewise showed variability between the assessed value and the purchase price. The roan horse that assessors considered to be worth £60 was sold to Gabriel Conser for £82.10.[75] As in the prewar years, the gap between appraised value and public sale price reflected local conditions—a context that now involved a politically invested community.

The reckoning and coordinating that the redistribution of loyalist property required burdened the commissioners in time, effort, and money, suggesting that revolutionary politics, not profit, was their motivation. The clothing, tools, and livestock sold at Commissioner George Palmer's Dutchess County, New York, auctions in 1777 and 1778 were old and went for small sums—such as Thomas Richardson's "Old Bust Collar" that Ephraim Andrews purchased for 8 shillings, or the 23 white shirts that he, multiple other men, and one woman bid on individually for sums ranging from 4 shillings to £4.5 on April 17. To collect, move, and sell the goods of just three estates that contributed to these auctions, Palmer had to make 93 payments, typically a couple of pounds each time, to the men who helped him assemble the sales. The £1.5 that George Riddle received for "picking up Jones irons" and bringing them to the auction was more than half the £2.6 that they fetched at the sale.[76]

It took work to turn enslaved people into cannons or turn bed curtains into a soldier's wages; paying for that work enabled revolutionary polities to bind a group of political supporters to the fledgling state. Vermont's state treasurer paid out a steady stream of receipts submitted by commissioners who had done the work of storing goods, attending court, escorting loyalist families (usually wives and children) to join relatives behind British lines, guarding prisoners, cooking meals, and pasturing animals.[77] The state further reimbursed people for labor involved in selling the goods, acting as clerks of the sale, and "attending" the vendues. Commissioners paid themselves as well, in the form of sales commissions, for the auctions that they oversaw.[78] The extensive operation of seizure, valuation, and sale amounted to a concerted investment in the government's relationship to its citizens that operated through the norms of commerce as patriotic ritual.

Bidders may have been drinking, but loyalist auctions were hardly a free-for-all. As in any public sale, there were multiple restraints on behavior, determining which people were allowed to bid and which forms of money were acceptable payment. Lawmakers set rules governing the lead-up to sale. For example, South Carolina in 1782 specified three months' preview time and established that land plats be lodged in neighborhood dwellings so that potential purchasers could review them.[79] Printers were required to publicly announce sales. In July 1781, the Pennsylvania Executive Council had to postpone a planned auction when they discovered that the printer had incorrectly stated the terms by which confiscated estates would be sold, "which has, and may again, embarrass the purchasers."[80] Authorities attempted to accomplish social goals through strategic manipulations of sales. In order to discourage speculators, in the fall of 1777, the Massachusetts General Assembly directed the committee of sequestration to divide goods into lots "not exceeding in each lott the sum of thirty pounds" and sell them in such a way that "no one person . . . shall be suffered to purchase more than one lott."[81] There were politically targeted rules as well. In Pennsylvania, only men who had taken the Oath of Allegiance were permitted to bid at loyalist auctions, along with their wives and children.[82]

In establishing the rules of the auction—who could bid, when they could bid, what types of property were up for bidding, and what forms of money they could use to pay for their purchases—patriot governments established the boundaries of the new polity, linking market and political participation as they sought to control the political accomplishments of the sales. Even the separating out of married women's claims to family property was part of this political covenant, not merely a paternalistic gesture. Grace Galloway was keenly aware that Pennsylvania's decision to grant her permission to bid on her family goods at auction came with the knowledge that such a purchase would place a political claim on her by making her "a subject to the state."[83]

Bidders hoping to buy a loyalist neighbor's beehives experienced auctions as the transfer of private property from one individual to another; patriot officials cast them as one step in the conversion of private goods into public ones. The State of Connecticut recorded horses and cattle taken from enemy troops and "converted" into "public property to be distributed to American troops in lieu of wages."[84] Committees of Confiscation talked about the "public" good and "public goods." The Worchester, Massachusetts, committee announced a series of auctions in January 1782 that would take place at the estates of "Absentees" and would include movable property and real estate. In describing the goods for sale, they used language commonly seen in advertisements—"good Pewter," "large quantity of valuable Household bedding." But the terms of the sale gestured toward a broader aim than a good deal for customers. James Putnam's valuable farm, for example, was to be "sold altogether, or in parcels, as the Committee may think most for the benefit of the public."[85] Here, the public had more than one meaning—both the public of consumers (a common usage in any advertisement) but also the patriot public who would benefit from the money collected. Backed by a legal system that supported private property, the auctions served the public by redistributing loyalist goods.

Each sale day, controlled in its form but highly particular in the way it transpired, broke apart an old organization of property and initiated a new material order. While purchasers liked auctions that allowed them to own a piece of a great person's estate and perhaps took pleasure in obtaining part of a loyalist neighbor's collection, loyalists regarded the proceedings from the outside and fretted about the related truth—that auctions exposed the fact that an estate was greater than the sum of its parts. As one letter-writer from New York put it in 1781, in response to Maryland's confiscation act: "In consequence of that act's taking place the finest landed estates, if ever they revert to their right owners, will be nothing but dismantled wastes, hardly capable of affording a bare subsistence to those who shall be constrained to set down upon them, and BEGIN THE WORLD AGAIN."[86] The author's invocation of Thomas Paine's famous statement from *Common Sense*, "We have it in our power to begin the world over again," recast it in a decidedly pessimistic tone.[87] The symbolic cost of dismantling a social order, like the financial cost of breaking apart an estate into individual lots for auction, was borne collectively and individually by those who opposed revolution.

Linking loyalist auctions in form to the estate auctions of the deceased, patriot commissioners sought the opportunity on a small scale to begin the lives of the living anew, cleared of past debts and supplied with new sets of objects and lands. Property targeted by law for public sale was property marked for continued life in the regenerative presence of new farm stock led home by patriot bidders. While war destroyed bodies, buildings, and belongings, auctions preserved them. The material persisted, even as its meaning was transformed in the public negotiation over value.

Loyalists, of course, were not literally dead. The auction could not clear the path for a new world of political and neighborly relationships when past associations clung to the goods and lands. Labeled an "absentee," a loyalist property owner typically left behind a web of financial and material connections that were very much alive. Those living connections frequently confounded the revolutionary governments' attempts to dictate the terms of value in its multiple senses.

Managing Wartime Economies

Over the course of a long, destructive, and expensive war, Americans wrestled with the problem of value in negotiating prices, taxes, and the form of money itself. States and the Continental Congress issued different types of paper money to pay suppliers and soldiers and enforced legal tender laws requiring residents to accept these bills at face value.[88] These paper bills circulated but lost purchasing power as confidence in the governments that backed them waned. States experimented with price controls on a range of domestic and imported goods to counteract the effects of inflation and depreciation and control the value of money itself. In 1777 New England states passed a group of acts setting price ceilings on imported goods, grain, and produce, forbidding hoarding, and restricting residents from transporting goods out of state in search of better markets.[89] Communities were expected to know and enforce these market controls in shops and other venues. In New Hampshire, bidders who called out prices above the set maximum for imported fabrics and groceries at commodity auctions were fined the amount of their illegal bid, if those present reported the violation.[90]

Public auctions of commodities and foodstuffs, like those described in the New Hampshire law, were one answer to the problem of fluctuating prices and unstable currency. In keeping with colonial practice, routine auctions were open to public scrutiny and followed rules about "fair prices" established within communities. Therefore, when the Continental Congress established a three-member Board of Trade in October 1779 to import goods on behalf of the American people, they reached for a familiar tool to assert the public benefit of their actions. Congress authorized each state to create its own Board of Sale to sell merchandise at public auction and "for the benefit of the purchasers, all articles shall be sold by retail or in the peice, and exposed to view several days before the sale."[91]

But such public auctions of imports set prices according to the logic of the community in attendance, not the best-laid plans of governments seeking to structure the market to be civic-minded. Recoiling from the effects of bidders' judgments on the broader economy, several states tightly confined routine public sales as a wartime measure. In Pennsylvania, for example, a 1777 law condemned "the practice of selling of goods, wares, and merchandises by public vendue," for tending "to raise the price of almost every necessary article, and to depreciate the current money of the continent."[92] It therefore banned public vendues as a way for residents to raise money, with key exceptions; auctions conducted by sheriffs, estate executors, or people selling property in order to move away could continue in wartime, along with auctions of loyalist goods. A subsequent bill, which established a single auctioneer for the city of Philadelphia, noted that, "although a monopoly of the sale of goods by auction or vendue, in a time of peace and order" would not be justifiable, the war changed the rules.[93]

In the specific case of auctions of loyalist property, the involvement of the state made such sales ideal venues for collecting and regulating government-issued paper money. In fact, part of the design of loyalist auctions was to call in these notes, many of which had been distributed to soldiers in lieu of pay, and some of which had ended up in the hands of speculators.[94] In April 1784, in spite of the terms of the Treaty of Paris ending the war, the Middlesex County agent David Olden announced the sale of nineteen confiscated loyalist house lots, specifying that he would accept in payment both in cash and in "officers' and soldiers' notes given for the depreciation of pay, contractors' certificates, or collectors' surplus certificates of the state of New-Jersey."[95] Three months later, the agent for Sussex County printed similar terms for the public sale of 121 confiscated estates.[96] These maneuvers removed paper currency from circulation, discharged government debts, and allowed holders of the notes to recover something of tangible value from documents many feared were worthless.

When a bidder called out a price for a confiscated lot or plow, the number reflected judgment about the security and value of circulating money, as well as the property under the hammer. The value of that money, in turn, reflected community confidence in the revolutionary government that was conducting the war and community members' willingness to trust that the money could at some point be turned into gold, buildings, cattle, or tea tables. Years after the war, when he reported on the prices that loyalist goods sold for and whether those prices could be considered a "true" measure of their worth, Duncan Ludlow claimed that "the desire of parting with their paper currency most probably overbalanced their reluctance to purchase confiscated articles. The price may therefore I should think be considered an Index of the value taking into the account the depreciated State of the continental Money at the time of Sale."[97]

If Ludlow was cynical about the link between price and value claimed by loyalists after the fact, Richard Cranch of the Massachusetts General Court believed that community collusion undercut the price of the goods to the detriment of the tax-strapped states. He complained that estates sold in the spring of 1780 in Suffolk County were auctioned "on very advantageous terms" and thought a conspiracy might be afoot.[98] When auctions permitted generous credit terms, bidders did not need to present cash in order to collect their goods. Given wartime depreciation, purchasers took advantage. In early 1780, the Pennsylvania government in council complained that "many of the purchasers of confiscated estates" were delaying in making their second and final payments "to the great injury of the State, and the embarrassment of the Sales," and planned to hold up the requests for deeds until the precise original terms were met.[99] But waiting contained its own dangers, given that these were property redistributions with a political as well as commercial purpose. Pennsylvania's 1779 revision of the seized estates law noted that any person who bought land at a confiscated estate sale, who was subsequently evicted by a court judgment that favored some other nonloyalist owner would be reimbursed the "value of such estate at the time of such eviction out of the treasury of this commonwealth."[100] They would not necessarily recoup the price they had paid.

The linkage of price and value perplexed rebel states at every turn as they sought out ways to fund the war. In the end, sales of loyalist property covered perhaps 15 percent of the states' military spending.[101] When they turned to other sources of money, by extracting taxes or extending loans to support patriot armies, governments yet again had to confront the problem of valuing the people's property. Some states had long histories of public valuation of privately owned property for tax purposes. Massachusetts, by the middle of the eighteenth century, had a property tax that depended on owners to report their holdings to locally elected assessors, who determined the value of that property and the tax to be taken.[102] Virginia, in contrast, had no tradition of such valuations. The colony collected a tithe and taxed the sale of liquor and enslaved people. To fund contributions to the Seven Years' War midcentury, the colony had added a flat, per-acre tax on land and tobacco. The high cost of the Revolution, however, forced Virginia to adopt a new tax of ½ of 1 percent on "Capital Articles of Property," including buildings, silver plate, and enslaved people. But the newly elected commissioners disagreed over whether values should be calculated in sterling or Virginia depreciated currency. They differed, too, over what would count as a market price. Was the price obtained at a forced sheriff's auction a fair judgment of a piece of property's value, or could only a voluntary sale determine a market price?[103] In a very short period of time, Virginia's leaders had to grapple with the same debates over how to value property that had taken place over the course of a century elsewhere.[104] They adopted and discarded solutions such as treating property in land and enslaved people differently, with a flat rate for human beings and a valuation rate for land; dividing land into categories and polling the assessors about the value; and trying to guess how much land would have sold for before the war.[105]

Managing a wartime economy pressed governments to invent new forms of money and then handle the unintended consequences of the schemes they put into place, many of which reverberated long after the war as paper money was bought up by a wealthier investor class who could wait to redeem it.[106] The Treaty of Paris negotiated at the end of the war included Article 5, which recommended to the state legislatures to return confiscated estates; Article 6 stated that there were to be no more political confiscations. But loyalists had little hope these would be observed, and in fact advertisements for auctions of confiscated estates continued for years.[107]

In a tumultuous civil war, many losses could never be known with precision. Enslaved people ran away, denying their bodies as sources of profit for enslavers. Enemies burned homes and razed fields, destroying not only current value but also future profits. Those who contributed to the war effort sought reimbursement when the fighting was over. They petitioned state legislatures and submitted receipts to regain the value of goods and money that they believed they had only been loaning to prosecute the war. Rachel Wells loaned money to New Jersey, was robbed by an army chaplain, and "what I had suffered by ye English . . . came to two thousand Eight hundred & five pound hard cash." Surely, she told the Continental Congress in seeking repayment of the loan, "there is gold enough and to spare" for her.[108] Given the upheaval in money and valuation systems, though, it was hard to determine, much less afford, a redemption of the debt the new nation owed its long-suffering citizens.

Proofs of Value

Long after the hammer had fallen and a person's property had been carted off to a new owner, the auctions of loyalist estates lingered in the public imagination and in the formal records of the British government as testimony to all that had been lost. Much would never be redeemed. When the British government pledged to reimburse loyalists who had fled into exile after the end of the war, many struggled to prove that they had owned anything. Stories and memories of suffering could not be monetized into compensation for loss without additional evidence. Expected to prove what they had owned and how much they had lost, petitioners submitted a range of evidence, many relying on the reputations of people who signed statements supporting their claims. Those with few connections faced the skepticism of a five-member board consisting of members of Parliament and war veterans. William Cooper, a free Black man, claimed to have lost a house and land worth £500. The commission retorted, "All these blacks say that they were free born and that they had property, two things that are not very probable; we did not believe one syllable of his case."[109]

Paper proofs were hard to come by for exiles who had been uprooted multiple times. The loyalist Richard Swanwick of Pennsylvania had hidden his valuable papers in an underground chest. When the patriot mob came to his house, they tortured the man he had enslaved to reveal their location.[110] Like Sarah Nichols, the exiled woman at the beginning of this chapter, most had to rely on the memories of neighbors who could be located and pressed to testify. Some of the best-connected asked neighbors who witnessed the auction of their property to appear before a notary to swear to the sale and its terms. Otherwise, loyalists could be left with no evidence beyond their memories. William and John Hopton reported that while a handful of their enslaved people had been confiscated and sold by South Carolina Commissioners, an American officer had told them that the others "were given to the American Soldiers, and by them carried over the Mountains."[111]

Ironically, those who had property confiscated and auctioned more often had the benefit of a paper trail proving the existence and value of their property, in contrast to those who lost land or goods to fires, floods, cannonballs, or spiriting away by American soldiers. A public auction, overseen by local courts and committees, linked each piece of property to a price, and it was the prices that the Loyalist Claims Commission used as a benchmark for evaluating the extent of a loyal subject's suffering. Once a loss became a price, it could be compared, discounted, and reimbursed.

The political context of confiscation gave the loss its validity, even though it meant that the British government relied on transactions that had taken place under the oversight and political logic of an enemy state to establish the validity of its own subjects' sacrifices. While anyone living in a war-torn area might suffer the death of valuable livestock or the destruction of a wharf, property targeted by law for public sale was targeted for explicitly political reasons. This second level of proof—that a person had lost property for his political commitments, as opposed to the vagaries of time and war, could best be verified with documents produced by an explicitly political process of seizure, assessment, and sale.

Timing and geography also influenced which losses were understood to represent meaningful political commitments and which ones came from bad luck or just desserts. The Loyalist Claims Commissioners explained early on in August 1784 that they had excluded losses of property sustained outside the newly drawn boundaries of the United States. They also disregarded land purchased after the beginning of "the troubles" unless it had been purchased in territory controlled by British authority. Without that political guarantee, they explained, the purchase had likely been speculative, given that "the value of the Property was fluctuating." Taking advantage of value fluctuations was not a political cost they were willing to repay; those losses represented suffering that could not be reliably quantified. Any loyalist who sought reimbursement for such a purchase had to prove it was paid for "in Money or Money's worth the real value of which is capable of being ascertained."[112]

In 1786 the commission sent the lawyer Jon Anstey to the United States to test the value of the submissions by checking up on the prices. Anstey began in New York City and traveled down the coast as far south as Charleston, South Carolina, speaking with officials in each location.[113] He relied heavily on the records of the American revolutionary governments to verify the value of the losses loyalists had suffered. It was their records of auctions and appraisals that he trusted to adjudicate the demands of the people who had opposed the revolutionary movement. Those auctions, which felt to loyalists like unjust public robberies, in fact produced some of the most convincing evidence that they had ever owned property worth seizing, and therefore worth compensating. In fact, Richard Swanwick, the man whose property deeds were lost after being hidden in a buried chest, eventually submitted a copy of the scheduled sale from the American Commissioners of Confiscated Estates to the Loyalist Claims Commission.[114] Enemy documents recorded, and therefore preserved, the value of his property because both the British and the American governments recognized the same legal testaments of that value.

Anstey's notes, grappling with the difficulties of judging value in a time of war, divided information about property values into three classes of different degrees of certainty. The first was "Matters capable of legal conclusive Evidence," the second "Matters of common Notoriety, universally assented to as Facts," the third "general Information upon Topics that dwell in opinion only."[115] Records from the sale of forfeited estates fit the first category in that they had been conducted through what he saw as "legal" structures and practices. Yet the appearance of legality came up against the diversity of federalism. Because each claimant might have property in different states, and because each state had its own laws and procedures regarding forfeited estates, Anstey noted, "it is impossible to finish each Man's case as you go, and wind off a Web so knotted, and intangled upon a single Thread."[116] Reporting from Pennsylvania, Anstey commented that verifying confiscation sales through the "best evidence"—namely, evidence provided by state judgment rolls of courts of common pleas—would be "tedious and very expensive to the Public." Happily, he had persuaded the U.S. Office of the Commissioners of Forfeiture itself to let him look at their record books. He copied their entries to send back to London.[117]

Loyalist testimony bolstering the legal records of sales deployed a rich language of valuing that drew on common terms from prewar economic culture. Jane Henderson reported a list of lost property with rounded-up values that were clearly estimated. Her last entry on the list was for "Household furniture and bedding and wearing apparel and Corn farming youtentials and Sundrey other things to tedous to mention."[118] In this testimony, she was echoing the language that retailers frequently ended their newspaper advertisements with—"etc." or "too tedious to mention"—demonstrating the way that those commercial notices taught Americans one way to understand their property. Commercial language had become integrated into daily life.

But the marketplace of revolution was filled with uncertainties and ambiguities. British commissioners were aware of the constructed nature of value judgments, beyond the immediate problem of potential fraud. They noted "the estimate of Value is the subject matter of Opinion in which the most upright must ever be liable to differ even concerning ordinary objects." North American land claims were even more susceptible to opinion "because it is reducible to no fixed Standard or mode of Estimate but the value of each Estate is so distinctly dependent upon its own peculiar circumstances in respect of local situation and state of cultivation or Improvement."[119] As Anstey himself commented about the problem of value, "The Answer is always in a Circle, it will bring as much as it is worth—and it is worth as much as it will bring."[120]

The ultimate job of the Loyalist Claims Commission was to assess the value of a person's "undoubted loyalty" in the value of her or his sacrifice.[121] And in the end, that assessment was profoundly uneven. For all the careful documentation, interviews, and investigations, the British government awarded £3,033,091 to loyalists who as a group had claimed £10,358,413.[122]

*   *   *

In their testimony to the Loyalist Claims Commission, petitioners presented themselves as victims of their own loyalty; they supported the empire and they suffered for it. In so doing, they participated in a political construction of victimhood, made material in contests over land and goods.[123] Auctions fixed a monetary value on property at a time when both the money system and the political importance of property were in flux.[124] Regulated by laws enforced by courts that had been created under colonial conditions, auctions fused publicity and legal structure to claim property for the new US state. By engaging in the familiar process of valuing, auctions of loyalist goods enforced one set of political values and dispossessed another.

Loyalist auctions, which dealt in property that already had an owner, enacted a process of collective remaking as much as the individual self-fashioning that was common to other forms of revolutionary consumer protest. Individuals and institutions did expand their material lives and influence. In Philadelphia, the University of Pennsylvania expanded with the proceeds from loyalist auctions.[125] James Milligan bought a new two-story house and lot on Charleston, South Carolina's King Street.[126] Vermont's John Downer acquired a pair of britches.[127] At the same time, loyalist auctions created categories of people through their relationship to seized goods. Loyalists in Britain became an interest group with political pressure because of the collective weight of their loss. William Pepperell, representing his fellow loyalists in London, referred to them as "Loyalist American Sufferers."[128] Patriots, in turn, became Americans, bound to the new governments by redistributed property and the fees they collected as they moved this property through the political system.

The value of the property, and the value of the suffering acknowledged, were key parts of the political project because they recognized degrees of deserving and reasons for exceptions. The new US government chose to uphold courts' centrality to securing credit through adjudication and recordkeeping. There was also nuance in the outcomes of loyalist auctions because there were competing interests and perspectives in the neighbors gathered as bidders and witnesses. Yet that nuance was little appreciated by most targets of seizure and sale. To their minds, the patriots had forged price as a weapon against political outsiders.

CHAPTER 4

Agents of Trust and the Cost of Character

To be a South Carolina auctioneer in the years after the American Revolution was to be a villain. Indebted white farmers who might recently have relished the chance to bid on a loyalist neighbor's livestock now found themselves at the mercy of a court-mandated seizure of their property to pay debts owed to British merchants. Governor William Moultrie saw economic and political danger in sheriffs' auctions that would "transfer the whole Property of your Own Citizens, into the Hands of Aliens."[1] At such sales, some in the crowd attacked the sheriffs themselves to stop the proceedings. Others foiled the work of auctioneers by bidding at the auction of their own property, failing to make the 10 percent security payment, and bidding again at the resale, all with the goal of frustrating their creditors. Neighbors refused to respond at all to the auctioneer's patter, in protest of the sale. At these court-directed auctions neither debtor nor creditor could win, the politician and historian David Ramsey concluded, because "property, when brought to sale under execution sold at so low a price as frequently ruined the debtor without paying the creditor."[2]

Commercial auctioneers in cities such as New York and Philadelphia faced friendlier crowds, but they also came under attack for betraying the newly independent citizenry. One critic bemoaned that auctions, formerly "confined to the sales that were occasionally rendered necessary or constrained by peculiar circumstances, such as bankruptcy, the estates of deceased persons, damaged goods, &c," had become "a regular system" that primarily benefited foreigners.[3] British exporters who were eager to restore sales to American customers used urban auction houses as a funnel for goods that the new nation could not produce but could not resist. In the eyes of alarmed observers, political dependence once again threatened through the consumer market as Americans fell under the sway of auctioneers and their enticing deals.

In locations across the United States, auctioneers convened regularly scheduled public enactments of the new nation's economic and moral crises. In addition to binding American markets to European creditors and producers, they bolstered the United States as an emerging empire committed to Indigenous dispossession and chattel slavery. Government officials surveyed and auctioned land west of the Appalachians taken from Indigenous people by treaty or seizure; public vendues replaced squatters' claims with "orderly settlement" that promised "revenue and stability."[4] Court-authorized auctioneers in South Carolina presided over what one historian has called the state's "largest slave auctioneering firm," when enslavers' debts forced a sale, confirming that in the republic as in the colonies people could be owned and exchanged, and their commodification underwrote geographic and economic expansion.[5] Auctioneers cemented the tight connection between the sale of enslaved people and the sale of Indigenous land by repeatedly exposing them in a context where they were already fungible and already commodified, with only the price as an open question.

Unsurprisingly, auctioneers saw themselves neither as villains nor as tools of an emerging US empire. Rather, in their newspaper advertisements they presented themselves as skilled and knowledgeable businessmen who engineered great bargains for attendees at their sales. They spoke with confidence about the items they had gathered for sale and promised customers "constant attendance." They repurposed an older language of patronage to indicate that in a democracy, buyers were the ones who held the power—in politics and in the marketplace. Their self-presentation tapped into early republic political sentiments of "free trade," meaning both unrestricted commerce and reciprocal international markets.[6]

While the moment of bidding appeared tantalizingly "free" from the outside, the auctioneer himself was keenly aware of the structures that underlay his actions. Auctioneers operated within a net of legal and commercial obligations that shaped the final outcome of the sale, and this reality was at odds with the language of choice and consumer freedom that came to dominate the culture of political economy in the postrevolutionary period.[7] Just as revolutionary-era printers publicized a "free press" as a canny business strategy, so too did auctioneers encourage the image of the auction as the embodiment of "free choice" to attract business.[8] Their advertisements presented lists of imported goods and collections of enslaved people, inviting spectators and purchasers in to evaluate for themselves.

The idea of consumption as an individual act that a shopper could imbue with personal or political meaning was a compelling narrative for a new republic, so compelling that it continues to shape historians' understanding of market behavior.[9] Aspects of purchasing enabled individual taste and self-fashioning. If the meaning of a commercial exchange was to be found in the mind of the purchaser, it would seem to be a particularly free and open-ended experience, filled with possibilities. Each bid was an individual claim on a possible material future for the buyer.

Yet, in the very way they operated, auctioneers were a living embodiment of an antithetical idea—that consumption was a cultural and political system of competing obligations that inevitably limited the possible outcomes of a sale, and in fact manipulated buyers to act counter to their own interests. An auctioneer's skills seemed inchoate to skeptical observers, especially as systems of authentication in matters of exchange came under pressure from political and economic transformations in the money supply. Into this uncertainty crept suspicion as the auctioneer joined a predictable roster of villains—the banker, the speculator, and the confidence man—blamed for the hard swings of capitalism. In the first decades of the nineteenth century, marketplaces and democratic institutions confronted the old problem of trust on a national scale. Face value, of ubiquitous questionable banknotes and of the men and women striking deals among new acquaintances, was frighteningly unreliable; fraud lurked at every turn.[10]

Where, then, did legitimate marketplace power come from? Was it bestowed by the state or accumulated over years of diligent work? Was it a skill or a stack of cash? Was it embodied in every free man, or was it held collectively among networks of patronage or citizenship?[11] Lawmakers, purchasers, sellers, and auctioneers themselves struggled to define what kind of commercial actor an auctioneer was, and in doing so, they debated who should have market power.[12] The struggle sat not within a binary of regulation on the one hand and freedom on the other but rather over who served whom in the early republic marketplace.[13] As nineteenth-century capitalism evolved into a cultural system in which the relationship of a commercial exchange came to be the measure of all others, debates about auctioneers—in their attempts to reconcile personal, political, and market relationships—revealed the potential for manipulation in the name of consumer service.[14]

The Character of a Commercial Agent

The United States in the early republic was in the process of postrevolutionary political and cultural reassembly, and it made sense that auctions would be a proving ground.[15] Auctions had long reassembled one person's material life to start new ones, transforming a rich man's estate, constructed over years of study and travel, into talismans of refinement for humbler bidders. In breaking the collection apart, an auctioneer suggested new meanings for the constituent pieces. Presiding over a public sale of books, he might decide to focus on the physical attributes of the volumes rather than their literary quality if he thought appearance mattered more to the judging crowd. How "disheartening" this reinterpretation of the books' value was, reflected one writer, imagining the "long lives of laborious study" behind a book quickly sold for what the auctioneer announced was "less than the cost of the binding."[16] Revaluing easily tipped into outright puffery: "Thus an ill looking volume is 'a rare book;' an old musty tome is 'a scarce book' . . . a mixed medley of nonsense is 'a fine book to read on Sundays.'" In short, the dejected writer noted, "a good joker is worth some dollars a month more than a dry husky crier who sticks to his text."[17]

Whether they joked or entreated, auctioneers narrated the transformation of marketable goods as they broke apart and reassembled worlds. The stories they chanted out loud, the stories they implied with carefully chosen advertisements, and the stories they forged by assembling groupings of goods and people presented statements of value. In their hands, the stories ultimately created value, at least insofar as it was validated through bidding. The dissonance that a beleaguered writer experienced between his years of toil on the one hand and the quick markdown sale of his efforts on the other became the routine, and disorienting, politics of exchange.

Printed notices frequently mobilized the past history of goods. The Charleston firm of Macomb and Taylor announced an auction of "SUNDRY articles of merchandize" by advertising them as "damaged on board the schooner Nancy, William Curran, master, from Norfolk."[18] Their notice acknowledged that there was a problem with these nails, corks, and twine—they were "damaged"—but offered a possibly dramatic backstory and promised a future utility for the buyers and for the voyage's underwriters, who were to collect the proceeds. Estate sales, too, connected a material past to a material future. The 1788 broadside announcing the estate auction of John Penn's goods was laid out room by room, and readers were invited, literally and via their imaginations as they read, to stroll through the house of one of the signers of the Declaration of Independence, admiring Penn's taste in furniture and dreaming of what it was like to sleep in the bed draped in blue and white calico curtains.[19] With a successful bid, they could perhaps turn their dream into reality.

Auction catalogs anticipated and simultaneously shaped the dynamics of the in-person sale by reframing goods and people in an anonymous status as

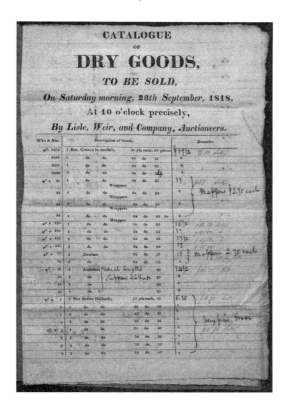

Figure 7. Printed auction catalogs circulated prior to sale; they were also places to document target or eventual sale prices. Lisle, Weir Auction Catalog. Mrs. Howard W. Lewis Collection of Early Philadelphia Businesses Papers (0367), Historical Society of Pennsylvania.

commodities.[20] Printed with lists and brief descriptions of the items to be sold, catalogs stripped away the history of goods in favor of a terse description that reduced a wide range of factors that might influence the meaning or value of a piece of property down to a few words.[21] They included a page of instructions for attendees about how to bid, which forms of money to use, and how to arrange for delivery of goods.[22] Bidders then filled in their own evaluations. In September 1818, the Philadelphia auction firm of Lisle, Weir & Co. paid John Binns to print 300 copies of an 11-page catalog for a dry goods sale, 250 copies each of a 3-page catalog of silks and nankeens, and a 3-page dry goods catalog (see Figure 7).[23] The catalogs themselves included marks, lot numbers, and a description of the goods in each lot. There was also a blank column for "remarks" where attendees could note the sale projections, prices, or other characteristics.[24]

In fact, purportedly neutral lot groupings themselves told powerful stories rooted in a commercial logic that applied to humans as well as to commodities. In Charleston the vendue master William Holmes's 1790 advertisement for the sale of three groups of enslaved people, he repurposed familial language into commercial idiom. Two groups were labeled "very likely families," and the third, "a wench and two children."[25] Holmes's advertisement implied that the first two lots, called "families," would be sold together; no such guarantees or implications existed for the last three people, who had come from the same estate that was being broken apart by the administrator. He presented the first family lot as explicitly connected by kinship, "a fellow and wench, in the prime of life, and their three children," and as possessing complementary gender-linked work skills. The unnamed "fellow" was a cooper, horse tender, a "tolerable good gardener," and all-around handy. "His wife" was a field laborer and "would make a good house servant, being sensible, cleanly, and honest."[26] Their children were identified by gender, perhaps to suggest how their labor could be used by a purchaser. Holmes structured his lot to draw on potential purchasers' ideas about gender and familial relationships, which he hoped would increase the price they were willing to pay. This was a strategic choice. The final three people in the advertisement, "a wench and two children," themselves had families, preferences, and work skills, but he chose not to keep them together in a salable unit with a comprehensible story, either framed around genuine family ties or an invented alternate reality.

For humans forced into it, the lot was a violent tool that reimagined familial logic as economic logic through the auctioneer's presentation. It was a kind of packaging that demonstrates what the historian Walter Johnson calls the "creative power of the traders' market practice" that acknowledged human individuality in order to reassemble it in new forms for sale.[27] The reassembly was often rendered in shorthand. In the same paper that Holmes presented the "likely negroes" in families, another auctioneer partnership promised "A FAMILY OF NINE NEGROES, ON a credit of 1, 2, and 3 years, a do. of 4; do another of 2, for cash, and a small gang of 14 part cash and part credit."[28] In all, twenty-nine people had been quickly sorted into familial and functional groupings that erased all other social and historical webs that each one had lived within.

The auctioneer's narrative was in competition with other stories and other possible past and future worlds. Human beings forced into lots had their own stories to tell, and enslaved people spoke directly to those who inspected them before sale, attempting to change the ways they were seen as property and thereby influence their own circulation.[29] Family members asserted kinship as they pleaded to be sold together. "I will not go without her," said one mother, of her child, who cried "mama."[30] Slave traders hoping for high prices attempted to wrest this interchange to their own purposes. They instructed the people they planned to sell to tell stories that they believed would imply high value, such as to "exaggerate their accomplishments."[31] Many cried instead, communicating the depth of their imminent loss, which could never be valued or repaid in monetary terms.[32]

Whether he was selling humans or inanimate property, the auctioneer's story was an alternate reality created for the purpose of sale, long before he mounted the stage. When bidders thought they could not judge the property by observation alone, his presentation was the basis of authentication. "We all remember," wrote the influential British jurist Lord Mansfield, "the sale of a gentleman's wines, where vast quantities had been sent in belonging to other persons; and also sold at a very high price under an idea that they were his. The consequence was, most of the buyers were taken in."[33] Open and socially leveling elements of auction sales, which permitted the diffusion of luxury goods to a wider public, were accompanied by ambiguous or misleading information about those goods that kept consumer knowledge dependent on the auctioneer's backstory.

His distinctive patter drew bidders from judgment to action. The practice of a seller employing a special "call" was well established in Europe and carried over to the colonies in the Americas, where vendors called out their products with recognizable melodies and repeated words. By the nineteenth century, North American printers were publishing illustrated volumes recording such cries ("Pepper Pot, smoking hot," "R-U-S-K. Fine light Rusk") as a recognizable component of the aural market culture of cities.[34] They also reproduced the auctioneer's patter, a style of talking about his collection and seeking bids from the audience of bidders. The practice of calling a sequence of ascending bids was by the nineteenth century familiar enough to audiences to be used in satires, such as this one parodying the sale of a worthless young beau, which lacks any hint of recognition for the real market in humans taking place every day in the early republic: "Three hundred dollars,—300 dollars once,—Five hundred dollars—1000 dollars, one thousand once, now bid ladies; he must be sold, and not him but thousands of the same species—They will be sold soon—and there will be more raised this long time to come. Fifteen hundred dollars, 1500 dollars, once,—Now is your time ladies—Two thousand dollars, 2000 dollars once, twice, three—gone, you have got him."[35] In adding a running commentary on the exchange itself, embellishing the goods as he went along and acknowledging the collective experience—"Now is your time ladies"—an auctioneer justified the connection among objects for sale, the opinion of the public, and a numerical price through group practice. His words in the heat of the moment served an essential economic function, even though when it came to final agreement, written conditions trumped verbal performance. "Men cannot tell what contracts they enter into, if the written

conditions of sale are to be controlled by the babble of the auction room," noted
one jurist in an 1812 English case cited by Samuel Livermore, American author of
an 1818 treatise on sales by auction.[36] If challenged, the printed conditions prevailed over what an auctioneer chanted out.

With personal charisma and rhythmic patter, auctioneers were selling their
reputation and trustworthiness along with the items they listed. John Gerrish,
the eighteenth-century Boston auctioneer, called constant attention to himself in his advertisements, referring to those who placed goods with him to sell
as "employers," to whom he would "endeavour to give satisfaction."[37] He drew
readers into his business successes and setbacks, asking for favor, "seeing he has
for a long Time past been struggling under a great Variety of Calamities and
Tribulations, and is *now* destitute of Ways and Means to support his Family."[38]
Evidently, he believed that strained personal finances enhanced his reputation
rather than undermining it, perhaps because he made it clear that sales were an
urgent matter of his own survival.[39] In highlighting his motivation, he converted
the potential liability of being a failed family provider into an asset. He was eager
to serve someone else's interests in exchange for financial reward.

In short, Gerrish was an agent. Agency was a long-standing model of hierarchical relationships fitted for commerce. Agents were more than employees,
given the level of trust and judgment the principal whom they served placed in
them. An agent was employed "to buy or sell goods, or transact any kind of business" for a commission, and in doing this business, had to "procure the best intelligence of the state of trade at his place of residence; of the course of exchange; of
the quantity and quality of goods at market, their present price, and the proba-
bility that it may rise or fall." He had to "pay exact obedience to the orders of his
employers" yet "exercise his discretion."[40] Some agents were connected to their
principal by personal ties—for example, mariners granted their wives power of
attorney to collect money and conduct business when they were at sea, thereby
turning them into agents. Others were hired for specific transactions. Business
manuals described how any man might need to appoint a range of agents across
his lifetime to conduct his affairs.[41]

The law formally acknowledged that the relationship between agent and
principal created potential conflicts of interest in commercial activity. Agents
were risk averse in serving the principal who hired them, which in the case of
auctioneers, conditioned the open-ended freedom implied in their promises to
sell "to the highest bidder."[42] Some auctioneers were agents of private interests;
others were agents of the courts, selling humans, goods, or land seized to pay
debts.[43] In both cases they were intermediaries whose control over transactions

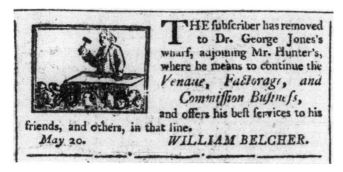

Figure 8. William Belcher used an image of
an auctioneer with his hammer raised to draw
attention to one of the services he offered to "his
friends." *Georgia Gazette*, June 27, 1799. Presented
online by the Digital Library of Georgia.

they had an indirect stake in made their motives suspect. The auctioneer Bart-
lett Still promised the people of Richmond to serve as commission agent,
tobacco broker, vendue master, and factor, vowing "every exertion and unlimited attention."[44] In each of these roles, he was acting on a third party's behalf,
pledged "faithfully to observe the interest of his friends, by giving them the
earliest information respecting the state of our markets." In seeking to please all,
Still raised the question of whose interests he was serving in any given transaction (see Figure 8).

Legal writers, emphasizing the contrast between producers and manufacturers on the one hand and agents and intermediaries on the other, highlighted
the particular obligations the latter had to the people who employed them. An
agent must "consult their advantage in matters referenced to his direction" or
be held liable for consequences.[45] Anglo-American law of principals and agents
focused on the ethical conduct of relations between suppliers and agents as the
mark of a good businessman. Customers, who relied on an auctioneer's business
ethics when he wrote down their name to confirm them as buyer, might ultimately be his dupes, as merchants and auctioneers ultimately answered to those
who supplied them, often on credit.[46] An auctioneer, one legal writer observed,
"is an agent to each party in different things."[47]

Suppliers at times did demand unethical behavior from agents that set them
against the interests of their customers, exhorting auctioneers to breathe new life
into old goods with tactics that ranged from puffery to outright fraud. The New

York merchants Crary and Babcock instructed their auctioneer to alter the distinguishing marks on three packages of brown linens "that some Philadelphians have seen in our store," so as to suggest they were different, newer goods when potential buyers came to preview them. Customers who discovered a bait-and-switch on the auction floor demanded restitution from the sellers. The case of printed fabric that the Baltimore merchants Bayard & Co. opened in March 1819 were "very different from the Sample Case" they had examined at the auction sale they had attended to acquire the goods. They complained that "those sent are very *small patterns*, and only *apart stripes*, & inferior quality also," while those they had bid on were "nearly all striped (two or three pieces only excepted) and *large patterns*, and better quality."[48]

The value of public sales to governments gave them vested interest in controlling who could undertake the job, which meant auctioneers' authority developed within a broader regulatory context. Colonies and then states developed licensing systems that either limited the overall number of people authorized to work as auctioneers, set conditions for who would be selected, or both. The goals of licensing laws in this period, as the scholar William Novack observes, were "mixed and sometimes confused, including prohibition, regulation, administration, and revenue," all under the general umbrella of serving the public good.[49]

Such laws often included a critical evaluation of the "character of an auctioneer" that Gerrish, the Boston auctioneer, had identified when he promised good service. In 1742 Pennsylvania, auctioneers were lumped together with peddlers as commercial agents required to obtain a recommendation of good character and purchase a license in order to conduct business. They were blamed for selling "small parcels" at "unseasonable Times" and luring "idle and disorderly persons" onto the streets at night.[50] Colonial legislation cast auctioneers as potential market troublemakers who needed to be controlled for the good of the public. In February 1773 the Massachusetts Legislature passed an Act for the Regulation and Limitation of Auctioneers, then amended the act and added more names in May. The law explained the need for limiting auctioneer permits by citing the growing number of "unsuitable persons" acting as auctioneers and vendue masters in Boston and other towns, in addition to the fact that they were selling in the evening, which tended to "corrupt the morals of youth."[51]

With licenses linked to moral probity, men denied a license took it personally. When the new Massachusetts law limited auctioneer licenses to a small group, the excluded A. Bowman went so far as to publish a black-bordered notice of his final legal sale in the style of a death notice. He declared in March 1773 that he would soon "be legally dead (the taking away a Man's Bread or his Life being synonymous)" having been "sacrificed for the *Good* of the province," and hoped his "Employers and Customers" would come and bid one last time, though his goods would be a mixture of the seasonable and the unseasonable due to the rushed nature of the sale.[52] Evidently they did because he opened a "Silent Auction Room" two months later and promised charm and results to those who stopped by as "he has a more convincing Way of proving his Articles to be Cheap than by a *common Blast* in the News-Papers."[53] He railed against the injustice of the license system's arbitrary decisions that left him "a Stranger here and without any Estate real or personal, without any natural Relations on this Side the Atlantick."[54] Those fortunate enough to receive a license advertised that fact as well.[55]

The idea that licensed auctioneers were agents of the state who served the community good rather than private gain persisted in many places in the early republic despite evidence to the contrary. Silas Weir, the same licensed Philadelphia auctioneer whom Crary and Babcock had asked to misrepresent their goods, piously exempted himself from jury duty in response to a summons, citing his "official duties" as auctioneer.[56] Maurice Viard, advertising to white Charlestonians who might have seen the woman called Sukey living "amongst her people" in town, directed them to capture her and deliver her to one of two public figures—the master of the workhouse or the vendue master.[57] In both cases, the public authority of the auctioneer was situated within a particular group of men with the potential to be jurors and slaveholders.

In another colonial practice that continued after the Revolution, revenues from auction sales remained critical for states to undertake public projects. In fact, as states sought a more active role in promoting and securing economic development, this source of revenue became increasingly attractive. New York State eventually funded the 363-mile Erie Canal with British loans, a lottery, and a tax on auction sales of goods. As they established tax rates on auction sales, states distinguished among different types of goods for taxation at differing rates. For example, South Carolina's 1785 law placed a 1 percent tax on ships, land, humans, and houses sold at auction, and a 2½ percent tax on auctioned horses, cattle, goods, wares, and merchandise; after three years, another law removed the tax on humans and land.[58] In 1794 the federal government passed a tax on sales at auction: twenty-five cents for every hundred dollars' worth of sales of lands, tenements, animals in husbandry, farming stock, and ships; fifty cents for every hundred dollars' worth of sales of all other goods and chattels (excluding court-ordered sales and those for people relocating).[59]

Tasked with generating public revenue, auctioneers were expected to keep the categories of goods separate, record the sales, and report and remit the proper payments to state authorities. The New York State comptroller collected reports and payments quarterly from auctioneers across the state. In the 1780s and 1790s, these were brief and straightforward as auctioneers sold two kinds of goods: those that were exempt from the duty (such as those sold at estate auctions) and those taxed at 2½ percent.[60] Several decades later, a more elaborate system of tax rates separated goods into those "free sold," those taxed at 1 percent, those at 1½ percent, and those at 2 percent.[61] Licensed auctioneers who had to maintain these recordkeeping practices ranged from smaller businessmen who held perhaps one auction each month to those who sold multiple times each week; all signed statements swearing that they had accurately reported the days of sale, amount earned, and taxes due.[62] State-to-state variability was significant enough that James Smith moved his auction business out of New York City to Bergen, New Jersey, where the combined duties and commissions were lower, and he skirted the law by encouraging potential sellers to forward him representative "samples" that he could use to auction off in New Jersey, while they kept the rest of the stock in New York, at a savings for all involved.[63]

As lawmakers adjusted the segmentation of auctionable goods, they sought to achieve a commercial public good with the blunt tool of tax. Governments in the early republic were drawn to projects that married public finance and social engineering, as with the parceling and sale of so-called public lands to individual white men who could become republican citizens.[64] Laws about taxes on auctioned goods, like other property laws, purposefully channeled property into a set of standardized forms in order to simplify and promote the circulation of real estate, animals, merchandise, and human beings.[65] Acknowledging variability would slow down exchange as sellers and buyers had to gather information about a packet of goods in order to agree on the value and the price. Determining which features to sort sales by was a political decision made in the interest of encouraging sales. Auctioneers' stories filled in the gaps between the unique characteristics of the property and the category of property, but the laws themselves also constituted economic narratives, as evidenced by the fact that state legislators changed their minds about the relative weight and composition of taxable types of property.

The mayor and City Council of Baltimore worked through several ordinances regarding auction licenses in the first years of the nineteenth century as they balanced social and commercial costs while gathering revenue. They also received multiple requests from auctioneers to shift the categories of auctioneer licenses and lower the fees. One group of petitioners pointed out that when it came to the auction of clothing, household goods, and working tools, "the Class of Citizens who sell such articles are generally poor and in the opinion of your memorialists entitled to the benevolent attention of the Corporation in providing such mode of Sale . . . as will afford a fair opportunity of disposing of them to the best advantage."[66] To the signatories, the "best advantage" meant that these goods, and the people associated with their sale, merited a separate, lower-cost auction because, when their clothing and household goods were placed in a general auction, they were "Scarcely noticed among the Valuable property" and as a consequence "Sold for less than their Value." Furthermore, the "Class of people who generally purchase Such articles" would find a separate auction of "Great Convenience." Debates over licensing levels and the tax rate associated with each were also debates over who should benefit from what kinds of economic exchange. The city council's decisions about how to divide salable items and the auction licenses linked to them into a set of categories were decisions about access to money and exchange, even as petitioners appealed in terms of the "benevolent attention" that the government should show to the "poor." Petitioners understood that moral judgments lay beneath the shifting percentages of auctioneer licenses.

To demonstrate that they were worthy of government trust, auctioneers were required to post a bond and, in some states, to demonstrate citizenship. South Carolina's 1783 law regulating vendue masters and auctioneers added the requirement that "he shall have been a citizen of this State, or was a citizen of any of the United States, twelve months."[67] Meeting these expectations typically required friends with money, connections that were more available to men than women, to white people rather than Black people, and to the wealthy rather than the struggling. The limitation was deliberate. In 1788, when the Pennsylvania Assembly debated the role of auctioneers in their state, James McLene advocated requiring a large bond, because "the man who has it in his power to procare [*sic*] that security depended upon the good opinion that his neighbors had of him, which gave the highest reason to believe him faithful to his trust."[68] A bond could do what a fee could not, because "many an unworthy person was possessed of ready money enough to lay down on any occasion they thought proper."[69] In this way, lawmakers hoped to ensure that an auctioneer was "worthy" and "respectable" since he handled "considerable sums of public money" and had "so much of other people's property constantly in his hands."[70] In other words, auctioning was an economic function that served the public, and as such, the privilege of conducting an auction was under government oversight. An auctioneer license was supposed to confer the state's imprimatur on the character of auctioneers, indicating that they had been vetted and were deserving of the public trust.

An Experiment in Democratic Patronage

By the second decade of the nineteenth century, most states no longer explicitly required proof of citizenship or moral probity to act as an auctioneer; rather, anyone who posted a bond, signed an oath, and purchased a license could take up the expanding business of auctioning. The licensing process filtered a range of public economic concerns through a set of proofs of probity—a bond, a set of guarantors, a financial down payment. As a growing US population supported commercial itinerants and secondhand economies, licensing was a key tool of local governments to keep promiscuous traders within established power structures through these pledges.[71] Peddlers, grogshops, and pawnshops all had to obtain licenses to operate, and in cities, many licensing regimes targeted industries and locations frequented by the poor and people of color. In the case of auctioneers, a streamlined licensing regime encouraged the growth of official auction businesses. According to directories, cities such as New York, Philadelphia, and Charleston had only two or three auctioneers each in the decade after the Revolution. Within twenty years, New York City alone listed ten auctioneers and Charleston twenty-four vendue masters, and the numbers continued to rise.[72]

In Pennsylvania, however, the governor had full right to select just seven men to work as auctioneers; patronage appointments were one of the perks of his power. The Pennsylvania governor William Findlay spent the early months of 1818, his first in office, commissioning flour inspectors, clerks of the court, and harbor masters, and sifting through at least forty applications from men who wanted to be licensed auctioneers. Selecting seven, he praised the "moral character and political standing" of successful candidates; he reported looking favorably on those "with wives and families" who had impressed other men of business. In bestowing patronage to such men, Findlay not only endorsed a particular model of commercial character but he also exhibited his own social power and ability to bind others to him through granting or withholding favors.[73]

Rejected applicants cried foul. Insisting the selection process was rigged, they prompted the state legislature to charge Governor Findlay and his secretary of the commonwealth with corruption for their patronage of the auction business. In a series of hearings, they uncovered the backroom deals and favors that had shaped the governor's choice of auctioneers. Just as nineteenth-century antigambling campaigns offered Americans opportunities to isolate the irrational and selfish aspects of gain from the productive and manly ones, the patronage inquiry strove to distinguish among commercial networking, customer service, and political corruption.[74] The potential for an open, democratic marketplace in the early republic depended on public reconsideration of the proper role of personal contacts in trading relationships. Putting patronage on trial gave the men of Philadelphia a way to talk about what a trader owed his customers, what a state owed its citizens, and whether those relationships should be analogous.

The committee's ethics investigation soon expanded into a broader inquiry about the political economy of influence, focusing on the discourse associated with patronage. On one level, "patronage" in early American statecraft had a straightforward meaning: the power of appointment. Governors by custom or law filled a number of specific state offices with longtime supporters or members of influential families. On a deeper level, "patronage" referred to networks of personal connections that shaped everything from economic opportunity to scientific knowledge to civic life.[75]

Flexible in its uses, early modern patronage depended on social hierarchies and gained its strength from exploiting unequal social positions. Historians of Anglo-American thought have therefore had little use for patronage as a typology for postrevolutionary social relationships, highlighting instead republicanism—in which citizens bound themselves together through virtuous sacrifice—or liberalism—in which competitive individuals struck bargains. But many late eighteenth- and early nineteenth-century thinkers, businesspeople, public servants, and ordinary Americans in fact operated in a patronage society, where generosity and gratitude were the social glue. They were acutely aware of the web of obligations that supported and ensnared them, even as patronage language—calling obligations "favors," for example—worked to conceal them.[76]

Commercial patronage ties between merchants funded the kinds of personal investment essential to the small scale of most business. A well-placed letter of introduction was the catalyst for opportunities that self-proclaimed independent men of business seized on; letter-writing manuals instructed men without patrons on how to use letters to get them. This kind of commercial patronage, in addition to serving a credentialing function among traders, was an essential part of a businessman's self-fashioning after the Revolution as before. Free American men who understood themselves to be pursuing "careers" in the early republic told stories of "standing alone" to face life's uncertainties, but they relied on patrons to create those careers. The rhetoric of work and manhood embraced independence, but the importance of supportive "friends" endured.[77]

This ability of patronage euphemisms to mask unequal relations may be why—at the same time that British Americans were voicing antimonarchical sentiments—the word "patronage" had gained new, broad use as a way to describe sustained commercial transactions. Auctioneers and others shifted the association of the term from its former aristocratic context to commercial undertakings providing a public service. Aristocratic patronage conferred authority through association with a person of high rank; democratic marketplace patronage conferred it through satisfied customers. The shift was a way to harness commerce to public service rather than merely promoting selfish gain.

Businesses with long-term relationships built into their commercial model were the first to adopt the term and concept. Newspaper editors began to thank subscribers and, importantly, "the public" for their "patronage" by the 1760s; within ten years, the term was in the solicitations of teachers, musicians, and physicians; by the 1780s, "patronage" emerged in reference to a wider range of goods and services. The new meaning was clear in the words of A. E. Lamot, advertising his brokerage office: "As a candidate for public patronage and favor, the subscriber well knows that the extent of his encouragement will be regulated by his exertions to please." By 1818, when Findlay was calculating his advantages and selecting auctioneers, "patronage" was ubiquitous in advertisements as a synonym for "custom" or "business" (see Figure 9). Even a retailer of hats "confident of giving satisfaction, both as to the quality and price of their hats . . . request[ed] a share of public patronage."[78]

This new usage gave the illusion of seller dependence on buyers, while strategically ennobling commercial business transactions. Immediately after Lamot identified his brokerage customers as patrons, he noted that giving "general satisfaction" would also "be his own interest, a tie which supercedes almost every other obligation."[79] The deployment of "patronage" in advertisements invoked a relationship that did not exist to frame one-time commercial transactions in a way that flattered and benefited the seller. Originally patronage had described an ongoing relationship of intimacy between unequal parties, in which one side gained financial support and the other cultural capital. In its revised commercial form, sellers cast customers as "public" patrons whose financial power rewarded

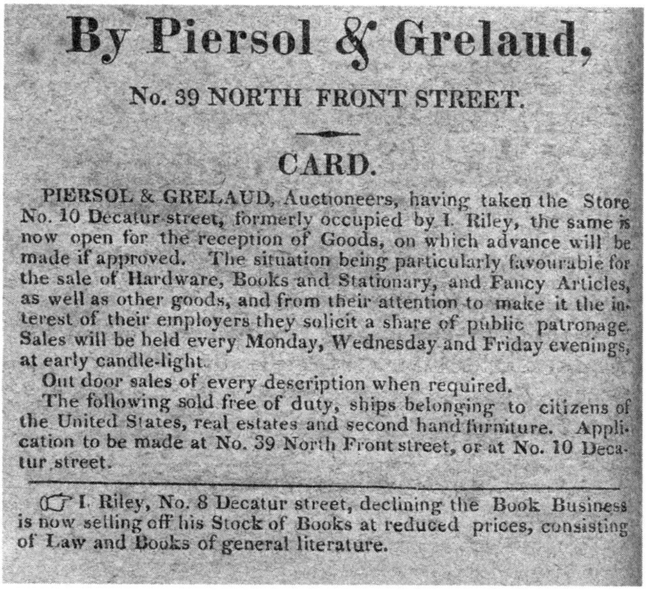

By Piersol & Grelaud,

No. 39 NORTH FRONT STREET.

___

CARD.

PIERSOL & GRELAUD, Auctioneers, having taken the Store No. 10 Decatur-street, formerly occupied by I. Riley, the same is now open for the reception of Goods, on which advance will be made if approved. The situation being particularly favourable for the sale of Hardware, Books and Stationary, and Fancy Articles, as well as other goods, and from their attention to make it the interest of their employers they solicit a share of public patronage. Sales will be held every Monday, Wednesday and Friday evenings, at early candle-light.

Out door sales of every description when required.

The following sold free of duty, ships belonging to citizens of the United States, real estates and second hand furniture. Application to be made at No. 39 North Front street, or at No. 10 Decatur street.

___

☞ I. Riley, No. 8 Decatur street, declining the Book Business is now selling off his Stock of Books at reduced prices, consisting of Law and Books of general literature.

Figure 9. Auctioneers such as Piersol & Grelaud advertised their services to "patrons" in city directories, with specific information about the types of goods and timing of sales. *Paxton's Philadelphia Advertiser* for 1819. Library Company of Philadelphia.

superior goods and services. If, as some writers complained, serving a single patron was debasing, serving "the public" was a broader civic good, much more than a run-of-the-mill exchange of money for goods.

The patronage model only went so far, however, in credentialing market actors whose skill was selling trust in uncertain circumstances. Auctioneers behaved both as brokers, hired to dispose of a distant merchant's or dead person's estate, and as businessmen, purchasing goods on speculation and repackaging them for optimal sale. Mobilizing their storytelling for multiple interests, they needed to convince those they worked with that they were agents of trust for information about the local scene as well as global markets.[80] Auctioneers' business correspondence reflected and helped produce a detailed knowledge of what would and would not sell in a particular city. The auctioneer's ability to know the "temperature" of a particular market for goods was essential to his value as a trustworthy businessman. In 1819 J. Schmidt & Co. had too many looking-glass plates to sell in New York, so they wrote to Philadelphia auctioneers, asking "what prospects there are" for selling such items "and on what prices we might calculate with some degree of safety. If you can hold out any encouragement we shall send you a parcel." Other traders, like New Yorker Francis W. Meriam, sent samples to help test market conditions in other cities.[81]

In building up expertise, auctioneers strove to distinguish themselves from clerks, a growing group of urban workers who took orders but had limited prospects for independence. In the Philadelphia patronage scandal, Samuel Fox, one of the men discussed in the behind-the-scenes conversations unearthed by the inquiry and son of an auctioneer, was finally placed not as a partner but as a clerk, paid $2,000 per year. The committee charged to investigate Governor Findlay's appointments was unclear on how clerks fit into the world of business. Was a clerkship a position for a promising young man or a gentle way to put an ineffective older man out to pasture? Was it reasonable for a clerk to be paid $2,000 per year, or did this salary clearly indicate corruption? They asked John Fox, Samuel's brother, "Is the situation of a first clerk or stageman in an Auctioneer's store considered a sinecure?" "Do its duties require experience, and are they arduous?" Appealed to in the debate over auction clerkships, the attorney Amos Ellmaker opined that a clerk was a tool, not a man of business. It was acceptable to hire a clerk or an auction crier who would assist with the daily sales activities, as long as he did not leverage his privileged position into a larger scheme by hiring deputy auctioneers to sell on his behalf. Such an employee, "properly speaking is not a *seller* of goods—no more than the Bell or Hammer which he uses. He merely calls the prices &c. for the seller." It was just as many clerks feared; they brought no more skill to the enterprise nor could they expect any more prospects within it than the common tools they wielded.[82]

Was commerce governed by favors and connections a relic of the past, in conflict with newer political ideals stressing manly independence? The men who initiated the petition against the Pennsylvania governor insisted that their complaint was not with influence per se but with patronage perverted, "to the base and dishonorable purposes of borrowing money and selling the offices on his gift with oppressive sinecures." This is why Samuel Fox's high salary for work that no one understood how to value rankled so strongly. The governor's "prostitution" of his power, they asserted, might be typical in Great Britain but in the United States would "with certainty lead to the sale of offices, and consequently to that corruption which must prove fatal to Freedom."[83]

In nineteenth-century politics, the term for such misuse of power was "monopoly," and opponents of licensing systems insisted that government favors did not belong in a democracy. The 1819 anti-auction pamphlet *Strictures on Monopolies* protested that such a system had no place "in a country in which the people take for granted they have a right to be free" and should leave unchallenged "the competency of any man to sell his own property, when necessity or inclination impel him to do so."[84] As "steady retailers" who previously depended on credit were edged out of the market by cash-based auctioneers, "a respectable body of people (lone women, widows, and families who were dependent for a livelihood on the regular prosecution of a fair customary retail trade)" went out of business and lost their ability to support themselves.[85] The authors argued that "respectable" people were best served by pursuing their own economic opportunities, not by being held captive to a privileged few with special commercial powers.

Those special powers of government patronage did not guarantee financial success, however. Auctioneers were not salaried placemen; they had to buy and sell and cope with the fluctuations of supply and demand just as any other man of business did. The inquiry into Governor Findlay revealed that the patronage system of licensing auctioneers failed to ensure stability or certify mastery. One of Findlay's original auctioneers, John Conrad, "although an upright and honest man" who fit the profile of respectable businessman, had to resign his post in October 1818 when his personal debts threatened to bankrupt the auction business he had forged with two partners. Nor did the governor's control over licenses imbue recipients with the judgment and rectitude lawmakers had hoped for. When a member of the House of Representatives asked John Jennings how he, a "man of upright mind," could accept an office from a corrupt officer, Jennings shrugged, concluding "that fact would [not] lessen the value of the commission,"[86] which had a value that Jennings calculated in primarily financial terms.

So in 1821 Pennsylvania rejected the patronage model in favor of the assumption that any man with financial backing could take a turn as auctioneer. Pennsylvania's new law divided auctioneers themselves into categories, much as auction tax laws established different rates for different classes of goods. Instead of an exclusive single list of chosen men, there was a three-tiered system open to those who could afford admission. "Auctioneers of the first grade," required to post a $6,000 bond, could subsequently sell anything by auction. Another group could sell hardware, books, stationery, paintings, prints, watches and jewelry after posting a bond of $3,000. Finally, those auctioneers who traveled to their product, selling "Household and Kitchen Furniture at the dwelling house of the owner thereof," "ships or vessels," or "real estate" needed only to pledge $1,000.

Auctioneers were no longer vouched for by the patronage of the governor but rather by the money they and their guarantors could post.[87]

The new system, modeled on Baltimore's, distinguished those goods on which duties must be paid (which required the attentions of an auctioneer with deep pockets and hefty bonds) from those sold duty-free (which were less directly tied to public interest), creating a kind of circular definition of commercial categories. One advocate of the new approach stressed that in addition to helping the state collect revenue, it would, by removing some of the uncertainty of business, encourage permanence and investment on the part of the auctioneers, who would "go to the expense of providing suitable accommodations, (rooms, storage, &c.) for the convenience of the public," which would "act as an excitement to a fair competition, by which the public interest would be promoted." If the public was the ultimate patron, auctioneers would serve their patrons better as entrepreneurs than as government agents.[88]

Not everyone was convinced that "fair competition" among vendues was the best way to serve the public interest because one fundamental problem with auctioneers—that they were agents who served the interests of sellers—could not be resolved through competition. Members of the public were not equally situated in terms of knowledge about goods and prices. In 1828 Hezekiah Niles, an auction critic and periodical editor, retold a story from Providence, Rhode Island, about frauds at auction in which "old trash" goods were doctored to appear to be from an esteemed British manufacturer. Niles claimed that "it is a well known part of every auctioneer's business, to conceal the names of those who employ him."[89] While any seller could exaggerate or obscure the features of the goods for sale, auctioneers had a particular incentive to do so.

According to their defenders, auctions had safeguards designed to combat the potential for fraud in exchanges between strangers. They were advertised in the newspapers as "public sales" and contrasted with the private sales that were ongoing in shops, warehouses, and streets around the city. Rules governed how they were publicized, how much auctioneers could charge clients, when and where they could sell, and how often they had to report duties to the state. The fact that potential bidders met at a single time, face-to-face, meant that negotiations were ostensibly subject to popular scrutiny and claims of genuineness verified by communal assent. On paper, at least, they were models of publicity and openness, qualities that made them appear uniquely democratic in the way they regulated economic behavior. One German observer suggested the predominance of this view in his description of Governor Findlay's 1820 reelection campaign, during which he made a point of being seen in the democratic activities of grocery shopping, shaking voters' hands, passing the whiskey jug, and attending public auctions.[90]

Critics frequently warned that auctioneers' cash (or short-term credit) business enabled them to operate outside of the most stable source of commercial authentication, which was a credit network. Personal and institutional networks of credit defined good business relationships for most merchants and, detractors insisted, auctioneers were not adequately enmeshed in those relationships. Instead, they saw auctioneers taking advantage of new sources of fungible value and mobile goods to speculate their way into business gains. In reality, the stability of credit networks themselves was under considerable pressure in the early republic, as older ideas about property accumulation contended with increasingly abstract understandings of commodities and the boom-bust financial cycles that resulted. Licensing and linking auctioneering explicitly to the governor's patronage were intended to keep the destabilizing possibilities of speculative pricing in check. Yet while Findlay's patronage, based on bribes and secrecy, might have created stability, it did so only by elevating the antidemocratic elements of favors over the promise of public service.

Celebrated freedoms to buy and sell were fraught with dangers of trust and problems of value, dangers illustrated dramatically by the public spectacle of auctions. Americans in trade who saw the potential of patronage to address these problems insisted that it must favor the worthy and promote the many rather than the few. Connections and favor were part of the economy, but only if they served to temper supply and demand in the interest of fairness for a larger public. Political patronage as wielded by Findlay elevated the unworthy and served personal greed. By twisting the liberality and generous investment that a gentleman was supposed to bestow, Findlay was a man without expertise or honor, an "auctioneer of offices" willing, like a prostitute, to sell intimate relationships for money.[91]

The Perils of Fraudulent Stories

As auctioneers battled the cultural perception that they were outsiders who disrupted and deceived, rather than essential distributors of goods who helped people get money quickly, they found themselves attacked in print as undeserving of the protected commercial status offered to other businessmen. In the decades after the American Revolution, lawmakers debated the proposition that a failed business should not land every person in jail, arguing that merchants and factors who took great commercial risks needed a way to wipe the slate clean and start over when they were dragged under by the vagaries of international commerce. States and the federal government experimented with new types of insolvency and bankruptcy relief, redefining debt as an economic, rather than a moral failure.[92] The auctioneer's risk, undertaken with someone else's property, was less obviously a necessary sacrifice to commercial growth.[93] An 1815 South Carolina law made it simpler for people who engaged auctioneers to sue for the proceeds of public sale of their goods if the funds were not forthcoming. Describing the money owed to the original property owners as "debts," the act further prohibited auctioneers from taking advantage of laws protecting insolvent debtors and allowing them to remain out of physical prisons.[94]

From the South Carolina lawmakers' perspective, auctioneers needed the motivating fear of imprisonment to conduct fair and timely transactions on behalf of community members who were often in dire straits. Auctioneer supporters, in response, decried the law as one that "sanction[ed] revenge, malevolence and oppression" and disregarded the obvious truth that "vendue masters, like every other description of persons engaged in commerce, are liable to losses, incident to the vicissitudes of business."[95] After asserting the idea that auctioneers were just like any businessman, this defender shifted to the ways that they were different: unlike a direct contract of sale in which the buyer fails to pay, a sale through an auctioneer was "only intermediate . . . and peradventure the vendue master never receives the money for the goods he sells, and is therefore in some degree *comparatively blameless*."[96] Governor Thomas Bennett, addressing the legislature in 1822, argued that auctioneers were unique only in being the target of punishment and they properly belonged in a more general category of agents. He pointed out that "the clerk, attorney, broker, factor and executor, necessarily exercise control over the property of others. . . . Yet vendue masters under the *degrading reflection* of being the only class of persons in society on whom the suspicions of the Legislature are implied to rest, are subjected to perpetual imprisonment for inability to meet the claims of creditors."[97] Eventually, lawmakers were convinced, repealing the penalty for auctioneers while at the same time requiring Charleston auctioneers to provide additional sureties to the City Council.[98]

Suspicion of the auctioneer as an untrustworthy political protégé subverting the public good had broad cultural resonance beyond Philadelphia and Charleston. The tools that auctioneers employed to attract bidders and shape their interactions had an artificiality that was easy to parody. Teague O'Regan—the central character in Hugh Henry Brackenridge's *Modern Chivalry* (published as a novel in 1815)—traded on patronage to become an auctioneer and found himself in a position far above his talents or capacity. In the novel, eager men "subjected him to flattery," to "compliment the strength of his voice, his vein of humour, which term they could give to his coarse jokes, and call it wit."[99] O'Regan demonstrated that patronage was no hedge against the infiltration of questionable outsiders into the marketplace; indeed, it could be a conduit. His ultimate ambition to be elevated to ambassador was only extinguished when his patron threatened him with forced circumcision. Lacking character or honor, the agent could not qualify as a proper man.[100]

The specter of the auctioneer as dangerous fraud soon expanded. Newspapers began printing stories about so-called mock auctions at which low-quality goods were fraudulently boosted by a group of confederates posing as auctioneer, clerk, and bidding audience members. Reporting on these enterprises was popular because it offered an exaggerated version of long-standing debates over the proper rules of exchange and touched, once again, on the tenuous connection between market value and market values.[101] Operating completely outside of licensing or patronage systems, a criminal gang used the familiar trappings of an auction to defraud gullible members of the public. The scam worked because city-dwellers relied on crowd endorsement of an auctioneer's tale to judge authentic value from worthless goods.

The mock auction was an economic fable with a new stock character—"Peter Funk," a false bidder whose choreographed enthusiasm was essential for egging on the marks who attended the sales. Funk appeared in accounts from New York to San Francisco throughout the nineteenth century. He and his confederates flipped the openness and interactivity of bidding on its head, and the cautionary tales popular in the press warned readers that they should not believe their experiences and judgments because matters in the market were not what they seemed. The auctioneer's skills could be deployed for sinister ends; his tools of organization, preview, and control enabled fraudulent manipulation that was all the crueler for purporting to honor the judgment of viewers and participants. "Even a prudent man may be influenced" by seeing others bid "to believe that the article for sale is in demand, and the judgment expressed by others of its value may have an effect on [the] estimate which he forms of it" warned *Niles' Weekly Register*.[102] Framed as criminal enterprises and targeted at one point by the mayor of New York with a poster campaign, "mock auctions" became shorthand for the swindles of the modern marketplace that everyday consumers were helpless to counteract.[103] Auctioneers insisted that "the publicity of their character, the Integrity of the individuals who conduct them, and their disinterested position between the buyer and seller, have a tendency to facilitate the discovery of fraud, and to insure its punishment."[104] Americans who followed the exciting tales of financial fraud in the papers, and even nonreaders who felt outmatched by the fast-paced sales they witnessed, were not so sure.

Derogatory stereotypes of auctioneers contributed to spreading fears about marketplace fraud. A limited group of stock commercial actors, such as the Jewish moneylender, had existed for centuries, and commercial personae expanded and found new forms in the nineteenth century. As access to money and goods expanded, the archetypal moneylender reappeared as the Jewish pawnbroker, ragman, labor broker, and auctioneer.[105] Indeed, O'Regan's threatened circumcision tapped into a current of antisemitism, and Peter Funk himself was depicted in the press as a German Jew.[106] Certainly, commercial communities of all sorts assembled around shared religious and familial ties. In early nineteenth-century Charleston, a network of Jewish men worked as auctioneers. They supported one another by forming partnerships and guaranteeing the bonds that auctioneers had to put up to obtain licenses to set up public sales. In 1808 Jacob DeLeon and Isaac C. Moses signed the £5,000 sterling bond of Jacob Cohen and Moise Abrams's firm Jacob Cohen & Company; in turn, Jacob Cohen and Isaac C. Moses signed the £5,000 sterling bond of Jacob DeLeon and Myer Moses's firm of Myer Moses & Company.[107]

Stock characters in popular culture staked out new ground, isolating aspects of the market economy that were especially troubling. The fictional O'Regan and Funk joined a new group of commercial personae that embodied the ambivalences of nineteenth-century capitalism, including the despised slave trader who served as a foil for supposedly honorable slaveholders, the pitiful seamstress who deserved charity but not equitable union wages, and the foolish merchant's clerk who embodied the degraded masculinity of urban life.[108] These types depended on crude binaries that denied the humanity of the individuals doing the work and the variety of experiences such workers had. They also limited the scope of the stories to be told about the economy by confining the protagonists to a familiar roster.

Because they were understood to be types, such stock characters in print played up the theatricality of market exchanges in place of their more complex social and economic function within communities. The auctioneer's tools of storytelling, for example, were created to respond directly to the people in front of him, who had their own ideas and often histories with the property being put up for sale. Storytelling had long been part of a communal interaction, mediated by law and social relations, in which competition was tempered with moral economy ideas about the proper distribution of goods. Abstracted from its social reality in newspaper tales of the duplicitous Peter Funk, the auctioneer's story came to seem like so many lies.

*   *   *

The rules governing auctions at one level appeared designed to establish a free market where people made price-setting decisions in an open competition. By the nineteenth century, auctioneers talked about their role in just this way. New York auctioneers insisted in 1821 that "public Sales in their general character, are no longer the resort of the necessitous, who are compelled to the sacrifice of property by the pressure of distress. Buyer and seller now meet on neutral ground for their mutual advantage. Auctions are employed as the most secure and convenient medium for the sale and purchase of merchandize at the current market rate."[109] In this formulation, auctioneers presented their sales as equivalent to markets and their prices as constituting the going rate.

Such claims were strategic rather than descriptive.[110] The reality of the auction was that individuals participating in it were not equally positioned, and the auctioneer was the one typically blamed for this imbalance. He misrepresented goods and cajoled and pressured people into making hasty and irrational choices at questionable prices. His expertise could not be situated in a long-standing network of patronage or a contemporary set of credit relationships. As such, he was a stand-in for larger transformations in market practices during the early nineteenth century, as migrants pushed onto land claimed by the United States and new commercial communities formed miles away from old familiar hubs.

In many senses an auctioneer's work followed the contours of other businessmen, whether brokers or merchants; they, too, established extensive commercial correspondence networks, advertised their products and services, and interacted with the civil court system. But the auctioneer also operated a set of distinctive tools—the catalog, the lot, the bid, the chant—that ultimately contributed to a commercial persona of a scheming businessman and likely fraud. Suspicions about his powers of manipulation had circulated for decades. In 1779 South Carolina legislators noted that "a practice has prevailed among vendue masters . . . to bid for the said goods, either with a view of enhancing the prices of the same, or of fixing the prices of goods of a similar kind."[111] Auctioneers had multiple practical ways to manipulate sales, and attending bidders could only keep them in check if they were knowledgeable.

By repeatedly targeting the auctioneer, laws and the print culture that lampooned or condemned him identified a shift in thinking about exchange. While auctions had always paired open, participatory elements with structures and assumptions that preordained outcomes, the same could be said of many kinds of marketplace experiences, including haggling and discounting on the one hand and government price controls on the other. The difference in the early republic "character of auctioneer" was that his manipulations were for the gains of unseen others as community interaction grew subordinated to a more anonymous system of capitalism.

CHAPTER 5

The Value of a Woman's Body,
the Cost of a Woman's Bid

In late spring 1816, two enterprising businessmen opened a "Ladies' Retail Auction Room" in New York City. They pledged to "offer a great variety of fancy articles" in a room fitted to an "elegant style."[1] By July they were under attack in the pages of local newspapers. One critic called the establishment "as novel as it is pregnant with mischief," painting in lurid colors the predicted race-mixing and sexual danger that would occur in a space of open bidding attractive to women.[2] He called immediately for a citizens' meeting to demand that the state legislature shut down the establishment. By the end of the year, an organized group of "Merchants and Traders" went further, penning a wide-ranging essay charging the state government to take action and restrict all kinds of auction sales in the name of morality, fair competition, and national commercial health.[3] The auction wars, which embroiled multiple eastern cities and culminated in a short-lived political party, were on.

The political auction wars of the early republic drew on long-standing suspicions that auctions were places of shady dealing and bad behavior that had hardened into public condemnation of auctioneers as frauds, illegitimately bolstered by antidemocratic patronage favors.[4] They gained momentum as postcolonial protests since many of the goods put under the hammer by those auctioneers had been "dumped" in American cities by British manufacturers at the end of the War of 1812.[5] And they voiced emerging ideas about civic engagement and consumer rights.[6] Like the so-called bank war of the early 1830s, participants in the auction wars battled over the proper role of the government in promoting commerce and protecting citizens.[7] Protectionists worried that auctions undermined national political economy and argued that taxation of auctions belonged alongside a strong tariff to nurture US manufacturing. A coalescing group of merchants and artisans believed that British-dominated auctions represented an unfair "monopoly" and petitioned Congress for greater regulation.[8] Attending to these political pronouncements, scholars have viewed the auction wars primarily as a contest among economic institutions, as commercial men pushed their government to actively balance the interests of farmers, merchants, and manufacturers in order to stabilize the new nation's place in the world.[9]

But there was also a gender problem at the heart of the auction debate that revealed a broader cultural transformation over the meaning of economic value. When the critic called the ladies' auction rooms "novel," he was in one sense correct—there was no tradition of auction rooms catering exclusively to women (or to men, for that matter), although women of all ranks had long participated in auctions as part of their economic lives. The "novel" gender problem of auctions was not the fact of women as market actors but rather the perceived mischief done at auctions. Many Americans were grappling with uncertainties over how to value objects or relationships in a monetizing culture. Expanding open markets presented a series of dilemmas around the instability of value. The fact that market valuation in the form of price could fluctuate challenged the possibility of shared community standards and the fixed worth of something like gold. At the same time, the reach of market relations into human domains threatened the conviction that anything, or anyone, could remain invaluable.

Female bids, female bodies, and female labor all became sites for securing value at a time when other measures seemed unstable, speculative, and constantly changing.[10] The flourishing of paper money issued by chartered and wildcat banks, import and export firms, and transportation companies undermined expectations of what money was worth. International credit relationships wove webs of indebtedness such that a panic on one side of the Atlantic rippled across the ocean to ruin lives on the other. Land speculation produced boom and bust valuations of parcels that had participants reeling. As one man claimed about the public sales of territory, "no certainty remains; two thousand dollars' worth of land may be struck off at vendue for the trifling sum of one hundred dollars."[11]

Against this unsettling backdrop, the auction wars jousted over the possibilities of fixed values in race and gender. Auctions had always operated as open venues for broad economic participation and simultaneously as performances whose outcomes were determined by community norms and institutional structures. Some prices and some distributions of goods were up for negotiation, but there were nonnegotiables, too. There were reserve prices that established the minimum bid and ticketing systems that sometimes limited who could participate. There were customary practices, such as the sense that a widow should have the winning bid on parts of her late husband's estate. And there was the fact that enslaved people were put under the hammer alongside land and dry goods, defining them as property before the bidding even began. In each of these cases, values created outside the marketplace—such as who deserved certain goods, or who could be entrusted to join a group of community bidders—filtered the valuation produced by the sale.

The place of women at nineteenth-century auctions—as commodities, as bidders, or as beneficiaries—became a focal point for gendering economic value itself. When the legal international trade in enslaved human beings closed in 1808, the reproductive value of enslaved women's bodies gained new economic and political significance.[12] The speculative value in a woman's body had been built into colonial laws underpinning American slavery, and the urgency of that investment pressed on early nineteenth-century slaveholders who planned to raise up the next generation of laborers rather than import them. The idea that enslaved motherhood was a source of capital growth was routinely enacted at public auctions that commodified female bodies' sexual and reproductive potential. The presence of free women's bodies in these same commercial spaces suggested that their sexuality could also be valued with a price and that their reproduction, too, supported economic growth.

An emerging middle-class ideal insisted on the opposite, presenting economic relationships and reproductive lives as "hostile worlds" for free families. In this formulation, the household intimacies of husband and wife or parent and child had emotional, spiritual, and social value as long as they were not coarsened by economic calculation. In turn, economic transactions were rational and fair insofar as they played no favorites and calculated value in dollars and cents rather than friendships forged or long-standing agreements jeopardized.

The conviction that love and money were opposites, which appeared in multiple forms in the popular print culture, pulled against lived experience. Intimate relationships were routinely and increasingly negotiated through money in the form of banknotes and insurance. Waged labor depended on familial forms.[13] City-dwellers paid boardinghouse keepers for food and cleaning that in another context would be considered caring labor. And day after day, traders and assessors priced enslaved motherhood.

Auction stories, frequently satirical, narrated intersecting definitions of what could and what should not be commodified by reinforcing markers of difference linked to race and gender as binary categories (Black/white, male/female). While auctioneers' critics focused on what they termed "fraud," the central problem revealed in ladies' auctions was not criminal but cultural. Anti-auction politics insisted on the need for shared, fixed standards and asserted the critics' claims of stability by invoking the supposedly natural attributes of race and gender. Ladies' auctions, ladies at auction, and women under the hammer, however, revealed the complex ways that the value of gender and race could be fluid even as the emerging capitalist economy reinforced them as binaries.

Auction Wars, Bargain Prices, and "Regular" Commerce

When P. B. Van Beuren and Elijah Mix launched their Ladies' Retail Auction Room in 1816, they were joining an expanding business sector in American cities at the close of the War of 1812. British manufacturers, eager to access American markets again to sell stockpiles of fabric and other dry goods, had discovered that urban auction houses, which were familiar vehicles to liquidate ruined shipments or ruined businesses, could distribute their goods for cash or short credit. American auctioneers such as those appointed by Governor Findlay of Pennsylvania, in turn, saw an opportunity to compete with import merchants, who typically sold merchandise on long credit, by instead turning imported stock over for immediate payment.[14] The businesses soon presented a visible claim on public commercial space. A reader had just to "cast his eyes on auction advertisements" in East Coast newspapers, one alarmed report asserted, and "he will frequently find a whole side of the paper filled with them!"[15]

As in the eighteenth century, nineteenth-century auctions promised bargains, and low prices became a political problem in the aftermath of the War of 1812. Auction opponents insisted that the low prices of public sales were not fair prices, either in terms of how they tracked with the true value of the items or in terms of how they came about. Writing under the pseudonym "COMMON SENSE," one insisted that the "system" of auction sales was "unquestionably demoralizing . . . for that which renders uncertain and unstable the mercantile course of things, more or less destroys those 'steady habits' which create confidence, and on which honor and honesty are based."[16] If that was the case, the writer continued, "of what avail has been your well-fought battles in the second war for independence"?[17] During the war, Congress had taxed goods sold at non-court-directed auctions at 3 percent in order to raise funds for the conflict. In peacetime, merchants in cities along the East Coast demanded that the tax be extended and increased to 10 percent, which would raise the price of goods sold at auctions of imports and make space for US merchants and shopkeepers to compete for customers.

American import merchants framed their opposition to auctions as one of regular commerce standing firm against irregular forms of buying and selling that threatened the stability of the local business community. They claimed that, as merchants, they served the public in well-informed, orderly market trans-actions, while auctioneers moved stock by duping hapless bidders to purchase goods no one could vouch for. The New York Society for the Encouragement of Domestic Manufactures, which entered the newspaper debate, charged that auc-tioneers, "whose office was formerly *subordinate* to that of the merchant," had, in recent years, received unfair preferences that would destroy both the merchant class and all those who, "without being commercial, depend upon commerce for their support. . . . The proprietor, the mechanic, the artist, the laborer follow in the train, and must seek elsewhere for subsistence."[18]

In truth, there was considerable crossover both in the manner of sales and who was doing the selling. As they had in the eighteenth century, businesses regu-larly advertised private sales on one day and auctions on another. Furthermore, men who obtained auction licenses had frequently been merchants themselves.[19] Merchants also depended on auctions. Their warehouses filled with goods that had customs bonds pledging the payment of import duties for those same goods. When those bonds came due, they needed to sell off stock, and they turned to auctions to sell quickly as public sales were their "only means of disembarrassing themselves."[20] Yet, over and over, opponents contrasted the secondary function of auctions with the primary function of merchants and shopkeepers, hoping to define regular trade in a way that benefited their own ledgers.[21] It was the irregu-lar auction trade, they contended, that moved quickly with cash and short credit sales and that created the low prices they could not compete with.

A group of New York merchants and traders insisted that, via auctions, "citizens are supplied with goods made not for use, but for sale," and thus the prices were lies.[22] Their charge was a direct blow against the idea that value was generated in the moment of exchange and in favor of an understanding of value that revealed itself in the use of goods over time. Newspapers circulated a story about a bundle of blue fabric sold to New York merchants in a private sale that turned out not to be the promised indigo but rather inferior, logwood dye. When the customers discovered the misrepresentation, they returned the fabric to the merchants, who in turn demanded repayment from the foreign agent. But this form of commercial check and balance was swiftly undermined

by the foreign supplier, who simply resold the fabric at auction instead, at a
30 percent markup. Who suffered when the supposed safety measures of regular
commerce failed? The "industrious farmer and mechanic of the north, and the
planter of the south," who attended the auction in search of bargains. Such men
bought fabric for "coat[s] for their wives and daughters" only to watch the articles fade, "blue one week and brown the next" due to deteriorating dyestuffs.[23]
The duplicitous foreign agent profited, and the auctioneers collected their fees.
And the lesson? "All's fair in trade." Yet the author rejected "buyer beware" as
an appropriate market ethic by insisting that indigo- and logwood-dyed fabrics
had intrinsic or true values that were fundamentally different because of how
they functioned as clothing.[24]

Speculation, as to whether bargain blue cloth would sell and whether it
would serve customers, involved risks around valuation that pervaded all forms
of exchange. By 1815 almost two hundred banks in the United States issued
forms of paper money, as did a variety of state-chartered companies, and these
paper bills circulated alongside tokens and various forms of domestically minted
and foreign coinage in a confusing array. Furthermore, while early nineteenth-
century banks pledged that their paper bills could be redeemed for gold or silver,
they issued more bills than they could redeem in precious metals through business and personal loans that they hoped would keep the money in circulation.[25]
A depositor, investor, or someone who accepted a note in payment was making
a gamble. If a bank closed, the notes still in circulation became pieces of paper,
nothing more. Likewise, if the note looked legitimate but was in fact a product
of the thriving counterfeit trade that agents pushed into ordinary transactions,
bringing it to a bank could reveal it was worthless. The value of a note therefore rested on parties' confidence in its ability to be exchanged. If the receiver
were unsure, either about the note itself, the bank it drew on, or the person who
passed it along, he would discount the value of the piece of paper—meaning that
a note that said ten dollars might only be worth $9.50.[26]

The pervasive uncertainty about the value of a dollar was evident in a series
of financial panics, the first in 1819, that overlapped with the auction wars. Communities had faced hard times and postwar depressions in the eighteenth century, but the 1819 speculative bubble spread bank failures, mortgage foreclosures,
and unemployment across regions. Expansive communication made possible by
new transportation and publication venues created the sense of a shared crisis in
value. In struggling to make sense of this peacetime financial panic, participants
blamed irrational speculators, greedy banks, and frauds. Restoring stability and
security, some claimed, would require rational, regulated daily exchange.[27]

The price fluctuations in the postwar years were not caused by auctioneers, but the experience of watching the same goods knocked down for different prices produced an unsettling shock that value, which supposedly underlay prices, was itself speculative. Auctions were guilty of "breaking up the very foundations of regular business, deranging all the calculations of those concerned in commerce . . . and doing away with the idea of a settled value to any species of property," as one pamphlet put it. In other words, calculations could manage change, whether that be predicting customer demands or factoring a reasonable profit on a new commodity, but not if every value was unknowable. One published memorial claimed that, because of the rise of auctions, "confidence is destroyed between the purchaser and the vendor, because there is no longer a fixed rule to which they can resort as the standard of a fair price."[28] The "fixed rule" was not necessarily a defined price but instead a set of business practices and social relations that auction opponents brought under the umbrella of regular business. In all of the ink spilled in the auction wars, the writers' rhetoric contrasted a fluid world of unstable values and calculations rendered moot by unpredictability with the purportedly sober, regular trade of merchants in which prices made sense and were fair.[29]

Auction critics—primarily white male traders and politicians—insisted that female customers were part of the scourge of irregular commerce, and that the permissive atmosphere of auctions encouraged the shedding of gendered ideas of proper market behavior. With no enforcement of a fair price, bidders were free to use auctions to pursue bargains at all costs, a situation that disordered the power dynamics between buyers and sellers (and free men and women more generally). Merchants huffed that spoiled customers, "too much in the habit of not purchasing unless they have a large abatement, whether the goods are at fair prices or not," resorted to tricks to obtain a deal, and "some, even females, are so lost to a sense of right as to tell fibs, saying they can purchase better goods for less money, &c."[30] Released from the stability—or rigidity—of conventional prices by the presence of urban auctions, female shoppers could, such critics feared, bluff a retailer into offering a bargain.

Auctions' defenders were quick to point out that competition based on price was not a nefarious manipulation but rather a practice encouraged by consumers themselves, and merchants' critiques of the dangers of fluctuating prices were in fact a lament that they could not compete. One writer quoted Adam Smith's *Wealth of Nations* in observing that "it always is, and must be the interest of the great body of the people to buy whatever they want of those who sell it the cheapest." Any challenge to this "commonsense" could only come from "the interested sophistry of merchants and manufacturers."[31] In other words, forcing consumers to reject imports because they were inexpensive was merely self-interest cloaked as patriotism. In that way, it was no better than the prewar embargo that had banned British and French imports and, when people purchased inexpensive left-over imports at auction anyway, punished them under a policy built for "entrapping the ladies and making them feel the vengeance of the law."[32]

"Ladies" as a Commercial Category

The commercial meaning of "ladies," a term used by the Ladies' Retail Auction Room to explosive effect, was in flux in the years of the auction wars. Far from a straightforward opposite to "gentlemen," the concept was deployed by sellers on both sides of the Atlantic to segment the market and encourage purchases. As a result, the designation of a "ladies'" auction was, like "auction prices," a marketing strategy. Presuming that gender identity was a main way that people experienced public life, sellers struggling to compete in an economy crowded with merchandise promoted the idea of "ladies'" goods or experiences as one of their strategies to move stock. When, in 1758, the first dedicated "auction rooms" were advertised in Boston, gender-linked amenities were part of the attraction. Space in that first auction room was identified as "commodious (both for Men and Women)." The auctioneer promised to behave so as to suit the supposed special needs of female bidders. He would act "with Honor and Fidelity, Decency and Decorum—So that even the Matron, or the Damsel, need not fear being offended."[33] Subsequent auction rooms in New York City promised that "proper seats will be reserved for the ladies," at a sale of dry goods.[34]

The concept of an overtly gendered market space appealed to auctioneers, and soon after Van Beuren and Mix opened their novel establishment, John Dorsey, a Philadelphia auctioneer, decided that he, too, would launch ladies' auctions because they "had been attended with merited success in New York."[35] Dorsey intended to focus on selling "very superior articles," whether supplied by agents, manufacturers, or women consigning "elegancies" to him. In Baltimore, S & J Cole tested the waters with a single "Ladies Auction" sale of "*Four superb PIANO FORTES*," which ladies could inspect and listen to the day before the sale.[36] Additional ladies' auction rooms emerged in locations around New York City, with auctioneers organizing sales of jewelry, tableware, and small pieces of furniture.[37]

The ladies' retail auction rooms in fact linked two groups of "ladies," by offering low prices to female buyers and also quick liquidation to female sellers.

Auctioneers promised "liberal advances" on goods "deposited for sale," provided they were fashionable and a good fit with the rest of the merchandise. They routinely placed enticements at the end of their advertisements, inviting "ladies and gentlemen" with articles they "wished to dispose of" to deposit them in time for the next sales catalog to be prepared.[38] By drawing on cultural ideas around refinement and free women's daily financial practices, auctioneers crafted customers who would keep them in business.

Creating new categories of goods and suggesting an appropriate clientele was a proven way to increase consumption. Furniture makers in Britain discovered this in the 1760s, when they started selling tables, desks, and cases "for the ladies" or "for a gentleman."[39] Consumer goods previously of undifferentiated status were reimagined as property for groups called "ladies" or "gentlemen" and advertised in US newspapers by the turn of the century. Customers agreed that some items were gendered. In 1816 John Pintard encouraged his daughter in New Orleans to pass along shopping requests to her mother, who was a regular at the city auctions. She could receive low prices for her daughter "for many articles in the female line" at auctions, he promised.[40] Typically, when consumers or sellers talked about "ladies" or female-gendered property, they were referring to goods associated with self-fashioning such as clothing, jewelry, and home furnishings. Such gendered designations were not limited to auction rooms; by the nineteenth century, advertisements from many different types of sellers routinely promoted "gentlemen's" and "ladies'" articles to be sold. Sellers therefore reinforced the idea that distinct groups of customers—in this case, ladies and gentlemen—existed and desired different kinds of goods. These categories were inventions, and yet attached to gender terms that implied an inborn basis to them.

Not all people born female were included when an advertisement called out to "ladies," because the term was intended to signal class and racial boundaries for potential shoppers. The auction-house operators Van Beuren and Mix were quickly accused of transgressing these boundaries by catering to a "motley group" of bidders, meaning one in which people of multiple races, classes, and genders intermixed. In their printed defense against this charge, they directed readers to judge them by the "ladies" present, who "have been the most respectable of our city."[41] The presence of respectable women, they believed, had the power to insulate their establishment from accusations of immorality. Their strategy was to make a tight and reinforcing connection between respectable female consumers and specific classes of ornamental goods and housewares, even if the actual clientele and the items for sale were, as with most auctions, far more diverse and varied. Early republic cities had growing free Black communities, for example, which in New York made up just over 8 percent of the population.[42] Yet these New Yorkers, who joined the ranks of urban workers and consumers, were excluded in the language of gendered gentility.

Auctioneers argued that the presence of ladies elevated commerce; detractors insisted that they degraded it, and in so doing, degraded themselves. Satires skewering the group of white women, Black men, and "gentlemen who wear corsets" at the ladies' auctions rejected the idea that a gendered marketplace could be orderly and even genteel. The innovation of celebrating a commercial space for "ladies" was undercut by its very novelty; it was, by definition, deviation from regular trade.[43] The fact that irregular trade was a fluid category that reflected power differentials rather than any particular law was evident in the way it was picked up by authors of divergent politics. A writer could in the same essay defend some kinds of auctions but still condemn the New York Ladies' Retail Auction Room as "a justly reprobated pest of regular trade."[44]

Controlling the physical presence of male and female consumers reinforced pretentions to gentility for auction establishments that did not stand up dedicated ladies' auctions, as when Cudworth, Waller, & Co. in South Carolina promised a dedicated auction room that would offer shelter for bidders "from the Inclemency of Weather in Winter, and the scorching Heat of the Sun in Summer."[45] In their stage managing, these advertisers sought to create a genteel consumer experience that still preserved the enticing promise of low prices and the enjoyable social drama of bidding. Jacob Mordecai, looking back on the Philadelphia vendue store of the early nineteenth century, reported that "it was the general custom for wives and widows to attend at auction stores, then called vendues, and purchase goods for their shop supplies. Benches were placed in rows in front of the vendue shelves. There a preference was always given to female purchasers to occupy the front seats. Goods were passed along, every body being seated."[46] Pragmatic women looking to stock their shops sat, as did ladies in search of a new tea table. The goods moved, but the women did not; there was no motley mixing, Mordecai insisted.

Efforts such as these to make some auctions genteel by marking goods, spaces, or bodily practices as appropriate for ladies and gentlemen were at odds with the enduring appeal of auctions as open-air opportunities for anyone to wander by and bid at or watch. Many sellers wanted to have it both ways, by appealing broadly and also in targeted ways to find their customers. Jacob Cohen in Charleston, South Carolina, used auctions to sell a wide variety of goods to the public, and he depended on holding auctions outdoors, in front of his store, to capture the attention of Charlestonians. But he was careful to separate the sales so as to serve distinct groups of buyers. In the early morning, he displayed "gentlemen & ladies gold watches" for bidders; at noon, he lined up five enslaved people, including women, children, and "an old man" in front of the store.[47]

Although advertisements like Cohen's were designed to suggest that sales of fancy accessories and sales of people were distinct, the truth was that a shopper at his establishment looking for a ladies' watch before breakfast could return to the neighborhood to bid on a child in the afternoon. The terms "ladies" and "gentlemen" in a commercial context worked to obscure the common humanity of the people who made purchases and the people who were purchased. These highly gendered words, designed to exclude on the basis of race and class, structured the terms of exchange and reinforced the notion that some people could be treated as objects for sale just as a fancy watch was. Advertisements and commercial notices did not have to mention human commodification explicitly to assert that some people acted in the economy and to imply that others were acted on.

Legal practice provided reinforcing justification for defining gender and race through commercial exchange. The types of items in advertisements for ladies' auctions—jewelry, clothing, trinkets, tableware—were those that even free married women, limited under the laws of coverture in their ability to claim property rights, could control within their families.[48] Free women of all backgrounds treated property worn on their bodies and property associated with housework as their own, to take with them, sell, or preserve from male family members' designs. In her published notice refuting her husband's claims that she had abandoned his household, a Vermonter Hannah West was willing to acknowledge that the "farm, horses, cows, hogs, etc." that she had shared with her husband were "his," but when he took "all my cloth that I had to clothe my family with . . . my flax, wool, and all the provisions which we raised on our farm the last year, which was enough to have supported our family, and to have sold to the amount of 200 dollars," he overstepped.[49] The textiles were hers, to support her family as she saw fit through sale, trade, or preservation.

Americans knew that the items they lived with every day could be turned into money, but they disagreed over who was allowed to benefit from that transaction, whether the debate was between a merchant and an auctioneer or a husband and a wife. Social and political power did not always translate into control over the value of goods. As the historian Laura Edwards has observed, "a handkerchief was better than a dollar bill" for women looking to secure value in objects that they could keep for themselves and plan to use in the future.[50] Dollar bills in the nineteenth century were ephemeral and often of questionable authenticity, but textiles were enmeshed in legal principles that supported ownership claims by white women and people of color in the face of challenges. Even enslaved women might expect to keep, and trade, their clothing and small accessories. Auctioneers benefited from these associations as they fashioned a gender-divided commercial world.

Trash to Treasure: Women's Work

The gender problem of auctions highlighted the challenges that a monetizing economy presented to everyday concepts of value. In a market economy, price— the public marker of value—was not fixed. As Adam Smith and political econo- mists who followed him suggested, rather, that value crystalized when an object was exchanged, with an explicit or assumed price attached. While Smith posited a natural link between the price of a good and the labor it took to create it, auctions challenged that connection by serving as a conduit for the regular revaluation of goods. At the ladies' auction, one writer complained, "refuse goods . . . in milli- ners' and jewellers' shops," "if boxed up and sold at auction, would be equally new and equally valuable" as the imports "hawked about" from city to city.[51]

What caused the transformation from trash to treasure? To critics, the answer was clear: "fashion, extravagance, speculation, and idleness."[52] With no value-adding work other than boxing up old goods to enact the transformation, there could be no rational explanation for bids that rendered the leftovers new. One satirical announcement promised to auction off the used gowns of French ladies to American consumers and presumed that the bidders did not care if a dress was made of woolen scraps if in the poor light of evening the mismatched pieces "will not be perceptible." Indeed, the fictional seller was confident that some ladies would "give more than three times the retail price" for the chance to be the winning bid.[53]

Free female bidders pushed the supposed vices of female shoppers into the limelight and raised the stakes in this environment of unstable value. While male competitiveness was gaining cultural acceptance as an economically bene- ficial force, female competitiveness at auction was assailed in print culture as the manifestation of the socially destructive impulses of rivalry and jealousy. A fictional Carolina Augustina Bluestocking satirically rated the establishment of ladies' auction rooms in Boston as "one of the best schools for *economy* that was ever invented," given women's willingness to give "three times the value of an article, in order triumphantly to out-bid some other lady"[54] As Bluestocking's satire implied, this was neither economy in the sense of prudent shepherding

of resources nor economy in the sense of the rational flow of goods from supplier to consumer. It was heedless behavior, made all the more galling because,
Bluestocking insisted, these free women lacked any real skin in the game. They
exploited their "father or husband's purse or imprudence" with the result of dis-
ordering the community price-finding function of a public sale.

With jealousy and vanity motivating bidding, women could easily be mis-
led to purchase heedlessly, at least according to their detractors. David Lewis, a
notorious criminal and counterfeiter, attended the Ladies' Retail Auction Room
with the express purpose of stealing from rich women. Dressed "like a 'gentleman in true dandy style,'" which he claimed was "the sure passport of admittance
into female society," he attended one auction and later reported finding himself
in the glittering company of ladies such as Sarah Todd Astor, married to the fur-
trading and real estate tycoon John Jacob Astor. Lewis described the auctioneer
as a like-minded scoundrel who knew that "the best plan for picking a lady's
purse was to dazzle her eyes" with fine lace and French jewelry.[55] Dazzled women
overspent and then, in the case of Astor, carelessly threw her reticule filled with
lace and jewelry on a bench; Lewis snatched it away.

The stream of satire that skewered every aspect of free women at auctions—
from their motivations to their behavior to their judgments—went beyond old,
familiar complaints about free women as irresponsible consumers. Rather, these
satires spoke to discomfort with the fluidity of market values and the financial possibilities this fluidity offered to people with unstable legal and political
power. When "Old Kaleidoscope" criticized the Ladies' Retail Auction Room,
he mocked the "wife who buys at one auction and sells at another" for acting
merely "to keep her[self] in pin money," using a term for female discretionary
funds that implied she was frittering away her profits on nonessentials.[56] But
salvaging value from used or surplus goods and putting that value back into the
economy was one of the unpaid tasks of nineteenth-century housewifery. As sellers, free women used auctions to liquidate household items for cash. Auctioneers
then advertised their sales "to housekeepers" looking to outfit their living spaces.
Despite detractors' assertions, the importance of this practice to free women's
solvency was evident when disaster struck. One widowed mother of five had a
purse with $157 in it stolen from Gammage & Cooper's Ladies' Auction Room
in 1818. The bills—mainly $20s, but also one each at $50, $5, and $2—represented her children's "support," according to the notice in the newspapers.[57]

Free women who used auctions to repurpose goods and recirculate value
joined a range of professionals who presented themselves as experts in valuing.
Pawnbrokers learned what objects were worth through daily appraisals.[58] Lawyers,

clerks, and so-called wreckers mastered the workings of complex new financial instruments, including paper money and stock certificates, then swooped in at bankruptcy proceedings to profit from their insider knowledge. The success of these professionals came in separating the exchange value of an object from personal or other values, then realizing that value in another market transaction. Because they did not create some new tangible good through their activities but "merely appropriated it," both male professionals and the women who repurposed goods alike were portrayed in popular culture as parasites, descending on a tragedy to benefit themselves like the men and women who waded out into the shallows to salvage what could be collected from a shipwreck.[59]

In truth, women at retail auctions were creating value. To see their salvaging and revaluing of material goods at auction as parasitic, critics had to reconceptualize their activities as nonproductive in the nineteenth-century business context. They did so by lampooning women's motivations and making arbitrary distinctions of scale. A male country shopkeeper attending an auction to obtain stock was praised for engaging in a productive endeavor; a widow bidding on lots sneered at as "infinitely small" was not. These arguments, designed to promote the interests of so-called regular traders, shaped the development of the auction wars into the 1820s by dismissing or ignoring the usefulness of auctions to those purchasing smaller lots.

The fight over scale in auction purchases fed a larger shift that began to devalue socially reproductive work undertaken by free women as noneconomic. Free women's work in making do, pawning, and selling and purchasing goods at auction was essential in supporting family existence, as free women mediated market and household economies with a variety of activities. These labors produced and sustained human lives—parents, children, husbands, sisters, neighbors—none of which were primarily understood to have a specific market value. The labor itself—of pawning, or borrowing, or patching up—earned no wages that could be measured, rendering it invisible in the historical record and difficult to characterize as having a certain value.[60] If you could not put a price on it, did it have value at all, outside of the realm of the heart?

Of course, urban people in the nineteenth century were thoroughly familiar with putting a price on the labor of free laundresses, cooks, and other sellers of service work.[61] An expanding urban service economy, often managed by women, helped commodify so-called domestic labor by putting a specific monetary value on it. The fact that it was feminized and closely linked to work that free women did without pay for their families made piecework sewing, for example, notoriously underpaid and "suffering seamstresses" objects of pitying charity.[62] Buying and selling at auction—like the seasonal pawning and redeeming of household goods—was a foundational economic practice of families, and married women retained claims on multiple kinds of goods, especially cloth and clothing, that they could circulate in this way.[63] Through this circulation of goods, mobilized in formal service work and informal making-do, free women of every status shaped the flow of value from one setting into another even as that value was seldom attributed to their actions.

For enslaved women, the value of labor, including borrowing and patching and extending to cooking, cleaning, and sewing, was firmly attached to the value of the worker herself and made manifest at auctions. Enslaved women with particular skills were expected to fetch a higher price when sold. Advertising a woman as a good "washer, ironer, and cook" was more than auctioneers' puffery in the eyes of the law—it was a pledge of skills worth perhaps 20 percent more than another woman without specialized skills. As a result, fraudulent representation of a woman's abilities had a measurable price when the buyer brought a seller to court.[64] Through the mechanisms of auctions and law, markets codified "women's work" performed by the enslaved as a field that allowed specialization and specific remuneration, though not for the benefit of the woman herself.[65] Because the market value of an enslaved woman was always present, even when she was not actively being bought or sold, her accumulation of feminized work skills added to her value under the "chattel principle."[66]

Even further, her domestic labors could be turned to support the commodification of other enslaved women. By the middle of the century, Richmond, Virginia, and New Orleans had become auction hubs for the interstate slave trade that moved human chattel from the East Coast to the Gulf Coast through purchase and coffle. At such sales, traders sold people to strangers rather than neighbors, which opened up possibilities for manipulating the way their bodies and abilities were presented. Auctioneers and slave traders in these southern cities compelled women they enslaved to fit up the exhausted new arrivals for sale. These women, held in bondage themselves, undertook the work of purchasing, altering, and sewing "sale outfits" that the displaced would wear to appear as "ideal slaves" and bring in the highest bids at public sale.[67] One enslaved woman's needlework propped up the valuation of other women, children, and men; the seller and auctioneer pocketed the proceeds.

An auction was occasionally the venue for monetizing the value of free women's work, but that did not mean working women reaped the rewards. Consider the "American grass bonnets" braided and sewn by the Woodhouse women of Wethersfield, Connecticut, which in 1821 were reported to rival the imported Leghorn style of Italian straw then being imported and sold for "twelve to fifteen dollars."[68] The Woodhouses entered their bonnets into a cattle show competition sponsored by a local committee that wanted to promote agriculture and handicraft by bestowing prizes on women and men who wove the finest flannels or constructed superior coverlets.[69] To turn political appreciation into economic energy, such goods needed pricing and distribution, and for this, boosters deployed auctions.[70] From this public sale, one of the Woodhouse women's grass bonnets traveled to London, where it was celebrated by the Society for the Encouragement of Arts, Manufactures, and Commerce.[71] Another sold at auction at the Tontine Coffee House in New York City to a member of Congress who presented it to Louisa Adams, wife of the secretary of state. In celebrating this purchase and subsequent political gift, the *Boston Recorder* commented on the lesson learned: "A grass, which until recently has been considered of no value, is probably now to constitute a most durable and elegant part of the dress of our ladies; to become a source at least of immense savings, if not of large income to our country."[72] Mary Woodhouse's labor had turned the wild weed into a fashionable accessory and the New York auction had located the price and the purchaser to publicly fix a value on it. Once it had a price, the grass bonnet could fuel dreams of a future "immense savings" for the female consumers of the nation. The rough hands of the Woodhouse women disappeared with the hammer strike.

Treasure to Trash: Women's Bodies

If trash could be redefined as treasure through auction pricing, the reverse was also possible. One English critic claimed that, by offering unbelievable bargains, auctions undermined not only a community's shared sense of value but also "destroy[ed] a person's reliance on his own judgment, and . . . reduce[d] him to a state of imbecility."[73] The dark side of "auction bargains" were those transactions that undervalued items which, in another context, would be understood as highly valuable. Even satisfied bidders had to wonder: How could something valuable be sold so cheap? And if it was sold cheap, had it any real value to begin with? Auctions were designed so that every item brought to the stage would leave with a price, and therefore they had the further potential to violate established understandings of what could be deemed truly priceless.

The transformation of nineteenth-century economic life visible in discussions about value involved a reshuffling of power that made questions about the origins of auction bargains newly fraught. From a world of exchange governed by social hierarchy, community constraints, and customary rights, people in the new United States were fitfully entering an era in which the economy might be an independent sphere of interaction among free agents. How, then, to account for those relationships—hierarchical, affectionate, or both—that still structured and supported material life and exchange? Could they be evaluated in monetized terms, or would monetization disrupt relationships? In Royall Tyler's play *The Contrast*, the heroine Maria van Rough's father celebrates her engagement by crowing that "hav'n't you every thing your heart can wish; an't you going to be married to a young man of great fortune; an't you going to have the quit-rent of twenty miles square?"[74] He is misguided on every front. His daughter, expressing proper sentiment, insists that only "a lease for life of the heart of a man I could love" is what matters to her, not a lease of property. Sadly for her, the fiancé in question is both a "depraved wretch" and deeply in debt, not at all what he appears to be and offering neither the financial windfall desired by the father's view of marriage nor the emotional bond wished for by the daughter. The economic relations taking shape in the early republic might not be what they appeared to be either.

Businessmen, middle-class wives, and political theorists read varieties of literature all promoting the same idea: that the family was a place of affection, not calculation. In fact, the ideal home was established in deliberate opposition to a workplace governed by money. Home and work, in the culture of domesticity, were separate, opposite, and even "hostile worlds" that needed to be kept apart for the sake of both the human heart and the family pocketbook.

The fear that money would pollute intimate relationships had circulated in the late eighteenth century in satirical literature about prostitution. In satire and in cautionary tales, women who engaged in sex work were "profoundly associated with the sacrifice of some part of the core self to the demands of the marketplace."[75] By the nineteenth century, the perceived threat of a transactional ethic in human interaction was pervasive, and to combat it, reformers and cultural critics agreed, the United States needed a society of middle-class homes presided over by self-effacing white mothers to act as bulwarks against the marketplace.

Yet money and affection collided in the daily experience of free women and men. Family survival strategies required the careful calculation of a daughter's labor or a husband's wages to make ends meet, especially in an urban setting, where men increasingly worked for wages and free women were largely confined to low-paid, temporary work. New industries, such as the for-profit life insurance industry, further embedded financial calculation in the family structure and put a price on intimate relationships. These companies enticed married men, whether

farmers or lawyers, to insure their lives to provide security for widows and father-
less children.[76] Life insurance did not formally put a price on the husband's
head—his family's financial interest in his life was not specifically enumerated—
but it offered middle-class men with a way to guarantee a fixed sum of money in
the event of their death for those left behind.[77] Companies thus profited from the
ways that the marriages of average free people were financial arrangements. Their
success came in their ability to finesse the crass calculations of life expectancy and
convince husbands and wives to use financial tools to preserve the affectionate
family from the harsh financial consequences of a father's death.

New legal and commercial structures joined familiar litigated debt to create
acceptable forms of calculating and pricing intimate relationships and free wom-
en's bodies. For example, parents brought civil suits against boyfriends who had
"seduced and abandoned" their daughters after promising to marry them. They
typically claimed that the injury was the parent's loss of their daughter's labor
services, under the legal concept of trespass. Yet, as judges began to observe in the
text of their opinions, the true loss was the young woman's "devaluation in the
marriage market."[78] An expanding popular press spread these stories, reinforcing
ideas about the value of white female virginity by paradoxically highlighting the
money this priceless possession could be exchanged for.

The idea that matching men and women in marriage took place in a "market" ran as a strong countercurrent to the "hostile worlds" rhetoric, with satirical
auction humor navigating the seeming contradiction. Satire used the auction's
function as a market matching tool to comment broadly on the potentially
dangerous intersection of sex and money in arranging a marriage. The farcical
auctioneer Peter Pennyless proposed to auction lusty widows to "keep-it-up
bucks," an indebted young woman to "a Member of Congress or a Jew," a "hack-
ney Writer" to any woman willing to feed him within the "less grievous yoke of
matrimony." He further proposed to use his auction to match "four dozen of
young Fellows, and one dozen of young Women, willing to marry to advantage"
to go settle in the Northwest Territory.[79] Another fictional auctioneer purported
to sell not one but two "homely" bachelors to a virginal Miss Tidkins who could
then keep one man at home and lend the other out to a friend "should she be
pressed for a beau."[80]

Faced with intimate relations that could be confused—such as marriage on
the one hand and sex work or slavery on the other—Americans employed auction stories to mark the boundaries of relationships that threatened to blur.[81]
Auctions worked in part by commodifying desire, and in the minds of critics,
sex was always on offer. One of the earliest attacks on the original Ladies' Retail

Auction Room featured Napan Woolyhead Chopsticks, a racist caricature in the *New-York Courier*. Though an eager customer of the ladies' auction store, he comically misunderstood the establishment to be a place where ladies themselves were sold at discount, "a mode of disposing of women," he claimed, "exactly to my taste." Chopsticks's "minute inspection" of the "tolerable assortment" of the evidently available ladies was quickly met with the shrill command from one of them to "keep your black paws off!"[82] Played for laughs, his was the "honest mistake" of a person who recognized the implications of a market where everything was for sale, racial hierarchies were unstable, and even a white lady's virtue held cheap. The tale bore a threatening role reversal in which a Black man could purchase a white woman, a dangerous usurpation in the minds of white men of their linked sexual and economic dominance. Stories such as this one teased a world upside down in order to underscore the potential racial power violations of an open market culture.

The trope of sexual commerce at auction appeared in multiple guises in the early republic, which collectively emphasized the uncertainties caused by linking desire and economic value when it came to free women's bodies. Fictional rogues, crassly arranged marriages, and other figures of transgressive sex populated these stories to warn readers that their judgments about value could be easily corrupted by lust. One frequently reprinted satire warning of the dangers of fraud when assigning value based on appearance used Herodotus's description of a Babylonian auction of brides in 500 BC to critique modern courtship. Since men were "so ill-advised as to place almost all value in the sex upon the outward form," one author claimed, a modern reenactment of the ancient auction, held in the light of day, was a fairer method for judging a bride's value than wooing in a candlelit ballroom. Furthermore, he suggested, perhaps the United States Treasury could benefit by placing a tax on goods sold at auction that included brides bought for their looks. Men who chose worthy plain brides could receive a rebate.[83] The true value of an object at auction—including a free wife—could not be judged by appearances because value could not be ascertained through the lens of desire.

Courtship satires played on the fact that many auctions were places to dispose of damaged or otherwise imperfect goods to unknowing purchasers. Multiple periodicals reprinted the satirical auction of a modish "first rate BUCK" with powdered and perfumed hair and a habit of cursing—a type, the article claimed, that flourished in times of war and speculation but not "in the neighborhood of industry." Initially addressed to "gentlemen," the piece was revised and "altered to fit the latitude of Saratoga" in 1812, when it was addressed to the

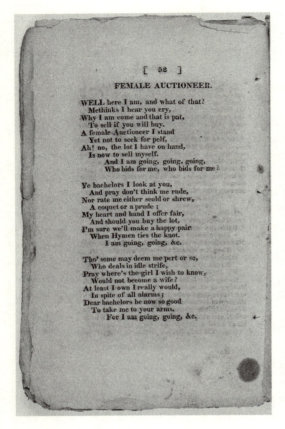

Figure 10. Comic songs
and satirical essays linking
auctioning and courtship
for free white people also
suggested the transgressive
possibility of commodifying
free white women's sexuality.
The mocking suggestion
that a woman could be an
auctioneer was a variation
on this theme. "Female
Auctioneer." *Comic songs,
as sung at the theatres and
principal concerts. To which
is added, an appendix,
containing a number of the
most celebrated popular
songs.* Courtesy, American
Antiquarian Society.

"ladies" to bid. While earlier iterations of the satire ended in failure—"Hand
him in then, let us put up something of some value"—the version with the bidding ladies resulted in a sale for $2,000 and a warning from the auctioneer that
the buck would be "the bane of your life."[84] The familiar dynamics of this economic institution could be readapted, but the underlying moral direction—to
laugh at and recoil from putting a price on free humans—sustained the utility
of the image. Humor about bidding for brides and bucks deflected uneasiness
about the intersection of economy and affection (see Figure 10).

Stories about auctions used free female bodies to discipline market practices by marking the limits of commodification in ways that could be deadly serious. One newspaper harshly critical of creditors claimed that there were some
who "would sell the widow's milk at auction, which nature had given her for
the support of her orphan child, if it were possible to do it."[85] The comment was

designed to shock readers with its cruelty and inhumanity, suggesting that such a claim on a free woman was unthinkable. Yet white and Black wet nurses commonly advertised in northern and southern newspapers, and informal networks of women circulated free and enslaved women with "a fresh breast of milk."[86] As enslaved women were rented out as skilled wet nurses, they retained their value as property for the owners capitalizing on their reproductive labor. The auction comment decrying the sale of a "widow's milk" argued that, for white women, such a claim on her was unthinkable, a bodily violation that demonstrated the monstrous heartlessness of the creditor-focused auction. The bereft mother in the tale owed her milk to her child, now that her husband, who had enjoyed almost unlimited access to her body, was dead.[87] To extract and sell her milk for a price was a profound misuse of the financial tools and logic of debt collection.

Auction stories, both satirical and serious, shored up the invaluable nature of free white female sexuality because auctions themselves routinely put a price on enslaved women's sexuality. In the former case, the price was a violation of the true value; in the latter, the price was the value. Laws governing slave sales, which were often covered by formal or conventional warranty, endorsed the idea that price determined value when it came to human bodies. In South Carolina, any enslaved person who was purchased for what was called a "full" or local market price was presumed healthy and could not be returned if the buyer was later disappointed unless he could prove that a fault existed at the time of sale. One owner claimed that an enslaved woman he purchased had spread a sexually transmitted disease on his farm and he wanted his money back. The court denied him, stating that he had paid a full price and had no basis for claiming that she was diseased at the time she was bought.[88] The price he paid was her value, regardless of any errors of judgment on his part.

Gender and sexuality were fundamental to the underlying logic of full prices and how they differed from person to person on the auction block.[89] Enslaved women who were fertile and still young enough to give birth were expected to fetch higher prices—a twenty-nine-year-old with three children was perceived as a different commodity than a forty-one-year-old who had given birth to ten.[90] Any seller who attempted to pass off an old woman as a young, fertile one was alleged to be misrepresenting her value—never mind what the woman's own intentions for her reproductive life were. The reproductive potential of her body was sufficient to warrant a higher price.

Enslavers since the eighteenth century had scrutinized enslaved women's bodies for signs of youth and fertility, developing a preference for women "without fallen breasts."[91] Slaveholders and aspiring owners in the nineteenth century, after the closing of the legal Atlantic slave trade, saw a woman's reproductive potential, read through her physical body, as an essential part of her value when connected to their plans for economic growth.[92] On the auction block as in wills, she represented more than one body—she was a worker and also a mother who would generate more valuable bodies. She was sold, bequeathed, or given together with her "future increase"; she was referred to as a "breeder." The paternity of such future children was an afterthought.[93]

The value of any human being as a producer and reproducer rested on more than physical capacity or particular training, though, and auctions, by taking place in a public setting, became sites for debate over the appropriate price for the emotional and psychological dimensions of humanity in enslaved women. Was a mother-and-child pair, sold as a "lot," worth more, less, or the same as the two individuals sold separately? One disgruntled creditor in Kentucky claimed that a sheriff had sold a woman and her child together for humanitarian reasons, rather than maximizing potential offers by selling them apart for what bidders would offer.[94] His lawsuit failed when the court devised its own evaluation on the price of sorrow, arguing that the mother's grief and the child's dependence would devalue them as separate products of sale. "The mother and child were indeed physically divisible, but morally they were not," wrote Judge John Boyle, "the sheriff in selling them together certainly acted in conformity with the dictates of humanity" and probably in "the interest of the owner."[95] In other words, it was economically profitable to take the moral and emotional dimensions of mothering into account because of the effects that emotion had on an enslaved person's "worth" as an investment.

This kind of calculation, which rested on the belief that the value of an enslaved mother's love could be determined through auction pricing and therefore considered rationally in setting up the sale threw into sharp relief the fact that the "hostile worlds" understanding of economy was a privilege of middle-class whites. Familial love could be turned into a commodity for the benefit of enslavers, but this was just one of several possibilities.[96] Judge Boyle's opinion about both "humanity" and "the interest of the owner" were not widely shared across slaveholding regions. The slaveholding class often paid lip service to preserving the family bonds of enslaved people even as they routinely violated them as a financial strategy for their own families.

Thomas Hinde's wife believed in the value of keeping an enslaved woman together with her children when they were placed up for auction, but the feelings validated in the course of bidding were hers, not those of mother and child. Bidding at the sale of a woman and four children she had thought she owned,

Virginia Hinde "seemed resolved to buy them at any price," even as a rival in the crowd countered her bids, higher and higher, to the final cost of "more than 5200 pounds of tobacco, confessed to be enormous."[97] In fact, the by-bidder had been put in place because the seller was concerned that "some people, disposed to favor" Virginia Hinde, "might decline bidding against her."[98] When the dust cleared, Thomas Hinde brought the case to the Virginia Chancery Court, arguing that the by-bidder, posing as a true competitor at the auction, was in fact an agent of the seller who had no intention to buy the woman and her children, but merely took advantage of the "solicitude of a distressed woman"—by which he meant his wife, not the desperate mother on the auction block—to goad her into overpaying.[99] The defendants countered that Thomas Hinde had failed to consider the "true value" of human bodies during the bidding, and that he had instead acted "to gratify a wife, for a family of servants, endeared to her probably by an intercourse of obsequious attention and faithful ministration."[100] Mrs. Hinde's alleged feelings for the woman who ministered to her, and her husband's affection for her, had produced a price grounded in irrational "phrensy." According to the defendants' view of financial decision making, in which value was measured by productive capacity, the Hindes should have known better (see Figure 11).

Irrationality in another form, of sexual fantasy, was a common feature of auctions of enslaved women. Slave traders who shopped at and supplied auctions expressed sexual obsessions about enslaved women in their letters. Buyers and sellers referred to "fancy maids," light-skinned women who sold for high prices allegedly for their domestic skills but also as objects of sexual exploitation.[101] Sexual and commercial desires met to serve dreams of power and domination by the men who bid outrageously high prices on women whom they targeted for abuse and display.[102] Those high prices revealed what the power of sexual violation and its display to other men was worth to those who bought "fancy" women, and it was a calculation built on fantasy. Yet sellers discussed pricing such women as if it could be soberly predicted for profit. Slave traders' correspondence served as market reports from interconnected regions, with information about the prices that "fancies" brought.[103]

Irrational sexual fantasies challenged the rationality of prices in multiple venues involving free and enslaved women, making the auction of human women the most tragic example of a broader truth. Shopping as a form of flirting had a long history in critiques of consumer behavior, reproduced and reinforced in literature and imagery that portrayed the shop as a crucible of sexual tension with shopper and salesperson gazing at each other, touching hands over the goods, and negotiating a transaction that might include sexual favors in addition to the

Figure 11. This nineteenth-century image of a New Orleans auction
illuminates white women's participation in the commodification of
enslaved people alongside artwork, real estate, and imported goods.
"Sale of Estates, Pictures and Slaves in the Rotunda, New Orleans."
Courtesy, Manuscripts, Archives and Rare Books Division, Schomburg
Center for Research in Black Culture, New York Public Library.

exchange of a material object. This intermingling of sexual suggestion and economic negotiation was often used to criticize consumerism itself as a frivolous
waste of time, contrasted to wholesome productive work. It operated whether
the seller was a female dressmaker appealing to a male customer in the late eighteenth century or one of the thousands of newly minted male clerks entreating
female shoppers in the nineteenth century.[104] The dynamic was not limited to
the fevered imaginations of critics, either; merchants who operated retail spaces
in the nineteenth century instructed their clerks to flatter and charm female
shoppers to entice them to make a purchase.[105]

The fact that prices, and therefore the settled value, of the objects and
bodies under consideration were being shaped by the sexual desires of buyer

and seller meant that those values were speculative, neither just nor fair. The idea of "hostile worlds" between the market and the heart was concerned with the thought that economic values could corrupt the moral purity of the home. The corollary was the belief that emotional or sexual desires could undermine the rationality of economic exchange.[106] If exchange was the crystalization of value, auctions turned sexual speculation into the true value of a person or an item under the hammer. Such an outcome threatened the security of local economic knowledge and the social stability in which it purportedly rested.

By the middle of the nineteenth century, department stores attempted to eliminate the irrational uncertainties of a sexualized consumer interaction through a "one-price policy," when A. T. Stewart instituted the practice at his Marble Palace of dry goods in New York City and others followed suit.[107] The move to a single, predefined price did not solve the problem of whether the price was correct, just that it was not subject to individual negotiation, favoritism, or enticement. From early in the century, "one-price" advocates had believed accepting value as speculative would have meant putting some customers and some sellers at a disadvantage. In 1817 the rural shopkeeper Robert Henderson acquired hundreds of pairs of shoes, barrels of coffee, and a vast array of fabrics at a city auction. Yet he announced in the Brownsville, Pennsylvania, newspaper that he was "determined to establish a regular system of doing business" in which "but one price will be asked, which will be extremely low; from these rules all persons will be treated alike."[108] Henderson's promise of equal treatment spread to the large department stores that defined urban consumerism midcentury.

In each of its manifestations, the logic of the anti-auction writers represented their efforts to convert what they claimed to be a moral wrong into a political wrong. In reality, the wrongs they decried were fueled by the uncertainties of judging price in the expanding market culture of the early republic. Low—or high—auction prices could be the fault of fraudulent marketing, unfair political advantages, foreign competition, frenzied women, or lustful men. Here was the dilemma that auctions posed, by enacting circumstances in which participants revealed what they were willing to pay. The so-called freedom of any person to buy or sell as he or she saw fit was linked to the price-setting function of a free market in which everything had a price, and the price confirmed the value. The only way to hold something in a fixed value was to deny its intersection with the market.

*   *   *

By the late summer of 1818, the fashion for ladies' auction rooms had faded. The pioneering ladies' auctioneer Elijah Mix was discharged as an insolvent debtor who, according to one clerk's deposition, had a character "held to be very bad . . . having practiced gross frauds in sales."[109] In New York, Mix's old location at Number 7 Broadway became the "late Ladies Auction Room," now promoted as a warehouse for selling tea, sugar, and fortified wines on merchants' terms.[110] Ladies' auctions in other cities failed to generate enough business to continue as standalone institutions, though specific auctions advertised as "for the ladies" continued over the ensuing decades.[111]

The anti-auction protests launched in reaction to the ladies' auction rooms were a failure, and in December 1817, Congress in fact abolished the wartime tax on auctions, along with a number of other "internal duties" used to fund the war.[112] Ubiquitous public sales of forfeited estates and British imports confirmed the profound economic influence Britain still wielded, causing Hezekiah Niles, an anti-auction leader, to rail against Britain's efforts to reduce the new country to its former colonial status. The quality of the goods in import auctions did not matter, claimed *Niles' Weekly Register*: "Glass beads are current coin among savages, and any thing is good enough for America."[113] Explicitly linking white Americans and Native people ("savages") through colonial manipulation by European traders, the author suggested that, just as it had done for centuries by trading worthless beads for valuable furs, Britain still called the shots by passing off damaged and poor-quality items at auction.[114]

The auction debates moved on, toward a more firmly masculine vision of marketplace politics. In the 1820s, auctioneers began to champion yeoman citizen-consumers as the primary beneficiaries of their sales. These productive male consumers' rights to low, tariff- and tax-free prices became a powerful rhetorical device, as the market became a place where men acted democratically, provided they were not swindled by special interests. Regular trade, the rallying cry of the auction wars, was defined as a form of political engagement by men who equated their commercial and civic selves.

In 1828 anti-auction drives delivered tens of thousands of male signatures on petitions to Congress. Emboldened by what they saw as a groundswell in public support for heavy taxation, New York City men organized an Anti-Auction Party to turn that support directly into political power.[115] But the Anti-Auction ticket did not succeed as the numbers of petition-signers had suggested it might; in the November election, one newspaper reported, the auction party had "about 4000 votes out of about 25,000 in the city of New York" while Jacksonian party support surged.[116] Despite its lackluster performance, the formation of such a party signaled the centrality of auctions to US political culture and its debates about the promises and perils of the nation's expanding economy. Backed by their concerns about corruption, anti-auction men kept up the political pressure undeterred, displaying "liberality in port and petitions, in memorials and madeira" in Washington, DC.[117] More successfully, the group lobbied the New York state legislature, which eventually increased criminal penalties for infractions of existing auction law.[118]

The market's gender problem, as debated in the contest over auction taxation, was not only that the expanding commercial economy—with its speculative investments, paper banknotes, and anonymous cities—enabled corrupt individuals to manipulate values and defraud a foolish, feminized public. The ladies' retail auction rooms raised troubling questions about the logical conclusion of permitting commercial exchange to determine value at all. The potential "mischief" of female bidders was that they embodied these problems of monetized value. By the end of the auction wars, the national politics deflected these concerns by promoting a vision of rights in the marketplace marked by individual property holding and masculine competition. With the crisis in value averted, one account reported, the newspaper pages containing "elaborate disquisition on the auction question" were torn into "little rolls" to support the curls in ladies' hairstyles.[119]

The sweeping national penalties sought by anti-auction politics did not take hold, but their efforts to define regular business by deploying ideas about gender had enduring consequences for the perceptions of value that women's work and women's bodies contributed to the economy. In their rhetoric and in their chosen remedy, anti-auction writers were creating a story of what the proper economy was for a national audience debating the new rules in contests over banks, tariffs, and Native land. The anti-auction vision of a regular economy excluded white women and people of color as not worthy of political notice from elected representatives nor deserving of protection through the tools of political economy.

CHAPTER 6

Economies, Families, and the Auction Block

In the end, Harriet Jacobs's grandmother insisted on climbing the auction block. Promised freedom upon the death of her enslaver, "Aunt Martha" was disgusted to hear that the estate's executor (and her enslaver's son-in-law), Dr. Flint, planned instead to sell her to settle debts. He first proposed to "dispose of her at private sale" to spare her "feelings" the shame of a public auction. Martha knew the shame was Flint's. As Jacobs wrote: "If he was base enough to sell her, when her mistress intended she should be free, she was determined the public should know it." Rather than allow herself to be sold by a handshake in a private parlor, Martha insisted that an audience bear witness to the injustice of her sale. According to Jacobs, the assembled bidders reacted as protesting neighbors long had done: by shaping the sale to their own sense of justice. There was only one bid, for $50, from her former enslaver's sister, and though the auctioneer waited, "no one bid above her." This woman bought Martha to free her, with the support of the assembled crowd.[1]

Jacobs's carefully crafted story of Martha and the auction block presented a scene that was central to abolitionist literature. The cruelty and incongruity of placing a human being in a public sale to be priced, along with the other "negroes, horses, &c." pinpointed the evils of slavery for reformers determined to end it. They hoped that by repeating this moment in capitalism—through reenactments, illustrations, and eyewitness retellings—they could invoke sufficient horror in white Americans to act against slavery. In so doing, abolitionists made it clear that auctions of enslaved people commodified those very entities and emotions—love, family, pregnant women—that white Americans had deemed properly outside the bounds of commercial valuation. Critics of the ladies'

auctions had insisted that commodification involving white women was prepos-
terous; abolitionists insisted commodification of Black women was a tragedy.

Images and narratives repurposed the "speculative gaze" of bidders at an
auction of human beings to call attention to the racial and sexual violence that
underpinned it.[2] Activists used the performative nature of an auction to enlist a
wider audience as witnesses, not to confirm the fairness of the sale—historically
a key role of auction attendees—but rather to call out its fundamental unfair-
ness to the humanity of the enslaved. "Shame! Shame!" the audience gathered at
Martha's auction reportedly cried out, "That is no place for *you*."[3] Readers were
expected to feel the same.

Frequently, as in the story that Jacobs chose for her book, the focus in abolitionist writing was on an estate auction, the institution that linked reproduction—of free and enslaved families—through property law and commodification
in order to sustain the free family and destroy the enslaved one. They flipped the
middle-class sense of "hostile worlds" to argue their case. The money motive that
was abhorrent in its violation of the enslaved family was simultaneously deployed
to shore up the free family, and these two aspects of capitalism could not be disentangled as long as chattel slavery was a legal cornerstone of white wealth and economic growth.[4] It was a complex point to make. While visual depictions of slave
auctions set up a contrast between emotional family values (of the people being
sold) and the crass competitiveness of market values (embodied in the audience),
the broader context was that the two could not be separated in a society that
relied on enslavement for capital. At the moment that these depictions depended
on stereotyped opposition between market and heart to make their moral point,
they also embodied the intertwined nature of family and finance, fixed firmly
within a racial hierarchy.

The details of auction scenes in abolitionist literature and images—the
stage, the leading-man auctioneer, the audience—sought to make the whole
enterprise a horrifying kind of theater and connected it to long-standing associations of market and theater in Anglo-American culture.[5] The slave auction
scene, therefore, was not only a deliberate distillation of the central dynamic of
enslavement but it was also a historically specific construction about the market.

Race and gender were central to depictions of an immoral market because
economic mastery was closely associated with white men, in popular culture and
in law. The same image that narrowed the experience of enslavement down to
its core evil of treating human beings as objects also narrowed the operation of
market valuation down to acts of individual competition between independent
male economic actors. In the morality play surrounding the slave auction, the

villains were the auctioneer and the male bidder, not the white woman who had motivated the sale by insisting on her rightful inheritance.[6] In such depictions, the economy as a realm to be managed and mastered was a white masculine one, supported by structural exclusions. The reality, of course, was more ambivalent, as auctions of enslaved people were always sites for the disruption of households, including patriarchal white households.

Representations of slave auctions—whether in pictures, stories, or testimony—were a key site for the taken-for-granted truths of American market culture in the nineteenth century. Auctions distilled household gender relationships, state efforts to control economic activity, and the development of race-based capitalism by the mid-nineteenth century, revealing the ways these disparate elements of American society joined together. Immoral markets abounded; whether any market could or should be moral was a contested question.

Seeing Markets

Markets in human beings had been part of colonial North America's commercial print culture since newspapers first emerged in the early eighteenth century. In runaway notices and sale advertisements, printed text trained potential customers to "see" markets in people as they did in other goods. The human bodies described on the page sometimes were attached to an enslaved individual's name, but they were always associated with money, either in the form of a reward for recapture or in the terms of a potential sale. All of these notices had practical commercial and political purposes in controlling enslaved people and facilitating profit from their labor. They also played a role in shaping readers' expectations of what commerce was. By presenting the "facts" of exchange, they shaped ideas about what to pay attention to and what to ignore in daily thinking about monetized value.

By the nineteenth century, newspaper advertising in the United States had increased its visual appeal as new printing techniques allowed advertisers to include more images to accompany the text. The development of lithography meant that authors and advertisers could publish detailed images of products for sale as well as shop interiors. Newspapers increasingly clustered public sales under eye-catching banners titled "Sales at Auction." To the extent that newspapers offered a visual representation of urban markets, this type of organization is notable. They did not present the urban marketplace geographically, based on the locations of shops, nor thematically, organized by types of goods. Rather, they depicted a market organized by the type of sale and visually separated out public sales by marking them as different. There were new regional differences in newspapers, as well. The end of legalized slavery in northern states meant that men, women, and children were no longer included in the auctioneers' columns of their papers, but in the South, the "Sales at Auction" columns of the paper included a mixture of human and inanimate property, frequently conducted by the same firms.[7]

Guidebooks and travel accounts augmented the commercial press in this robust print culture of the market by turning commercial exchange itself into a subject of study and curiosity. Their reports featured images of retail display windows and promenading shoppers in commercial districts, all designed to give outsiders an introduction to the local marketplace. Accompanied by ample commentary, these depictions aimed, implicitly or explicitly, also to shape the "normative model" of shoppers and their expectations of exchange, much in the way that advertisements long had done so.[8]

Such depictions were deliberate efforts to make shoppers see or feel markets in a certain way, rather than faithful representations of the activities of buying and selling. Retailers who promised "orderly commercial abundance" in their printed advertisements indicated that order and predictability were desirable features of market exchanges.[9] The reality was that most Americans in the mid-nineteenth century obtained goods from crowded general stores, traveling peddlers, and a bustling secondhand trade whose unpredictability was a feature of the flow of its inventory. Thus, depictions of commercial exchange aimed to connect commerce with a series of feelings that expanding trade could invoke rather than to faithfully depict the details of the experience. In a fancy goods store, the mood was elegance; in the shadow of imposing, newly constructed docks, the mood might be awe.[10] In the former, power was in the hands of the consumer; in the latter, power was in an anonymous, monumental system of transatlantic trade and pooled investments in construction.

Visual art that took commercial transactions as its subject had a critical take on human motives built into its spatial mapping of economic power, and depictions of auctions were no exception. For British satirical artists, that power was expressed not through order and predictability but rather through personal charisma. In Thomas Rowlandson's 1808 etching "Christie's Auction Room," the auctioneer, a central figure elevated above the bidding crowd, channels attendees' energy toward where he wants them to look (see Figure 12). The audience, crowded together, is curious about the art for sale—gazing upward at it, consulting their catalogs, discussing the merits of pieces with one another, and perhaps too eager to believe the words of the man calling the bids. The paintings for sale are indistinct, but their gilt frames indicate an atmosphere of money.

CHRISTIE'S AUCTION ROOM.

London Pub. Feb. 1 1808. at R. Ackermann's Repository of Arts 101 Strand.

Figure 12. An etching of the famed London auction house
depicts a curious crowd deep in multiple conversations and an
auctioneer gesturing for their attention. Christie's Auction Room.
Designed and etched by Thomas Rowlandson (British, London
1757–1827), February 1, 1808. Metropolitan Museum of Art.

The crowds, their speculative gaze, and the directing power of the seller were
a frequently invoked dynamic in nineteenth-century depictions of retail spaces
as well. Inside the dry-goods or department store, a clerk—often derided as a
"counter-jumper"—held up fabrics for the inspection and encouragement of an
assembled group of female shoppers. Like the Rowlandson auctioneer image,
depictions of a transaction across the sales counter selected the most theatrical,
and potentially sexually charged, moments of consumerism to stand in for the
act of purchasing.[11] The more mundane processes of budgeting, arranging for
credit payments, and even waiting and making do with repaired and borrowed
goods—all essential to the transaction of purchasing—were left out of such
tableaux entirely. In visual culture, the market was narrowed to the interaction
between buyer and seller over goods.

So powerful was the print culture of the market by the nineteenth century that abolitionists chose to mobilize it as a trail of evidence in the 1830s when they began to develop an extensive library of publications written to influence white northerners. Coordinated media campaigns of reproduced print and visual presentations strove to establish the "facts" of slavery, believing that if white northerners knew the facts, they would move swiftly to end slavery's evils.[12] They gathered and reprinted runaway notices and columns of advertisements for the selling of people; taken together, this evidence supplied the detailed calculations of enslavement in order to condemn the application of financial calculation to human experiences and bodies. In their collection of the print culture of slavery, abolitionists exposed the depth and variety of connections between abstract numbers and human capacities that slavery entailed. Newspaper advertisements, posters, and broadsides listed the physical attributes and special skills of the people up for sale, suggesting a link between work capacity and value. They often included potential pricing information, such as appraisal values or opening bids, and typically listed the financial terms that would be accepted for sale, in some combination of "cash," bonds, and other credit arrangements.[13] Finally, they advised potential purchasers where and when to appear in order to make a purchase.

In the hands of abolitionists, the print culture through which systems of slavery operated became evidence of the cruel monetization of human beings under enslavement. The American Anti-Slavery Society, in *American Slavery as It Is: Testimony of a Thousand Witnesses*, collected and reprinted runaway notices to train northerners in how to read the clues hidden in plain sight about the brutality of enslavement. It turned classified advertisements focused on locations and rewards into a mountain of evidence that the "neutral language of commerce" in fact cloaked the torture of Black people.[14] An 1837 Georgia advertisement promising $100 for the return of a twenty-three-year-old man named Perry included the words "one under front tooth missing" when it appeared in the *Pensacola Gazette*, a seemingly straightforward mark of identification.[15] The editors of *American Slavery as It Is* extracted this sentence and presented it as "testimony" of "punishment—mutilation of teeth" alongside twenty-four other examples of teeth "out," "missing," or "gone" from multiple papers in a two-year period. The abolitionist Sarah Grimké, the daughter of slaveholders and one of the editors, added her personal knowledge from her Charleston, South Carolina, childhood that enslavers broke people's teeth deliberately. Her testimony moved a "fact" about property from its commercial context to restore it to its embodied, personal origins. In this way, an advertiser's convention in describing certain features of human property became damning evidence of the violence at slavery's core.

White people's eyewitness testimony of the southern market in humans was another essential piece of context for how abolitionists wanted northerners to see and react to the printed evidence compiled by the American Antislavery Society. Accounts penned by northerners who traveled south related their emotions at seeing enslaved people tied together in coffles and also those put up for public auction. The New Yorker Silas Stone's description of slave sales in Charleston, South Carolina, in 1807 was of a social space and a heartrending emotional experience. He described slave market sales as a chaotic event akin to the selling of horses, and the public auction, staged "in front of the noble 'Exchange Buildings' in the heart of the city," as a scene of public pain. Stone told of one woman and her eight children set up on the stage. As each child was sold away, one by one, Stone "watched their emotions closely, and saw their feelings were in accordance to human nature." The mother, knowing she was being permanently separated from her family by sale to the highest bidders, gave "the most agonizing sobs and cries." Stone reported that he cried, too.[16]

Stone's tears were expressions of empathy and also a commentary on circulating ideas about American commerce that set rhetorics of emotion and rights in conflict. He reported an emotional response to the public sale to demonstrate both his own sentimental identification with the woman on the block and to mark his recognition that the value of a mother's love was violated by the value of the marketplace. Sentiment in nineteenth-century American consumerism lifted up the potential of commerce to increase people's sense of connection with others through exchange of both goods and feelings.[17] At the same time, a flourishing national discourse considered markets as venues for "citizen consumers" to assert their political rights through unfettered trading.[18] The auction effect of colonial economies, in which the repeated exposure of human beings to public valuation, price, and sale normalized economies of capital over economies of personal meaning, bore fruit in this nineteenth-century tension.[19]

By juxtaposing the deal-seeking buyers on one side and family-focused enslaved people on the other, abolitionist auction narratives underlined the idea of property as a question of rights for white men rather than interdependent relationships across a community. Abolitionist images and texts, rich in stories of violence, defiance, and flight, presented enslaved people—sometimes in their own words—as humans with complex motivations and familial relationships. Imagery and language depicting those conducting and bidding at slave auctions, in contrast, were of calculation and cruel disregard for human pain and personal relationships.[20] Created to make viewers feel the inhumanity of selling human beings, these depictions paradoxically drew on, and solidified, the facts of the economy as an impersonal place where calculation trumped relationships. Buyers and sellers were the subjects who drove economic activity; enslaved laborers and families were its object.

In truth, enslavers used the threat of auction as an "emotional bludgeon" to compel obedience in the people they held in bondage.[21] Enslaved people, in turn, deployed emotions—such as an enslaved mother's tears and Aunt Martha's public shaming—to influence auction purchases and prices. The potential for monetizing emotional displays did not mean those emotions were false. Rather, slavery in the nineteenth century operated through an "emotional politics" where all parties struggled for mastery in the control and display of their emotions.[22]

The white male auctioneer was a central figure in visual representations of slave sales, with the audience ranged around him in a structure that recalled depictions of an evangelical preacher and his congregation. Henry Watson, a man who escaped from slavery and became an abolitionist and published his life story, made the parallel directly. His *Narrative* reproduced a previously published image with the caption "The Author upon the Auction Block" (see Figure 13).[23]

The Author upon the Auction Block.

Figure 13. *Narrative of Henry Watson, a Fugitive Slave* featured an illustration of Watson's sale, surrounded by bidders and witnesses. "The Author upon the Auction Block" (1848). Courtesy, Manuscripts, Archives and Rare Books Division, Schomburg Center for Research in Black Culture, New York Public Library.

The Author in attendance on Public Worship.

Figure 14. Henry Watson's published narrative included an illustration
of a white preacher speaking to a congregation of Black witnesses.
"The Author in Attendance on Public Worship" (1848). Courtesy,
Manuscripts, Archives and Rare Books Division, Schomburg Center
for Research in Black Culture, New York Public Library.

In this engraving, the man on the raised stage is a white auctioneer, his arm with
an auctioneer's hammer in it, raised over a Black man in front of an assembled
white audience. Later in the book, when Watson describes attending a Methodist
church service, the accompanying image is an echo of the auction scene. A white
preacher stands on an elevated pulpit, with his arms in the air, speaking to a Black
congregation (see Figure 14).

The visual focus on the forceful speaker pointed to specific forms of power
and authority in the nineteenth century that were embodied in the compelling
evangelical preacher. Clergymen themselves called their conquests over sinful
souls "the art of knocking them down," an expression of authoritative, even violent conclusion that auctioneers also used.[24] White men's mastery—expressed
in courthouses, politics, and the pulpit—was deployed to reinforce hierarchies,
a point Watson made clear by quoting the sermon delivered by the preacher
illustrated with outstretched arms. The white minister announced to his Black
congregation that "it is the will of God, who hath by his wise providence made
you servants, because, no doubt, he knew that condition would be best for you

in this world."[25] The Protestant institution building of the nineteenth century, signified by the Methodist minister with his hands in the air, fostered "spiritual economies" with a national reach that trained Americans to conceptualize the markets around them in parallel terms.[26]

So successful was this identification of religious and commercial markets, abolitionists claimed, that slaveholding communities in the South mobilized spiritual economies for capitalist ends. The abolitionist Lewis Tappan, speaking at the Female Wesleyan Anti-Slavery Society in 1841, reported that when a recent Virginia slave auction was disrupted by a storm, the whole group decamped to a local church. "The auctioneer ascended into the PULPIT and made it his stand, and there struck off under the hammer, using the cushion for the Bible as his bench, the souls and bodies of men."[27] Two decades earlier, Tappan had been a leader in opposing a different set of auctions—those of British imports that merchants like he had decried as "irregular commerce." Now a founder of the American Anti-Slavery Society, he saw in auctions of people unchecked power through the familiar mechanism of the public sale. It was the evil of monopoly turned to its most devastating ends.

The minister's hands were empty; the auctioneer's were not. The hammer in the hand of the auctioneer underscored the violence of commodifying human beings. An illustration in Henry Bibb's autobiography used another visual parallel to comment on power at the slave sale. It showed multiple Black women pleading on their knees as the auctioneer raised his hammer in one hand and a tiny baby by the wrist in the other (see Figure 15). To the left, another white man raises a whip over a pleading Black woman, making the visual parallel explicit. Antislavery writing, too, called out "the auctioneer's hammer" as the tool that linked violence, family separation, and the evil of human commodification.[28]

Building on an earlier transatlantic use of images of the supplicant enslaved mother and the enslaved person enduring torture, American abolitionists depicted the auction block as a site where family separation and emotional pain were bound by the incongruity of putting a monetary price on a human being.[29] The masthead of William Lloyd Garrison's *Liberator* newspaper included an auction vignette with pleading enslaved people under a poster announcing the sale of "Slaves, horses, & other cattle" (see Figure 16). To sell human and animal property in the same manner was to deny those family connections that white Americans understood to be central to their humanity. Frederick Douglass decried a setting he witnessed "where the victims are to be sold like horses, sheep, and swine, knocked off to the highest bidder . . . the tenderest ties

Figure 15. Henry Bibb's narrative is filled with damning, emotional details of the feelings of Black families. Illustration from Henry Bibb, *Narrative of the Life and Adventures of Henry Bibb, an American Slave, Written by Himself. Documenting the American South*, the University Library of the University of North Carolina at Chapel Hill.

ruthlessly broken, to gratify the lust, caprice, and rapacity of the buyers and sellers of men."[30] The "tenderest ties" embedded people in kinship and community that were disregarded in selling them as property. Instead, the auction embodied slavery's evils by making the monstrous seem routine—just another form of sale of living goods.

The audience of bidders and spectators heightened the cruelty of a slave auction image, as these men and women actively engaged in a barbarous sale of human beings were dressed in the trappings of middle-class respectability. The white women were properly covered in the bonnets and long skirts of feminine propriety, a contrast with enslaved women on the block, who were often bare-breasted. The men were neatly attired in clean clothing, unlike the typically ragged men placed for sale.[31] Middle-class readers of abolitionist texts were positioned to join the spectators in the bidding audience as peers but expected to draw the opposite conclusion about the respectability of slave sales. Like the southern white attendees who witnessed and did not bid, they participated in racial privilege but were instructed to mobilize it for benevolence.[32]

Visual depictions flattened the motivations of the audience by presenting them as a collective, but abolitionist writers used text to fill in the gaps, often

Figure 16. The abolitionist newspaper used an auction scene
to encapsulate the moral horrors of human commodification.
Liberator masthead, April 23, 1831. Boston Public Library.

presenting the interactions between purchasing men and the pleading enslaved
people on the stage. An 1844 antislavery account in the *Christian Reflector* narrated an auction on the Raymond, Virginia, courthouse steps during which an
enslaved husband and father urged his purchaser to bid on his wife and children.[33] The purchaser, "a gentleman of high character, and whose bid was made
without a knowledge that he [the enslaved man] had a family" declined to do
so. Instead, he chose to "relinquish" his purchase, due to his "unwillingness to be
the means of separating the man from his family."[34] Another bidder had no such
qualms, and the family was separated regardless.

By centering on the auctioneer as prime agent and the audience as essential
foil, visual depictions typically left the seller absent entirely. This tactic heightened the illusion that the performative bidding was the sum total of the exchange,
rather than just one moment in a series of economic and social calculations. It
was, of course, a deliberate distillation of the evil of slavery, and one of several
that abolitionists used to call out the dehumanizing impact of the institution.
This formulation was also, however, a deliberate construction about the market.
Slave auction imagery narrowed enslavement down to what abolitionists saw as
a core evil—treating human beings as objects or animals. The imagery also used
auctioning to narrow the social and personal structures that shaped the economy
down to a public competition between buyer and bidder.[35] Such narrowing paralleled familiar narratives about auctions that made the imagery legible to white
readers whom abolitionists hoped to convert to their cause.

The hard reality was that sellers—those who set a sale in motion but did
not actively participate in the calling out of lots or bidding—had all kinds of
ideas about what the auctioning of human property would do for their lives

and pocketbooks, and these desires shaped the timing and conduct of sales. R. V. Tiffey wrote to the auctioneers R. H. Dickinson & Brother about an enslaved woman named Susan: "I saw Susan's master the day after I recd. your note, & he requested me to say to you, that it is his wish that you would sell Susan the first opportunity, whatever you can get for her, as she is making so many complaints and says she is not sound, he is not willing to warrant her sound for fear that she may be returned in his hands or there may be some difficulty about her, all of which he wishes to avoid, but warrants the right & title to be good."[36] Referring to his reluctance to offer warranty for her health, Susan's enslaver was keenly attuned to the legal expectations of sale.

Susan, like other people held in bondage, was likewise an "economic thinker" as well as someone who sought to honor the social and emotional value of her relationships with family.[37] She insisted to the man who enslaved her that she was "not sound," using the terminology of economic evaluation that would shape her sale. He, in turn, perceived her words not as realistic self-evaluation but rather as cover for her valuing of kin: "I believe it is all pretentions & false representations she is making with the hope of returning to King Geo to live with her husband which she will never do." For him, an auction transaction was the solution to his own fraught personal interactions with the woman he held in bondage over her desire to return to her home and family: "You will please sell her at once & send me a check for the money."[38]

The theatricality of the slave auction was part of its power for participants as well as for abolitionists emphasizing the tragedy of human commodification. American auctioneers of enslaved people used showy humor to attract crowds to bid on humans, and laughter became another expression of economic power that silenced personal pain. Amusement, in the "theater of the marketplace," was central to the flow of capital in the sale of human beings as much as at any other auction. Cato Carter, formerly enslaved, remembered of one sale "The cryer was a clown and made funny talk and kept everybody laughing."[39] Their aim was to tame the violence and suffering of slavery with the tools that auctioneers used to entice crowds by linking bidding with entertainment. The audience came together as a local public, in the same way that they had since the eighteenth century at a variety of public sales, but they came together specifically to participate in the racial commodification of Black people through the shoring up of white familial property relations.

By capturing a single, deliberately framed moment of commodification, the auction accomplished for participants what the auction image did for

abolitionists—simplify complex financial and personal interactions in order
to ratify one version of a larger truth. The consequences of that simplification
radiated across generations and contributed to the long-term processes of exclusion that marked parts of human experience as noneconomic. Buyers and sellers depended on the formal structures of public sales to bolster their particular
framing of economic issues. Sellers planned auctions that would allow them to
restructure debts, or they arranged deals with buyers in advance of the public
sale and expected the auction to convey the title only.[40] The dramatic moment
of the auction enacted a transfer that purportedly resolved, at the same time that
it obscured, the difficult intersecting realities of economic life. Those realities,
including the seller's intentions, could remain hidden, unless a subsequent lawsuit challenged the sale, in which case the messier truth was exposed.

The legal wranglings of two generations of one slaveholding family exem-
plify what such exposure meant. Early in the nineteenth century, Daniel Haddix's widow attended the sheriff's auction held to resolve her late husband's debts
and bid on an enslaved woman.[41] When decades later the Haddix sons insisted
in court that the same enslaved woman and the children she had subsequently
borne belonged to them as part of their inheritance, the case hinged on how their
mother had presented herself at that sheriff's auction. Years before, had she participated in the auction on her own behalf or as administrator of the family estate?
The court looked to the sale price, $210, as validation of legitimate exchange,
noting that "the negro was actually sold at public auction, for as much as she
appears to have been really worth," even though the widow had to borrow money
to make the purchase and later struggled to repay the loan.[42] Her sons, who saw
the enslaved woman as their inheritance from their father, could expect nothing.
The enslaved woman and her children, now legally the property of someone else,
would not be moved again to satisfy them.

The Haddix boys had no visible role in the original auction that settled their
father's estate, nor did the children of the woman sold that day and born after the
sale. Yet the younger generation on both sides had profound investment in the
interaction of the auction because of the way that economic practices supported
or undermined families. Free white families were economic units that sought to
preserve members collectively, but they were vulnerable to the boom-bust debt
cycles of the nineteenth century. Enslaved people labored under enormous pres-
sures of white Americans to treat them as individual units of value rather than
as members of social collectives. The auction that had appeared to consist of
one individual bidding on another individual to clear the debts of a third was

in many ways a show, staged to simplify the profound role of reproduction and family among the free and unfree people involved. The public sale created a market that prioritized one definition of property that governments had been developing from their colonial origins. In focusing on auctions, abolitionists focused on the show. A successful auction drew on the personal relations among and between buyers, sellers, and the people being sold, but it ultimately affirmed a vision that linked markets with the property rights of white families.

Moral and Immoral Markets

Although opponents of slavery used auction stories and images to call attention to the immorality and violence of slavery, they did not believe commerce as a whole was necessarily evil. In fact, several movements attempted to create "moral markets" that would harness the cultural and economic power of exchange to combat enslavement. Beginning in the mid-1830s, antislavery fairs sold food, fashion, and household goods, as well as antislavery items such as pincushions printed with the image of the kneeling bondsperson in chains, all to raise money for the cause of antislavery. They were advertised as "holy festival[s] of Freedom," linking the sentimental materialism of nineteenth-century gift purchasing with the emancipatory promises of consumption.[43] It was a "deferred" method of achieving freedom for enslaved people, given that the profits were used to manufacture more antislavery banners, pamphlets, and pincushions aimed at changing the hearts and minds of white northerners.[44]

Free produce—a transatlantic movement growing out of the British sugar boycotts of the 1790s—sought more direct applications of market mechanisms against slavery: boycott and competition. Activists contrasted an evil market that rested on the exploited labor of the enslaved with the supposedly uncoerced labor of free people, and individuals committed themselves to abstaining from slave-grown sugar and cotton. Their intention was to make slavery unprofitable for enslavers by cutting off demand and encouraging competition from producers who would commit to free labor. Abstaining from slave-produced goods allowed middle-class women in the North, especially Quaker women, to claim moral authority for themselves and their families.[45] In "free produce" stores, Black and white antislavery entrepreneurs offered an alternative to a US economy thoroughly interconnected with slavery, by selling ice cream flavored with fruit juice rather than cane sugar and boots "entirely free from the contamination of slave labor."[46] Many also believed that bringing free labor into direct competition with enslaved labor would reveal, through low prices, that the former was more efficient. Market rules, they argued, were neutral, and economic power could be employed to support or to tear down an evil institution.[47] Theirs was an argument about fairness that the anti-auction writers had made in insisting that something called "regular commerce" existed, uncontaminated by undemocratic designs.

The free produce movement, with free Black activists as some of its most prominent leaders, rested on the conviction that the consumer was the ultimate driver of economic production because she or he created the demand to which producers responded. By the 1840s, the political and economic power of consumers was a regular part of national discussions, appearing in debates about free trade policies; all purchases, it became clear in these debates, were political acts.[48] Free produce advocates believed that consumers could be motivated by more than price, utility, or abundance, and these other motivations should be encouraged to create a marketplace that rewarded antislavery values. They mobilized a broadly shared understanding of the connection between supply and demand to enjoin consumers that by purchasing products produced by enslaved people, buyers were turning slaveholders and those who sold people at auction into their own agents, and thereby they were responsible for sustaining slavery.[49]

Black Americans did not believe the market was moral, but they did use it in a third way to oppose slavery: by redeeming their kin out of enslavement and into freedom, one purchase at a time. Attempting to turn the racial domination of capitalism on its head, they bid, or more commonly negotiated, in order to reconnect families.[50] They participated in estate auctions that threatened to separate families by mobilizing free members of those extended families to put their capital toward purchasing partial family restoration in freedom.[51] Black and white abolitionists debated the practice of purchasing people out of slavery, because the act both compensated the enslaver and also participated in the commodification of the purchased human.[52] At the same time, most abolitionists contributed to efforts to ransom enslaved people out of the South as a pragmatic, urgent intervention in individual lives.[53]

Antislavery publications highlighted stories of a free Black person redeeming an enslaved Black person as evidence of moral character in the purchaser. Rather than conceding the limited and compromised opportunities for acting within an evil system of human commodification, these publications reiterated the idea of the morally righteous consumer, but with a twist. While free produce advocates strove to create alternatives to slave-produced goods and economic networks, those who celebrated the purchasing of people from slavery believed that direct involvement in the sale of human beings could be redemptive. The *African Repository and Colonial Journal* reprinted a piece from the *New York Observer* with the headline "Benevolence of an African," which retold the story of "an aged colored woman, far gone in a consumption" who years before had purchased her own and her husband's freedom in New Orleans.[54] According to the article, "She heard one morning that a number of servants were to be sold at auction" and resolved to purchase one, "saying to herself, this done, I can depart in peace." She bought a woman for $250, then brought her to New York as a free person, with the understanding that she would commit herself to Christianity. "A striking example of the power of religion," commented the *Observer*.

Some antislavery activists presented Black people purchasing family members as exemplars of financial independence as well as of "moral elevation."[55] An 1840 report in the *Colored American* on the free Black community in Cincinnati emphasized that the thrift and hard work of the formerly enslaved yielded them significant financial gains, putting the lie to the insistence of whites that they "cannot take care of themselves." One man's ascendance to financial independence began on an auction table in Lexington, Kentucky. The man, called only "No. 6," appealed to bidders "not to bid a high price, for he had a friend ready to purchase him." He pointed to his weeping wife and daughter and begged the auctioneer not to sell him to a southern man. According to the account, "his appeals so affected the by-standers" that they allowed him to go for a low price to his friend. He subsequently repaid the friend and, as a free man, bought four other family members out of slavery. By 1840 he was a property-owning taxpayer.[56] In other words, his skill in managing his own self-commodification prefigured a more general financial savvy that served him well as a free man. Once he had navigated the crucible of the auction, he paid off debts, purchased property, and successfully participated in the political economy that simultaneously kept his family enslaved until he used the mechanism of the auction to liberate them.

But could an economy that rested on human commodification be redeemed within its own rules of operation? The flip side of bringing family members out of enslavement through a morally motivated auction purchase was the routine violation of family ties through auction purchases. An address to "Free Colored People At the North" listed the many ways that a free Black man in the North was secure in his familial relationships as head of household in a way no enslaved man could be. His children were protected in his home, his rights to his wife were inviolable, and "the virtue of his daughters is safe."[57] His family was the mirror image of those within slavery and the evidence was crystalized at an auction. The author, who celebrated the patriarchal rights of a free Black man, described an acquaintance's trip to New Orleans, where the contrast was pointed. The traveler was accosted by an auctioneer: "Do you wish to buy a wife?" The auctioneer leered "as he invited his attention to the personal charms of the girls thus offered to the licentiousness of the highest bidder."[58] The meaning of this exchange for the Black newspaper was clear: no moral intentions on the part of the purchaser could turn this transaction into a morally responsible encounter. The auctioneer's suggestion that a wife could be bought revealed the fatal flaw in the structure itself.

The powerful feelings that abolitionists evoked around slave auctions—of pathos, sympathy, and disgust—did not lead even sympathetic white Americans necessarily to call for abolition, and this was a weakness in their focus on the theater of auctioning. Some white commentators responded to the horrors of the auction block by condemning the manner of sale rather than the fact of human commodification itself. At the turn of the nineteenth century, for instance, the British politician Bryan Edwards recalled the 1732 Debt Recovery Act, a law applying only in British colonies, which had mandated that land and enslaved people could be seized and sold at court auction to satisfy litigated debt, alongside personal property. Edwards argued that the law, passed in response to pressure by British creditors, had damaging long-term effects for those men and women enslaved in the new United States. Yet his solution was not one the abolitionists would have condoned. Rather, in his bid to repeal the law, he suggested Black laborers should be "attached to the land, and sold with it."[59]

As Edwards explained his thinking, he took for granted that the sale of a human was a transaction impersonal and unyielding as the purported laws of the marketplace; it was only the auction that made it needlessly cruel. Edwards used an emotionally charged story that became familiar in antislavery literature to make his point. He described a hypothetical "good negro" who over time "gets comfortably established, has built himself a house, obtained a wife, and begins to see a young family rising about him. His provision-ground, the creation of his own industry, and the staff of his existence, affords him not only support, but the means also of adding something to the mere necessaries of life."[60] Suddenly, due to his enslaver's debts, he is seized by the sheriff, "forcibly separated from his wife and children, dragged to a public auction, purchased by a stranger." This misery, Edwards pointed out, "occurs every day." In his depiction, the enslaved man forced to the auction block had all the traits that would make him sympathetic to male lawmakers as a potential head of household, including a wife and family and the spirit of material self-improvement. The injustice of his situation was to have his efforts disregarded in a public auction all because "his master is unfortunate."[61] In Edwards's retelling, no one was to blame for his suffering except the law of creditor protection. The injustice, and the emotional pain, was best addressed not by freeing Black families (which would deprive white families of their wealth in property) but rather by modifying the law to bind them to the land, kept together, but in perpetual bondage.

Newspaper advertisements primed white northerners in the United States to draw similar conclusions by presenting the legal executions behind slave sales as settled law. Laws that treated people as property, which of course had a specific history and social context, became, in the seemingly neutral language of commercial print, unchangeable facets of economic life and the meaning of the economy more generally. An article in the *National Gazette* began by quoting an advertisement from another paper: "for the sale at auction of a negro girl of seventeen years of age taken in execution for taxes due by her master to the Corporation of Washington."[62] The *Gazette* author used this legal notice not to condemn slavery itself but to seek a kinder way of perpetuating it. To be torn from family at a public sale, asserted the *Gazette* author, was "a worse execution than death itself." Slavery was "inevitable," as was the need to sell property, but "if real estate in some parts of the Union is safe from the auctioneer or the sheriff, why may not human flesh be?" The author felt the "unoffending fellow creature" deserved kinder treatment but not release from the "inevitable" institution of slavery. The seventeen-year-old's status as human property and status as a family member could not be resolved within this limited economic imagination.

Some white Americans who sought amelioration of slavery rather than abolition went as far as to insist that an auction was a neutral tool, not a uniquely cruel spectacle. If handled correctly, they argued, an auction could be used by benevolent patriarchs for the moral purpose of keeping enslaved families together. The New England minister Nehemiah Adams began his book's chapter on "Slave Auctions" with an emotional scene—a one-year-old child, wrapped in a blanket, on the courthouse steps, awaiting sale. It was a narrative that resonated with abolitionists' portrayals of the grotesque violations of family that auctions of enslaved people made possible, and Adams claimed he could not bear to watch the sale unfold. But as his visit progressed, he wrote, the "estimable gentlemen" of the southern town explained the sale had been a performance to reunite the enslaved mother, who had been sold while pregnant, with her child, who was born belonging to the former master. The sheriff who presided over the sale was in fact the "avenger and protector" of the little girl, controlling the bidding so that she was reunited with her mother through purchase by her mother's enslaver, a case of "slavery restoring a child to its mother . . . redressing its own wrong."[63]

Adams repeated the self-justifying explanations of white enslavers in a fashion that made even the public sale of a baby evidence of paternalistic care. In his telling, the individual manly heroism of the all-powerful sheriff auctioneer who directed the sale and the morally motivated bids of the white purchasers who planned to reunite the baby with her mother stripped the auction of its economic context and significance by obscuring them in a drama of consumer and salesman. As a minister who had formerly spoken out against slavery, Adams was convinced by the narrowing of economic issues down to individual transactions to believe that his moral compass—which had initially recoiled at the prospect of a child for sale—had pointed him wrong. Purchasing commodities, in this understanding, was a neutral act that only gained meaning from the intent of the buyer, even if that intent was fantasy.[64]

The Public Sale

Attention to the auction block as the stand-in for immoral markets made it harder to see that the theatrical, competitive consumers who supposedly drove sales were a product, rather than a cause, of commercial development. From their earliest days in British colonial America, auctions operated alongside other means of selling humans, and public sales had disposed of property both human and inanimate. In the nineteenth-century South, sales of enslaved people were "a regular part of everyday life" through auctions and private sales, and discussions of prices of human workers and financial value in human bodies formed the backdrop of daily conversation.[65] After the closing of the Atlantic slave trade in 1808, some sales activity moved from East Coast wharves to the docks where river-cruising steamboats unloaded their goods, but courthouse steps and farmyards remained just as common sites of sales, with enslaved people cycling through public auction and private transaction over the course of their lives. The commercial auction block was one venue among many circulating human beings alongside many other goods through the economy.

The symbolic power of the auction block, from the perspective of abolitionists, was that it offered a focus for conversations about the commodification of human beings. The spread of investment and financial tools in the nineteenth century supported an understanding of the market that was an abstract one. Calculating financial risk for the purposes of future profit on a cotton crop abstracted the relationship of the purchaser to what she or he purchased.[66] Financial instruments played with time, requiring people to make judgments now for some undetermined moment in the future. The auction block, however, was a place, and it was a time. Dates and hours featured prominently in any auction advertisement; in fact, an advertisement did not even need to use the word "auction" to identify it as such. The statement indicating "this day at three o'clock in the afternoon" was enough to signal a public sale. Auction advertisements placed the most visible and specific temporal markers on a newspaper page that was otherwise marked by terms such as "this day" or "lately." Some of this specificity was dictated by law. For example, an 1806 Pennsylvania law required trustees of a new academy in Beaver, Pennsylvania, to sell land lots at the courthouse "on or before the first Monday in August next, having previously advertised the same for three weeks in a newspaper published at Washington, one in Pittsburgh, and one in Meadville."[67] But temporal specificity was also part of the design of a public sale, in order to bring all interested buyers into a head-to-head competition.

With its emphasis on location and timing, the auction block sale provided a ready-made tableau for abolitionists, a set piece of individual transactions that was immediately legible in linking violence, money, and sin. The abolitionist preacher Henry Ward Beecher held mock auctions of beautiful light-skinned enslaved women in his crowded Brooklyn, New York, church to raise money to pay off the people who claimed to own them.[68] One admiring minister even commented that Beecher "would have made a capital auctioneer if he had chosen that business."[69] In raising money on women who had already reached a free state, but not freedom from recapture, Beecher sought to shock northern congregations with the debasing sexual violence of slavery by forcing them to participate in looking at, and bidding on, "a marketable commodity" who looked like them. The financial arrangements could have been conducted privately, as most slave redemptions were, but Beecher wanted publicity.[70] The auction block, or auction stage, provided market specificity as much as market spectacle.

Scholars have followed the metaphorical lead of abolitionists by invoking the auction block as the ominous site of the sin of human commodification. For some, the physical location is the foundation of critical historical understanding because—unlike the domesticated environment of a plantation or small farm—the auction block was a raw expression of racist power and profit seeking and a better starting point for understanding the capitalist dynamics of slavery.[71] For others, it is a more implicit auction block that centers the understanding that at all times an enslaved person had a potential price on her head and a potential sale threatening her family ties. The "chattel principle" of enslavement meant that human bodies were collateral that could be liquidated and made manifest at any time.[72] Enslaved people strategized where they could to avoid specific sales that would separate them from family members, but they could only escape the pervasive commodification of their bodies in their relationships with each other and their own "soul value."[73]

Certainly, the public nature of an auction mattered. Some formerly enslaved people even related that they were forced to participate in the publicity of their own sale. Stephen Dickinson Jr., reported that an auctioneer in Vicksburgh "paraded us about the street for about an hour, offering us for sale, compelling one of us to carry a red flag, and another of us to ring a bell."[74] Defenders of slavery insisted that such publicity was legally and financially useful. Nehemiah Adams insisted, "Slaves are allowed to find masters and mistresses who will buy them. Having found them, the sheriffs' and administrators' sales must by law be made public, the persons must be advertised, and everything looks like an unrestricted offer, while it is the understanding of the company that the sale has really been made in private."[75] In fact, he claimed, such publicity was a financial legality that confirmed the emotional desires of the enslaved themselves, when they sought out purchasers to keep their families together.

But such participation was by the power of the state. Adams's reference to "sheriffs' and administrators' sales" is a reminder that on the auction block, enslaved people were deeply and directly embedded in the very social and political relations that their commodification, in the abstract, denied. When communities responded to the bell, or to their knowledge that it was a court-ordered sale day, they were often coming to bid on human beings they knew or thought they knew. Auction attendees on courthouse steps placed their bids in a "high information environment" in which a human being's personal history and physical capacity could be displayed and evaluated.[76] This reality—that humans were not standardized objects—meant that auctions of enslaved people were necessarily different from auctions of animals and inanimate goods, in spite of efforts to treat them in the same way. That reality necessitated state authorization and the repetitive deployment of the auction effect to achieve its goal of commodifying people.

White residents of Charleston, South Carolina, debated the politics of the auction block by contesting the proper visibility of the sale in people, but not sale itself or the key role of lawmakers in perpetuating those sales. In 1839 the City Council passed an ordinance that made it illegal to sell enslaved people anywhere but at a purpose-built "mart" established at the city workhouse, a site deliberately at a remove from the commercial center of the city.[77] The law sought to centralize the sale of human beings and bring them off the city streets and under cover. The council also petitioned for a state law requiring that all auctions of enslaved people be moved to the slave mart, to join the individual private sales housed there. Notably, they included in their petition those public sales conducted under the authority of the sheriff and the master in equity, which were court-ordered auctions that had historically been treated separately in auction licensing and tax law.[78] In response, the judiciary committee agreed that "the daily sales of slaves at auction which take place about the exchange in the midst of the greatest thoroughfare of business in the City may be and no doubt are a source of annoyance," but they argued that the same could not be said of court-ordered auctions. Drawing a distinction within the category of public sales, the committee insisted that auctions by law generally were "made only on the first Monday in each month, and it is not often that many sales of slaves are made in any considerable numbers by them." Furthermore, it was inconvenient to separate the auctioning of humans from the auctioning of other forms of property that were taking place at the courthouse. Chairman William DeSaussure explained: "By the law of the land all judicial sales must be made at the court house; this system has prevailed for more than half a century; it has been found beneficial to the country, and your committee are not satisfied with the reasons offered for the proposed change."[79]

South Carolina lawmakers perpetuated a misrepresentation made repeatedly by the powerful to explain away the politics of enslavement. Yet court-ordered public sales were foundational to the story of American capitalism. In fact, half of the sales of enslaved people in South Carolina took place under court authority.[80] The courthouse steps were as representative of the sale of human property as a commercial auction block.[81] State courts and state law provided the force behind the transactions, a point that is lost in accounts that highlighted the individual evil, compassion, or scheming of individuals in a competitive marketplace. By dismissing the number of court-ordered auctions of human property as "not considerable" in numbers and only periodic in terms of frequency, lawmakers denied their role in sustaining the destruction of enslaved families as a basis for their legal, political, and economic system. It was a denial that echoed across the nineteenth century in every region of the United States and benefited from the belief that the market's rules were intrinsic rather than political.

*   *   *

Harriet Jacobs wrote the account of her grandmother on the auction block from a refuge of freedom she had found in New York. She hoped "to arouse women of the North to a realizing sense of the condition of two millions of women at the South, still in bondage" by exposing the evils of "demon Slavery" even though it meant exposing her own sexual history in a culture with a fierce racial double standard when it came to female sexuality.[82] She crafted her autobiographical account in dialog with abolitionist literature and in conversation with other abolitionist activists; she intended her account "to be useful in some way" to the abolitionist cause.[83] With her recounting of Aunt Martha on the auction block, she connected personal details to a well-used trope of immoral markets. In her hands, the exposure of an auction was not its primary evil, but rather its saving grace, in that white people—both southern neighbors and northerners who assumed they had no stake in the matter—could not look away from the reality of the trade in families.

Jacobs's brother, John, published his own account of the auction-block sale of his family by the "hungry heirs" of their former enslaver. In his account, penned for British Antislavery activists, the mood of the sale is misery, from "the old slaves," sold first "as rubbish" for a dollar, to the young carpenter sold for $1,600.[84] His grandmother (the same "Aunt Martha") is not the defiant community matriarch of Harriet Jacobs's tale but rather a thrifty businesswoman who "possessed a tried and trusty friend, in whose hands she placed the savings of thirty years, that he might purchase her and her son Mark."[85] In her brother's version, the charitable female bidder in Harriet's tale is replaced by the man of business who acted "very honorably," purchased mother and son, freed the mother, and placed her son under her ownership. Keeping their small family together would require continued thrift on Martha's part, as Mark "could be sold any minute to pay her debts." In John's telling, Martha could manage her presence in the marketplace but never be free from the tyranny of property law and debt collection.

Both Jacobs siblings presented auctions as rituals of loss rather than rituals of profit, though they used different tropes about marketplaces to make their points. For Harriet, the exposure of her grandmother's sale allowed righteous intervention by the crowd. For John, concealed prearrangements with a bidder ensured that his grandmother's thrift was rewarded with freedom. In both their reconstructed memories, white families scrambled to hold on to value being stripped from them by the state by destroying the valuable community lives of the people they priced. The public sale offered rules and witnesses, which could be mobilized on behalf of individuals by trusted friends or loving relatives. But the auction itself was relentless. The only way to be free was to remove human beings from the category of property.

Conclusion

Marketplaces are designed to sort out who gets what and why; they distribute goods and simultaneously create a rationale for that distribution. Looking at eighteenth- and early nineteenth-century North America through auctioning reveals the dense meanings behind these seemingly straightforward transactions. Over and over, Americans deployed auctions to convert complex familial, labor, or diplomatic relationships into an exchange of goods for money. Auctions served as tools of settler colonialism, mechanisms for favoring creditors over debtors, community rituals of establishing political power over rivals, and ruthless assertions of racial hierarchy.

To expose, price, and value an object was a social and political act, not the outcome of an invisible law of the market. Auctions were potent sites of knowledge production because they were organized around powerful features that included the backing of the law, the oversight of a commanding director, and the presence of an invested audience. In the collective problem-solving of an auction, participants used the mechanism of price to sort out their ideas about value. In this way, the price of the object was always about the bidding community's values as well as their thoughts about the usefulness of a particular good; each shaped the other.[1]

Understanding the nuances in how institutions such as local courts and households shaped prices means understanding the social origins of economic norms. Power infused each purchase of a human family, a broken tool, or a riverfront acre, as contending voices used buying, selling, and witnessing to express their own allegiances and ideas about hierarchy. To attend to these voices places value, and values, in historical context, and therefore in historical relationships of power, rather than in the realm of financial abstraction and models removed from their social contexts. The daily, often mundane nature of these transactions meant value was embodied and familiar rather than abstract, and in that familiarity came its power. Moreover, in understanding the creation of value, we gain insight into American societies' attitudes and ideas about material objects and other human beings.

Supply and demand, productivity and consumption: these are the concepts that dominate economic models, with objects, people, and land flowing freely into a market exchange, as if they were already part of the realm of the priceable and exchangeable. But auctions represented a pause in the life of an exchangeable good, revealing the social forces that had shaped its sale. "It is a mournful thing," observed the author of the nineteenth-century novel *It Is All for the Best*, to have a home "invaded by the crowd of careless strangers who attend an auction, and above all when death and ruin have opened the doors to them; yet there is a great deal that is entertaining, too."[2] The uncomfortable intersection of loss and entertainment was a hallmark of auctions in the eighteenth and nineteenth centuries, from the mundane losses of damaged shop goods to the catastrophic losses of enslaved families, and those who came to witness or bid were often coming to be entertained as well.

The now-familiar idea that price and value are connected and that competition best reveals the true price was just emerging in the early eighteenth century when the group of white petitioners on the banks of the Rappahannock River sought a way to turn contested land into private property constituting a town called Fredericksburg, Virginia. The early land auctions legitimized this transformation by bringing the transaction into the open, where neighbors could keep track of one another's aspirations and validate them. To expose a transaction was to bring it under public scrutiny and the explicit backing of the legal system. Yet much in those land auctions remained concealed. Every bidder in attendance was aware of the history of loss that was taking this riverbank away from Indigenous people who also claimed it, but that knowledge was not recognized by the day's transaction. The settlers engaged in the ritual of the auction to acknowledge some communities and relationships and to deny others.

Across the eighteenth and into the nineteenth century, the dominant American culture developed the idea that open competition made a transaction fair, often in contrast to other types of selling, such as monopolies and patronage schemes. Competing ways to measure fairness in exchange, including Christian morality, or alignment with local customary practices, never fully disappeared, but the politics of publicity and print, along with the institutional weight of the law and court system, made these competing systems alternatives to what appeared to many to be settled rules of the economy.

In creating objects with value, auctions frequently rehearsed a construction of race and gender that was binary and hierarchical. As Americans debated the dimensions of human experience that should not be monetized, although they could be exchanged—such as household labor, sex, patronage support, modesty, and virtue—some used auctions to try to make these distinctions. Selling a Black woman was common; selling a white woman was a crime, and the distinction of which woman was sellable embedded notions of race and gender into emerging market logics.

Which was not to say that auctions imposed hierarchies from without. The participatory nature of public sales meant that audiences could work collectively at cross-purposes to government officials, or alternatively use legal structures for their own ends. Auctions could salvage the value of items otherwise spoiled or lost. Families frequently used them to renegotiate relationships at a crisis point of death or financial failure. It is in these details that we can understand the social and cultural shifts that supported the emergence of the commonsense link between price and value.

By tracking the multiple uses of one type of exchange—auctioning—the chapters of this book demonstrate that the transformation was not about freedom in opposition to regulation but rather cycles of exposure and concealment, of goods and relationships. By the middle of the nineteenth century, a result of the rise of market exchange as the dominant paradigm of the economy was that white women were both restricted from forms of economic power and also not judged accountable for its abuses. At the same time, for white men, economic failures were ascribed to individual lapses in character rather than in the structure of banks or capitalism; economic victories were their own.[3] Abolitionists saw these paradigms and endeavored to expose their contradictions. As they discovered, the moment of exchange certainly crystalized key dynamics in a capitalist economy, but taking exchange to stand in for the whole of how people organized their lives and family subsistence yields more information about the consequences of economic structures than the causes of how such divisions came to be.

In the twenty-first century, markets remain a powerful tool for exposing some relationships and concealing others. The city of Fredericksburg, carved out by the eighteenth-century bidders on the Rappahannock, itself had to confront its own history of exchanges when, on June 6, 2020, the town removed the "slave auction block" at the corner of William and Charles Streets and relocated it to the Fredericksburg Area Museum. The removal took place during a summer of protests over police violence against Black people in the United States, but it had also required a long local governmental and legal process of study, consultation, and court decisions.[4] The heavy sandstone block, originally installed in the 1830s or 1840s, was likely not a literal auction block on which enslaved people stood; rather, it was associated with the neighboring United States Hotel, an establishment at which public auctions and the sale of human beings took place prior to the Civil War.[5] Its removal to a museum, to be displayed in fuller historical context, was part of nationwide debates over the proper way to confront the history of slavery and racism in the United States.[6] As part of the 1619 Project of the *New York Times*, scholars and artists demonstrated multiple sites of slave auctions that had been integrated into the American landscape in the eighteenth and nineteenth centuries and then obscured in the years after the Civil War.[7]

Auctions integrated human enslavement into the American economy; they also installed fundamental concepts of capitalism in the American social and cultural landscape. The economic ideas enshrined in that block of stone in Frederickburg—that any entity can be coded as property, priced through market competition, and therefore fairly valued—received little explicit attention in the debate over moving it because they have become the commonsense of modern thinking about markets. The logic of the auction block still shapes the way people in the twenty-first century understand the justice or injustice of economic systems, and this logic conceals what we might do to create an economy and culture that work for all.

NOTES

INTRODUCTION

1. Henry A. M. Smith, "The Ashley River: Its Seats and Settlements," *South Carolina Historical and Genealogical Magazine* 20, no. 1 (January 1919): 3–51, 24–25; "Inventory and Appraisement of the Goods and Chattels of Richard Baker of Charlestown," 460–66, "Sales of Sundry Goods and Chattells belonging to the Estate of Capt.n Richard Baker Deceased sold by order of Mrs. Sarah Baker Administratrix, 512–16, "By Virtue of a Warrant of Appraisement to us directed bearing date the twenty Sixth day of December last we whose names are hereunto subscribed have viewed and Appraised all the Personal Estate of Richard Baker late of Ashley Deceased . . . ," 526–30, all in *Inventories, Charleston County, 1751–1753*, vol. 79, South Carolina Room, Charleston County Public Library, Charleston, South Carolina; "Will of Richard Baker," 35–42, *Charleston County Wills*, vol. 7, Charleston County Library.

2. Free married women in British North America and the early United States lived under the legal conventions of coverture, which limited their formal rights to property ownership and their ability to sign contracts. Scholars have emphasized, however, that coverture's principles varied by region and period. See, for example, Sarah Damiano, *To Her Credit: Gender, Law, and Economic Life in Eighteenth-Century New England Cities* (Baltimore: Johns Hopkins University Press, 2021); Laura F. Edwards, *Only the Clothes on Her Back: Clothing and the Hidden History of Power in the 19th-Century United States* (New York: Oxford University Press, 2022); Cornelia Hughes Dayton, *Women Before the Bar: Gender, Law, and Society in Connecticut, 1639–1789* (Chapel Hill: University of North Carolina Press, 1995); Linda L. Sturtz, *Within Her Power: Propertied Women in Colonial Virginia* (New York: Routledge, 2002); and Serena Zabin, *Dangerous Economies: Status and Commerce in Imperial New York* (Philadelphia: University of Pennsylvania Press, 2009). For an analysis of the legal history of coverture and how it came to be taken as a rigid system, see Holly Brewer, "The Transformation of Domestic Law," in *Cambridge History of Law in America*, ed. Christopher L. Tomlins and Michael Grossberg (New York: Cambridge University Press, 2008), 288–323.

3. Washington wrote to Tench Tilghman "At what prices the enumerated articles will sell or the terms proposed can only be known from the experiment." "Letters Selected from the Ferdinand J. Dreer Collection of Manuscripts," *Pennsylvania Magazine of History and Biography* 40, no. 4 (1916): 458–71, 459.

4. As Alvin E. Roth writes, auctions use prices and a "structured matchmaking environment" to shape and satisfy human desires. Alvin E. Roth, *Who Gets What—and Why: The New Economics of Matchmaking and Market Design* (New York: Houghton Mifflin Harcourt, 2015), 5 .

5. See Rebecca L. Spang's discussion of the human creation of value and its relationship to forms of money in *Stuff and Money in the Time of the French Revolution* (Cambridge, MA: Harvard University Press, 2017), 14.

6. Joshua R. Greenberg, *Bank Notes and Shinplasters: The Rage for Paper Money in the Early Republic* (Philadelphia: University of Pennsylvania Press, 2020), and Stephen Mihm, *A Nation of Counterfeiters: Capitalists, Con Men, and the Making of the United States* (Cambridge, MA: Harvard University Press, 2009), discuss the problems of reliable information in navigating the paper money landscape of the eighteenth and nineteenth centuries.

7. Economists have wrestled with the link between value and price, most familiarly in classical and Marxist approaches. Modern scholars frequently discuss prices as markers of information about seller and consumer preferences, suggesting a way of thinking about markets as notional places where dispersed buyers and sellers make individual decisions. For one historical analysis of price theory and its relationship to eighteenth-century economic thought, see Glory M. Liu, *Adam Smith's America: How a Scottish Philosopher became an Icon of American Capitalism* (Princeton, NJ: Princeton University Press, 2022), 200–206.

8. Sarah Barringer Gordon, "The African Supplement: Religion, Race, and Corporate Law in Early National America," *William and Mary Quarterly* 72, no. 3 (July 2015): 385–422, 411–13. Richard S. Newman, *Freedom's Prophet: Bishop Richard Allen, the AME Church, and the Black Founding Fathers* (New York: New York University Press, 2008), 164–66.

9. *American Telegraph*, August 20, 1817.

10. For the political and social possibilities of consumption in eighteenth-century North America, see T. H. Breen, *The Marketplace of Revolution: How Consumer Politics Shaped American Independence* (New York: Oxford University Press, 2004); and Ann Smart Martin, *Buying into the World of Goods: Early Consumers in Backcountry Virginia* (Baltimore: Johns Hopkins University Press, 2008). Work with an explicit material culture focus has some of the most interesting explorations of the uses and meanings of purchased goods. See Zara Anishanslin, *Portrait of a Woman in Silk: Hidden Histories of the British Atlantic World* (New Haven, CT: Yale University Press, 2017); Jennifer Van Horn, *The Power of Objects in Eighteenth-Century British America* (Chapel Hill: University of North Carolina Press, 2017); Sophie White, *Wild Frenchmen and Frenchified Indians: Material Culture and Race in Colonial Louisiana* (Philadelphia: University of Pennsylvania Press, 2014); and Laurel Thatcher Ulrich, *The Age of Homespun: Objects and Stories in the Creation of an American Myth* (New York: Vintage Books, 2002).

11. Anne Bailey, *The Weeping Time: Memory and the Largest Slave Auction in American History* (New York: Cambridge University Press, 2017). Bailey uses the concept of the Butler slave auction being a breach in the lives of the people who were sold and in historical memory; see chapter 2.

12. Nicoline van der Sijs, *Cookies, Coleslaw, and Stoops: The Influence of Dutch on the North American Languages* (Amsterdam: Amsterdam University Press, 2009, 236; "Reports," *American Journal of Philology* 27, no. 4 (1906): 461–78, 477; entry for *vendue, Oxford English*

Dictionary Online, accessed September 26, 2013. As the dictionary entry suggests, colonial North America and the West Indies shared a vendue culture. See Trevor Burnard, "Collecting and Accounting: Representing Slaves as Commodities in Jamaica, 1674–1784," in *Collecting Across Cultures: Material Exchanges in the Early Modern Atlantic World*, ed. Daniela Bleichmar and Peter Mancall (Philadelphia: University of Pennsylvania Press, 2011), 177–91, 187–88.

13. Important explorations of Indigenous land and the colonial project of property making include Allan Greer, *Property and Dispossession: Natives, Empires and Land in Early Modern North America* (New York: Cambridge University Press, 2018); Lisa Brooks, *Our Beloved Kin: A New History of King Philip's War* (New Haven, CT: Yale University Press, 2018); and Christine DeLucia, *Memory Lands: King Philip's War and the Place of Violence in the Northeast* (New Haven, CT: Yale University Press, 2018).

14. Transatlantic trade and connected colonial economic activities have been explored in numerous studies. For some North American examples, see David Hancock, *Oceans of Wine: Madeira and the Emergence of American Trade and Taste* (New Haven, CT: Yale University Press, 2009); and Peter Coclanis, ed., *The Atlantic Economy During the Seventeenth and Eighteenth Centuries: Organization, Operation, Practice, and Personnel* (Columbia: University of South Carolina Press, 2005). For examples of merchant responses, see Cathy Matson, *Merchants and Empire: Trading in Colonial New York* (Baltimore: Johns Hopkins University Press, 1998); Sheryllynne Haggerty, *The British Atlantic Merchant Community, 1760–1810: Men, Women, and the Distribution of Goods* (Leiden: Koninklijke Brill NV, 2006); and the classic Thomas M. Doerflinger, *A Vigorous Spirit of Enterprise: Merchants and Economic Development in Revolutionary Philadelphia* (Chapel Hill: University of North Carolina Press, 1986). For local market responses, see the still-influential scholarship from Christopher Clark, *The Roots of Rural Capitalism: Western Massachusetts, 1780–1860* (Ithaca, NY: Cornell University Press, 1990); and Daniel Vickers, *Farmers and Fishermen: Two Centuries of Work in Essex County* (Chapel Hill: University of North Carolina Press, 1994).

15. Emma Hart places auctions alongside other colonial adaptations to British marketplace practices in *Trading Spaces: The Colonial Marketplace and the Foundations of America Capitalism* (Chicago: University of Chicago Press, 2019).

16. Mihm, *A Nation of Counterfeiters*; Greenberg, *Bank Notes and Shinplasters*.

17. Hannah Ferber, *Underwriters of the United States: How Insurance Shaped the American Founding* (Chapel Hill: University of North Carolina Press, 2021); Jonathan Levy, *Freaks of Fortune: The Emerging World of Capitalism and Risk in America* (Cambridge, MA: Harvard University Press, 2014); Sharon Ann Murphy, *Investing in Life: Insurance in Antebellum America* (Baltimore: Johns Hopkins University Press, 2013). See also Jessica Lepler, *The Many Panics of 1837: People, Politics, and the Creation of a Transatlantic Financial Crisis* (New York: Cambridge University Press, 2013).

18. This scholarship is rich and expanding. For leading examples, see Caitlin Rosenthal, *Accounting for Slavery: Masters and Management* (Cambridge, MA: Harvard University Press, 2019). See also Edward E. Baptist, *The Half Has Never Been Told: Slavery and the Making of American Capitalism* (New York: Basic Books, 2016); Walter Johnson, *River of Dark Dreams: Slavery and Empire in the Cotton Kingdom* (Cambridge, MA: Belknap Press, 2017); and the essays in Sven Beckert and Seth Rockman, eds., *Slavery's Capitalism: A New History*

of American Economic Development (Philadelphia: University of Pennsylvania Press, 2016). Daina Ramey Berry examines the commodification of humans yet offers a sustained concept of "soul value" maintained by the enslaved people themselves in *The Price for Their Pound of Flesh: The Value of the Enslaved, from Womb to Grave, in the Building of a Nation* (New York: Beacon Press, 2017).

19. See discussion in Seth Rockman, *Scraping By: Wage Labor, Slavery, and Survival in Early Baltimore* (Baltimore: Johns Hopkins University Press, 2009). Caitlin Rosenthal argues that standard price lists for enslaved people in the middle of the nineteenth century marked the end point of standardization of human "value." Caitlin Rosenthal, "Capitalism When Labor Was Capital: Slavery, Power, and Price in Antebellum America," *Capitalism: A Journal of History and Economics* 1, no. 2 (Spring 2020): 296–337.

20. Several influential works look at the centrality of "marginal" and "informal" economic actors to colonial and nineteenth-century North American commerce, including Serena Zabin's *Dangerous Economies* for eighteenth-century New York; Seth Rockman's *Scraping By* for early republic Baltimore; and Brian P. Luskey and Wendy A. Woloson's introduction to *Capitalism by Gaslight: Illuminating the Economy of Nineteenth-Century America* (Philadelphia: University of Pennsylvania Press, 2015) and the essays in that volume explore different facets of such economies.

21. Stephanie E. Smallwood, "The Politics of the Archive and History's Accountability to the Enslaved," *History of the Present* 6, no. 2 (Fall 2016): 117–32, 126.

22. Some of the most influential writing on prices of enslaved people in the nineteenth-century United States includes Berry, *Price for Their Pound of Flesh*; Baptist, *Half Has Never Been Told*; and Walter Johnson, *Soul by Soul: Life Inside the Antebellum Slave Market* (Cambridge, MA: Harvard University Press, 2000). The topic has been investigated by scholars of Atlantic World slavery for decades.

23. E. P. Thompson, *Customs in Common: Studies in Traditional Popular Culture* (New York: New Press, 1992), presented an early modern moral economy that influenced scholars of colonial and revolutionary North America, including, among others, Daniel Vickers, "Competency and Competition: Economic Culture in Early America," *William and Mary Quarterly* 47, no. 1 (January 1990): 3–29; Ruth Borgin, "Petitioning and the New Moral Economy of Post-Revolutionary America," *William and Mary Quarterly* 45, no. 3 (July 1988): 391–425; and Barbara Clark Smith, *The Freedoms We Lost: Consent and Resistance in Revolutionary America* (New York: New Press, 2010). Intellectual and political historians studying Western Europe and North America found a shift in mentalité in the seventeenth and eighteenth centuries. See, as examples, Albert O. Hirschman, *The Passions and the Interests: Political Arguments for Capitalism Before Its Triumph* (1977; Princeton, NJ: Princeton University Press, 2013); and Joyce Appleby, *The Relentless Revolution: A History of Capitalism* (New York: W. W. Norton, 2011). For a useful discussion of the scholarship on economy and morality, see Christopher Clark, "A Wealth of Notions: Interpreting Economy and Morality in Early America," *Early American Studies* 8, no. 3 (Fall 2010): 672–83, and the articles included in that volume.

24. For a recent discussion, see the special issue of *Humanity: An International Journal of Human Rights, Humanitarianism, and Development* 11, no. 2 (Summer 2020). For the

nineteenth-century United States, see William J. Novack, *The People's Welfare: Law and Regulation in Nineteenth-Century America* (Chapel Hill: University of North Carolina Press, 1996); and Joanna Cohen, *Luxurious Citizens: The Politics of Consumption in Nineteenth-Century America* (Philadelphia: University of Pennsylvania Press, 2017).

25. Edward J. Balleisen, *Navigating Failure: Bankruptcy and Commercial Society in Antebellum America* (Chapel Hill: University of North Carolina Press, 2001); James W. Cook, *The Arts of Deception: Playing with Fraud in the Age of Barnum* (Cambridge, MA: Harvard University Press, 2001); Scott Sandage, *Born Losers: A History of Failure in America* (Cambridge, MA: Harvard University Press, 2006); Luskey and Woloson, *Capitalism by Gaslight*.

26. *The Lilliputian Auction: To Which All Little Masters and Misses Are Invited* (Philadelphia, PA: Jacob Johnson, 1802). An earlier (and still available) choice might be religious catechism. See, for example, John Cotton's *Spiritual Milk for Babes*, listed in Wilberforce Eames, *Early New England Catechisms* (Worcester, MA: Press of Charles Hamilton, 1898), 24–25.

27. Historians and literature scholars have both explored the connections of print, economy, and the definition of a "fact." For some of this literature, see Christine Desan, *Making Money: Coin, Currency, and the Coming of Capitalism* (New York: Oxford University Press, 2014); James Thompson, *Models of Virtue: Eighteenth-Century Political Economy and the Novel* (Durham, NC: Duke University Press, 1996); Mary Poovey, *A History of the Modern Fact: Problems of Knowledge in the Sciences of Wealth and Society* (Chicago: University of Chicago Press, 1998); Mary Poovey, *Genres of the Credit Economy: Mediating Value in Eighteenth- and Nineteenth-Century Britain* (Chicago: University of Chicago Press, 2008); Mark O'Malley, *Face Value: The Entwined Histories of Money and Race in America* (Chicago: University of Chicago Press, 2012); Jeffrey Sklansky, *Sovereign of the Market: The Money Question in Early America* (Chicago: University of Chicago Press, 2017); Greenberg, *Bank Notes*; and Spang, *Stuff and Money*.

28. Some important examples include Judith Carney, *Black Rice: The African Origins of Rice Cultivation in the Americas* (Cambridge, MA: Harvard University Press, 2002); Sidney W. Mintz, *Sweetness and Power: The Place of Sugar in Modern History* (New York: Penguin Books, 1986); Molly A. Warsh, *America Baroque: Pearls and the Nature of Empire, 1492–1700* (Chapel Hill: University of North Carolina Press, 2018); Jennifer L. Anderson, *Mahogany: The Costs of Luxury in Early America* (Cambridge, MA: Harvard University Press, 2015); and the classic Harold A. Innis, *The Cod Fisheries: The History of an International Economy* (Toronto: University of Toronto Press, 1978).

29. See, for example, David Hancock, *Citizens of the World: London Merchants and the Integration of the British Atlantic Community, 1735–1785* (New York: Cambridge University Press, 1995); Matson, *Merchants and Empire*; Jacob M. Price, *Overseas Trade and Traders* (Aldershot: Ashgate, 1996); Simon D. Smith, *Slavery, Family and Gentry Capitalism in the British Atlantic: The World of the Lascelles, 1648–1834* (Cambridge: Cambridge University Press, 2006); Richard L. Kagan, and Philip D. Morgan, eds., *Atlantic Diasporas: Jews, Conversos, and Crypto-Jews in the Age of Mercantilism, 1500–1800* (Baltimore: Johns Hopkins University Press, 2009); and Robin Law, *Ouidah: The Social History of a West African Slaving 'Port,' 1727–1892* (Athens: Ohio University Press, 2004). For a shopkeeper's perspective, see Patricia

Cleary, *Elizabeth Murray: A Woman's Pursuit of Independence in Eighteenth-Century America* (Amherst: University of Massachusetts Press, 2000).

30. In addition to Hart's *Trading Spaces*, this scholarship includes marketplaces in North American ports, including Emma Hart, *Building Charleston: Town and Society in the Eighteenth-Century British Atlantic World* (Richmond: University of Virginia Press, 2010); Ellen Hartigan-O'Connor, *The Ties That Buy: Women and Commerce in Revolutionary America* (Philadelphia: University of Pennsylvania Press, 2009); Robert Olwell, "'Loose, Idle, and Disorderly': Slave Women in the Eighteenth-Century Charleston Marketplace," in *More Than Chattel: Black Women and Slavery in the Americas*, ed. David Barry Gaspar and Darlene Clark Hine (Bloomington: Indiana University Press, 1996), 97–110. Another set of studies considers marketplaces away from port cities, including Ann Smart Martin, *Buying into the World of Goods: Early Consumers in Backcountry Virginia* (Baltimore: Johns Hopkins University Press, 2008); Kathryn Holland Braund, *Deerskins and Duffels: The Creek Indian Trade in Anglo-America, 1685–1815*, 2nd ed. (Lincoln: University of Nebraska Press, 2008); and Susannah Shaw Romney, *New Netherland Connections: Intimate Networks and Atlantic Ties in Seventeenth-Century America* (Chapel Hill: University of North Carolina Press, 2014). Scholars of secondhand trade and marketplaces who focus on areas outside of North America have begun to explore certain types of auctions. See the essays in Jon Stobart and Ilja Van Damme, eds., *Modernity and the Second-Hand Trade: European Consumption Cultures and Practices, 1700–1900* (New York: Palgrave Macmillan, 2010).

31. The tendency to treat British colonial and United States history as divided and distinct has obscured important continuities. With a few important exceptions, scholarship on the history of capitalism does not connect the eighteenth to the nineteenth century, in terms of market culture or methods of distribution. For key exceptions, see Hart, *Trading Spaces*; and Sven Beckert, *Empire of Cotton: A Global History* (New York: Alfred A. Knopf, 2014).

32. Greer, *Property and Dispossession*, introduction and chapter 8.

33. Beckert and Rockman, *Slavery's Capitalism*, 11.

34. The records of the Loyalist Claims Commission are preserved at the National Archives (United Kingdom). The Audit Office (AO) records are available on microfilm at libraries in the United States, identified either as AO 12 (film 263) or AO 13 (film 264), followed by volume and page or folio number. I accessed them at the David Library of the American Revolution. AO 12/10723.

35. AO 12/107/92.

36. K-Sue Park argues that American property law itself was marked by a "reliance on racial violence to produce value." Park, "The History Wars and Property Law: Conquest and Slavery as Foundational to the Field," *Yale Law Journal* 131, no. 4 (2022): 1062–153.

37. *The Ruinous Tendency of Auctioneering and the Necessity of Restraining It for the Benefit of Trade, Demonstrated in a Letter to the Right Hon. Lord Bathurst, President of the Board of Trade* (New York: Eastburn, Kirk, 1813), 47.

38. Classical economics rests on the idea that people are motivated to participate in markets because they are in search of "useful goods." For an interesting discussion and critique, see André Orléan, *The Empire of Value: A New Foundation for Economics*, trans. M. B. DeBevoise (Cambridge, MA: MIT Press, 2014), 3.

CHAPTER 1

1. *A collection of all the acts of Assembly, now in force, in the colony of Virginia* (Williamsburg, VA: William Parks, 1733), 411–12.

2. Charles E. Kemper, "The Early Westward Movement of Virginia, 1722–1734. As Shown by the Proceedings of the Colonial Council," *Virginia Magazine of History and Biography* 12, no. 4 (April 1905): 337–52, 338–41, 344–45.

3. *Collection of all the acts of Assembly, now in force, in the colony of Virginia*, 413.

4. Marylynn Salmon, *Women and the Law of Property in Early America* (Chapel Hill: University of North Carolina Press, 1986); Holly Brewer, "The Transformation of Domestic Law," in *The Cambridge History of Law in America*, vol. 1, *Early America*, ed. Michael Grossberg and Christopher Tomlins (Cambridge: Cambridge University Press, 2008); Kathleen Brown, *Good Wives, Nasty Wenches, and Anxious Patriarchs: Gender, Race, and Power in Colonial Virginia* (Chapel Hill: University of North Carolina Press, 1996).

5. The term "borders of belonging" here comes from Barbara Young Welke's study of law in the nineteenth-century United States, which traces the ways fundamental assumptions about race and gender were embedded in law and political membership. It is a useful concept for understanding economic participation in this earlier period. Welke, *Law and the Borders of Belonging in the Long Nineteenth Century* (New York: Cambridge University Press, 2010).

6. Claire Priest, *Credit Nation: Property Laws and Institutions in Early America* (Princeton, NJ: Princeton University Press, 2021), 3. For a discussion of colonial and Indigenous property practices, see Michael Blaakman, *Speculation Nation: Land Mania in the Revolutionary American Republic* (Philadelphia: University of Pennsylvania Press, 2023), chapter 1.

7. For property as a "social phenomenon," see Allan Greer, *Property and Dispossession: Natives, Empires, and Land in Early Modern North America* (New York: Cambridge University Press, 2018), 12.

8. Jennifer Morgan, *Reckoning with Slavery: Gender, Kinship, and Capitalism in the Early Black Atlantic* (Durham, NC: Duke University Press, 2021), 8–9. I thank Kathy Brown for coining "auction effect" and its opening up of interpretive possibilities.

9. Exploration of the "public" in terms of an eighteenth-century public sphere has often taken Jürgen Habermas's work as a point of departure. For one such set of essays, see Craig Calhoun, ed., *Habermas and the Public Sphere* (Cambridge, MA: MIT Press, 1992). Mary Beth Norton discusses "public" and "private" as increasingly dichotomous and linked to gender difference in the preface to *Separated by Their Sex: Women in Public and Private in the Colonial Atlantic World* (Ithaca, NY: Cornell University Press, 2014). Norton's work touches on one early dimension of the so-called separate spheres idea of a feminine private and masculine public, which is covered extensively in Amanda Vickery, "Golden Age to Separate Spheres? A Review of the Categories and Chronology of English Women's History," *Historical Journal* 36, no. 2 (1993): 383–414; Linda Kerber, "Separate Spheres, Female Worlds, Woman's Place: The Rhetoric of Women's History," *Journal of American History* 75, no. 1 (1988): 9–39; and Joan B. Landes, "Further Thoughts on the Public/Private Distinction," *Journal of Women's History* 15, no. 2 (2003): 28–39 and the forum in that journal.

10. John Warner and Thomas Fairfax, *A survey of the northern neck of Virginia, being the lands belonging to the Rt. Honourable Thomas Lord Fairfax Baron Cameron, bounded by & within the Bay of Chesapoyocke and between the rivers Rappahannock and Potowmack: With the courses of the rivers Rappahannock and Potowmack, in Virginia, as surveyed according to order in the years 1736 & 1737* (n.p., 1747?), map, https://www.loc.gov/item/99446122/.

11. Allan Greer discusses emerging surveying and "lot laying" practices in colonial British America in *Property and Dispossession*, 346–54. On regional differences in the method of distributing land and creating towns, see Bruce Mann, "Transformation of Law and Economy in Early America," *The Cambridge History of Law in America*, vol. 1, *Early America*, ed. Michael Grossberg and Christopher Tomlins (Cambridge: Cambridge University Press, 2008), 365–99, 367–68. In Virginia, land early on was distributed through the headright system, which allotted each householder fifty acres for himself and his dependents. Later, they turned to auctions, as in the case that opened this chapter. For the example in estate administration, see *Collection of all the acts of Assembly, now in force, in the colony of Virginia*, 444–45.

12. Beverly Lemire discusses ships on transatlantic journeys as "spaces of compound and at times conflicting economic cultures," following Fernand Braudel's model of a "triple division" of economic culture including international capitalism, local market economy, and a "shadowy zone" of barter. Lemire, "'Men of the World': British Mariners, Consumer Practice, and Material Culture in an Era of Global Trade c. 1660–1800," *Journal of British Studies* 54, no. 2 (April 2015): 288–319, 293; Emily Erikson, *Chartering Capitalism: Organizing Markets, States, and Publics* (Bingley, UK: Emerald Group, 2015), 181; K. G. Davies, *The Royal African Company* (London: Longmans, Green, 1957; repr., New York: Atheneum, 1970), 296.

13. Accompt of the Limits & Trade for ye African Company, National Archives, CO 268/1, ff. 5–6, https://www.nationalarchives.gov.uk/pathways/blackhistory/africa_caribbean /britain_trade.htm, accessed November 29, 2020.

14. Quoted in David W. Galenson, *Traders, Planters, and Slaves: Market Behavior in Early English America* (New York: Cambridge University Press, 2002), 82.

15. Quoted in Galenson, *Traders, Planters, and Slaves*, 83.

16. *Journals of the House of Commons*, vol. 11 (1693–1697) (London: His Majesty's Stationery Office, 1803), 281. George Cherry discusses how these petitions shaped a so-called free-trade movement in Parliament in "The Development of the English Free-Trade Movement in Parliament, 1689–1702," *Journal of Modern History* 25, no. 2 (June 1953): 103–19.

17. Quoted in Cherry, "Development of the English Free-Trade Movement," 114.

18. Defenders of monopoly presented various arguments about how they served the public good by restricting individual interests or by providing the governing structure that ensured continuous, consistent trade. See William Pettigrew, "Political Economy," in *The Corporation as a Protagonist in Global History, c. 1550–1750*, ed. William A. Pettigrew and David Veevers (Leiden: Brill, 2019), 43–67, 49–50, 59.

19. Brian Learmount, *A History of the Auction* (London: Barnard and Learmount, 1985), 18.

20. Virginia Bever Platt, "The East India Company and the Madagascar Slave Trade," *William and Mary Quarterly* 26, no. 4 (October 1969): 548–77, 553.

21. Steve Pincus, "Rethinking Mercantilism: Political Economy, the British Empire, and the Atlantic World in the Seventeenth and Eighteenth Centuries," *William and Mary Quarterly* 69, no. 1 (January 2012): 3–34, 21.

22. William A. Pettigrew traces some of the scholarship on this intellectual development as it pertained to corporations in Pettigrew, "Political Economy," 43–67; Smith quotation on 44. On the philosophical debates concerning the harnessing of private interests for the public good, see Albert O. Hirschman, *The Passions and the Interests: Political Arguments for Capitalism Before Its Triumph* (Princeton, NJ: Princeton University Press, 1997).

23. Sheryllynne Haggerty, *'Merely for Money'? Business Culture in the British Atlantic, 1750–1815* (Liverpool: Liverpool University Press, 2012); Margaret C. Jacob and Catherine Secretan, *The Self-Perception of Early Modern Capitalists* (New York: Palgrave Macmillan, 2008).

24. Arthur Meier Schlesinger, "The Uprising Against the East India Company," *Political Science Quarterly* 32, no. 1 (March 1917): 60–79, 69. Els M. Jacobs describes warehouse auctions of the Dutch East India Company in *Merchant in Asia: The Trade of the Dutch East India Company During the Eighteenth Century* (New Delhi: Dev, 2017).

25. Philip J. Stern calls the chartered corporation "a typically early modern fusion of private capacities of property ownership and legal personality mixed with the responsibilities and rights to govern over a particular form of public and its well being"; the colonists' challenge to the East India Tea corporation initiated from their own corporate sense of governance. See Stern, "'Bundles of Hyphens': Corporations as Legal Communities in the Early Modern British Empire," in *Legal Pluralism and Empires, 1500–1850*, ed. Lauren Benton and Richard Ross (New York: New York University Press, 2013), 19–48, 23.

26. Michael D. Bennett, "Migration," in Pettigrew and Veevers, *Corporation as a Protagonist*, 68–95, 74–75. Bennett highlights the dual governmental and commercial roles of chartered companies as well, demonstrating the overlapping public and private interests of these corporations as represented in their constitutional structures and in the careers of leading factors-turned-colonial governors. For a description of the private ventures of officers' "privilege trade," in the East India Company, see Huw Bowen, "Privilege and Profit: The Commanders of East Indiamen as Private Traders, Entrepreneurs, and Smugglers, 1760–1813," *International Journal of Maritime History* 19, no. 2 (December 2007): 43–88.

27. Lemire, "Men of the World," 297–98.

28. Lemire, "Men of the World," 304, 307.

29. K. N. Chaudhuri, *The Trading World of Asia and the English East India Company, 1660–1760* (Cambridge: Cambridge University Press, 1978), 131. Jane Merritt notes that company agents also participated in a "fictitious export trade" to avoid the public sales for their own profits. See *The Trouble with Tea: The Politics of Consumption in the Eighteenth-Century Global Economy* (Baltimore: Johns Hopkins University Press, 2017), 24.

30. Chaudhuri, *Trading World*, 133, 135.

31. Morgan, *Reckoning with Slavery*, 172.

32. Galenson, *Traders, Planters, and Slaves*, 83, 84.

33. William A. Pettigrew, *Freedom's Debt: The Royal African Company and the Politics of the Atlantic Slave Trade, 1672–1752* (Chapel Hill: University of North Carolina Press, 2013), 84.

34. "An Act for Establishing Vendue Masters Throughout This Colony," in Rhode Island, *The Charter Granted by His Majesty King Charles the Second, to the Colony of Rhode Island, and Providence Plantations, in America* (Newport, RI, 1730), 111. South Carolina's first vendue master was charged with similar duties. See Thomas Cooper and David J. McCord, eds., *Statutes at Large of South Carolina*, 10 vols. (Columbia, SC: A. S. Johnston, 1836–1841), 2:348.

35. *Charter Granted by His Majesty King Charles the Second, to the Colony of Rhode Island, and Providence Plantations*, 111–12; *The Laws of the Province of South-Carolina, in Two Parts. The First Part Containing all the Perpetual Acts in Force and Use, with the Titles . . .* , vol. 1 (Charles Town, SC, 1736), 171.

36. Emma Hart, *Trading Spaces: The Colonial Marketplace and the Foundations of American Capitalism* (Chicago: University of Chicago Press, 2019), 71–81; Justene Hill Edwards, *Unfree Markets: The Slaves' Economy and the Rise of Capitalism in South Carolina* (New York: Columbia University Press, 2021), chapter 1.

37. *The colonial laws of New York from the year 1664 to the revolution, including the charters to the Duke of York, the commission and instructions to colonial governors, the Dukes laws, the laws of the Donagan and Leisler assemblies, the charters of Albany and New York and the acts of the colonial legislatures from 1691 to 1775 inclusive . . .* , vol. 1 (Albany, NY: J. B. Lyon, 1894), 790, https://hdl.handle.net/2027/umn.31951002158537d.

38. See, for 1715, *Colonial laws of New York*, 863–64; for 1717, *Colonial laws of New York*, 905–6; Cooper and McCord, *Statutes at Large*, 2:348–49. On the location of the public vendue house, see Cooper and McCord, *Statutes at Large*, 4:260–61.

39. "An Act to restrain and prevent the too frequent Sales of Goods, Wares and Merchandize by public Auction or Outcry in Charles-Town; And for the better Regulation of such Sales," in *Acts Passed by the General Assembly of South-Carolina* (Charles-Town: Peter Timothy, 1751), 10–11.

40. Hart, *Trading Spaces*, 75–80.

41. Cooper and McCord, *Statutes at Large*, 2:693.

42. *Pennsylvania Gazette*, June 7, 1759.

43. Peter Charles Hoffer, *Law and People in Colonial America*, 2nd ed. (Baltimore: Johns Hopkins University Press, 2019), xix.

44. *Acts and Laws, Passed by the General Court of Assembly of Her Majesty's Colony of Connecticut in New-England . . .* (New London: Short, 1712), unnumbered page.

45. "Acts Passed by the General Assembly of Her Majesty's Colony of New-Jersey, in January 1709," in *Acts of the General Assembly* (New York, 1710), 28–38, 31.

46. New Jersey, *Acts Passed by the General Assembly . . .* , 1718 (New York: W. Bradford, 1720), 97; *The Acts of the General Assembly of the province of New-Jersey, from the time of the surrender of the government in the second year of the reign . . .* (Philadelphia, PA, 1752), 88, 358, 449; all in Eighteenth-Century Collections Online, accessed May 24, 2012. See also *Acts Passed in the General Assembly of the Province of Pennsylvania . . .* (Philadelphia, PA: Andrew Bradford, 1729), 355.

47. Scholars have investigated multiple dimensions of money in the seventeenth and eighteenth centuries. For British colonial America, see John McCusker, *Money and Exchange in Europe and America, 1600–1775: A Handbook* (Chapel Hill: University of North Carolina

Press, 1992); Jennifer J. Baker, *Securing the Commonwealth: Debt, Speculation, and Writing in the Making of Early America* (Baltimore: Johns Hopkins University Press, 2005); and Jeffrey Sklansky, *Sovereign of the Market: The Money Question in Early America* (Chicago: University of Chicago Press, 2017).

48. Tawny Paul, *The Poverty of Disaster: Debt and Insecurity in Eighteenth-Century Britain* (New York: Cambridge University Press, 2019), 67–71.

49. Cooper and McCord, *Statutes at Large*, 2:673.

50. Cooper and McCord, *Statutes at Large*, 3:164.

51. These were trends beyond colonial North America. See Randall McGowen, "The Body and Punishment in Eighteenth-Century England," *Journal of Modern History* 59, no. 4 (December 1987): 651–79. Cornelia Hughes Dayton found that punishments for nonmarital sex in colonial Connecticut divided over race at the turn of the eighteenth century, with whipping reserved for Black people. See Dayton, *Women Before the Bar: Gender, Law, and Society in Connecticut, 1639–1789* (Chapel Hill: University of North Carolina Press, 1995), 185–86.

52. The intertwined nature of the social and financial dimensions of credit relationships is explored in numerous works, including Bruce Mann, *Neighbors and Strangers: Law and Community in Early Connecticut* (Chapel Hill: University of North Carolina Press, 1987); Craig Muldrew, *The Economy of Obligation: The Culture of Credit and Social Relations in Early Modern England* (New York: Palgrave Macmillan, 1998); Sara T. Damiano, *To Her Credit: Women, Finance, and the Law in Eighteenth-Century New England Cities* (Baltimore: Johns Hopkins University Press, 2021); and Paul, *Poverty of Disaster*.

53. Barbara Clark Smith, *The Freedoms We Lost: Consent and Resistance in Revolutionary America* (New York: New Press, 2010), 75.

54. Sean Condon, *Shays's Rebellion: Authority and Distress in Post-Revolutionary America* (Baltimore: Johns Hopkins University Press, 2015), 30. See also Howard Pashman, *Building a Revolutionary State: The Legal Transformation of New York, 1776–1783* (Chicago: University of Chicago Press, 2018), 23–26.

55. Cooper and McCord, *Statutes at Large*, 2:671.

56. Margaret Ellen Newell, *Brethren by Nature: New England Indians, Colonists, and the Origins of American Slavery* (Ithaca, NY: Cornell University Press, 2015), 168.

57. Newell, *Brethren by Nature*, 175.

58. Virginia General Assembly, "An Act, for the better Security of the Country, in the present Time of Danger," in *Session Laws* (Williamsburg, VA, 1740), 4.

59. *The public acts of the General Assembly of North-Carolina / Rev. and published, under the authority of the legislature, by the honorable James Iredell . . . and now revised by Francis-Xavier Martin*, vols. 1–2 (Newbern, NC: Martin and Ogden, 1804), 1:66.

60. Hoffer, *Law and People*, 97; Mann, *Neighbors and Strangers*, chapter 1. Hoffer argues that, ultimately, debt litigation spiked as competing ideas about the nature of exchange grew out of an expanding, increasingly diverse population in the early eighteenth century.

61. *Weekly Rehearsal* (Boston, MA), July 23, 1733.

62. Damiano, *To Her Credit*, 106–11. Paul, *Poverty of Disaster*, 61, discusses women as "the brokers of moveable property" in a household.

63. See, for example, *Acts and Laws of His Majesties colony of Rhode-Island, and Providence-Plantations in America* (Boston: John Allen for Nicholas Boone, 1719), 21–22.

64. "An Act for the Tryal of small and mean Causes; and for repealing the several Acts now in Force which relate to the Recovery of small Debts," in *Acts Passed by the General Assembly of South Carolina* (Charles Town: Peter Timothy, 1747), 12.

65. "An Act Declaring the Law Concerning Executions; and for relief of Insolvent debtors," in *The Statutes at Large; Being a Collection of all the Laws of Virginia*, ed. William Walter Henning, vol. 5 (Richmond, VA: printed for the editor, 1819), 533. In Rhode Island, court officers held the goods for ten days before sale. "An Act for Regulating the Proceedings on Executions, and Distraints on Goods and Chattels," in *The Charter Granted by His Majesty King Charles the Second, to the Colony of Rhode-Island, and Providence-Plantations in America* (Newport, 1730), 14.

66. *American Weekly Mercury*, July 6, 1727. The sale was by a writ of *venditioni exponas*.

67. Thomas Russell points out the way the courts shaped "transactional life" more broadly in "South Carolina's Largest Slave Auctioneering Firm—Symposium on the Law of Slavery: Criminal and Civil Law of Slavery, *Chicago-Kent Law Review* 68, no. 3 (1992): 1241–82, 1277. For an example, see the public auction of imported cloth sold "*before the* Long Ordinary *door*, in Frederickburg, *on* Thursday, *the 15th instant, being* Spotsylvania *court day*," *Virginia Gazette*, November 8, 1770.

68. Katharina Pistor, *The Code of Capital: How the Law Creates Wealth and Inequality* (Princeton, NJ: Princeton University Press, 2020), chapter 2.

69. "In Louisiana slaves were designated as 'immoveables,' although sometimes the phrase 'real estate' was used." Thomas Morris, *Southern Slavery and the Law, 1619–1860* (Chapel Hill: University of North Carolina Press, 1996), 64.

70. Henning, *Statutes at Large*, 3:333.

71. K-Sue Park, "Race, Innovation, and Financial Growth: The Example of Foreclosure," in *Histories of Racial Capitalism*, ed. Destin Jenkins and Justin Leroy (New York: Columbia University Press, 2021), 27–52, 37. See also Newell, *Brethren by Nature*, 128–29.

72. Park, "Race, Innovation, and Financial Growth," 29–36.

73. Claire Priest, "Creating an American Property Law: Alienability and Its Limits in American History," *Harvard Law Review* 120, no. 2 (December 2006): 385–459, 411–12.

74. Priest, *Credit Nation*, 8–9. One hundred years later, state legislatures passed "homestead legislation" that once again protected real estate specifically from seizure and sale by the courts to pay creditors. Priest, "Creating an American Property Law," 394.

75. *South Carolina Gazette*, June 17, 1751.

76. K-Sue Park, "Conquest and Slavery as Foundational to the Property Law Course: Notes for Teachers," *Georgetown Law Faculty Publications and Other Works* (2020), 20, https://scholarship.law.georgetown.edu/facpub/2298/.

77. Kathleen Brown, *Good Wives, Nasty Wenches*, 118.

78. "An Act Concerning Negroes & Other Slaves," in *Archives of Maryland*, Vol. 1, ed. William Browne (Baltimore: Maryland Historical Society, 1883), 533–34. For attempts in multiple colonies to regulate intimate relationships as part of establishing racial slavery, see Brown, *Good Wives, Nasty Wenches*; Kirsten Fischer, *Suspect Relations: Sex, Race, and*

Resistance in Colonial North Carolina (Ithaca, NY: Cornell University Press, 2002); Jennifer M. Spear, *Race, Sex and Social Order in Early New Orleans* (Baltimore: Johns Hopkins University Press, 2010); and Jennifer Morgan, *Partus sequitur ventrem*: Law, Race, and Reproduction in Colonial Slavery," *Small Axe* 22, no. 1 (2018): 1–17.

79. *Boston News-Letter*, July 8–15, 1717.

80. Carl Robert Keyes, "Early American Advertising: Marketing and Consumer Culture in Eighteenth-Century Philadelphia" (PhD diss., Johns Hopkins University, 2007), makes this point, that advertisers were not responding to pent-up demand but rather producing and inciting demand. See chapters 1 and 3.

81. Keyes, introduction to "Early American Advertising."

82. See, for example, *Pennsylvania Gazette*, May 16, 1745; *South-Carolina Gazette*, August 27, 1748; and *New-Hampshire Gazette*, July 11, 1760. For colonial market regulations, see "At a Meeting of the Freeholders . . . April 24, 1734 . . . For setting up, and regulating a Public MARKET" (Boston: Gerrish, 1734), 4. In 1775 a regulation in Philadelphia concerning the assize of bread made reference to "all Kinds of Bread to be made for Sale, sold, or exposed to Sale," "Anno regni Georgii. Regis, Magnae Britanniae, Franciae & Hiberniae, decimo quinto. At a General Assembly of the Province of Pennsylvania, begun and holden at *Philadelphia . . .* (Philadelphia, PA: Hall and Sellers, 1775), 456. See definition 7a: "To offer publicly, 'put up' for (or to) sale," "expose, v.," OED Online (Oxford University Press), accessed June 8, 2021, https://www.oed.com/view/Entry/66705?rskey=B93nwO&result=2&isAdvanced=false

83. *Boston Gazette or Weekly Journal*, February 18, 1746.

84. Ruth Bloch, "The American Revolution, Wife Beating, and the Emergent Value of Privacy," *Early American Studies* 5, no. 2 (Fall 2007): 223–51, 225. Mary Beth Norton uses the *Oxford English Dictionary* as a starting point for her investigation of the gendering of the terms "public" and "private." Norton, *Separated by Their Sex*, xiii. See *OED*, s.v. "public" and "private" for the details of these terms' meanings.

85. Norton, *Separated by Their Sex*, 148.

86. *New-York Gazette*, January 7, 1760.

87. *Pennsylvania Gazette*, January 24, 1760.

88. *South-Carolina Gazette*, February 8, 1748.

89. Michael Harris notes that seventeenth-century London book auctions that failed to sell all their items later advertised that their goods could be purchased in private transactions at local shops. See Harris, "Newspaper Advertising for Book Auctions Before 1700," in *Under the Hammer: Book Auctions Since the Seventeenth Century*, ed. Robin Myers, Michael Harris, and Giles Mandelbrote (London: British Library Board, 2001), 1–14, 8.

90. Johann Martin Bolzius, "Reliable Answer to Some Submitted Questions Concerning the Land Carolina," trans. and ed. Klaus G. Loewald, Beverly Starika, and Paul S. Taylor, *William and Mary Quarterly* 14, no. 2 (April 1957): 223–61, 256.

91. *The Interesting Narrative of the Life of Olaudah Equiano, or Gustavus Vassa, the African, Written by Himself*, reprinted in Henry Lewis Gates Jr., *The Classic Slave Narratives* (New York: Penguin Books, 1987), 37. For another discussion of the "scramble," see Morgan, *Reckoning with Slavery*, 174–76.

92. Nicholas Radburn, "Guinea Factors, Slave Sales, and the Profits of the Transatlantic Slave Trade in Late Eighteenth-Century Jamaica: The Case of John Tailyour," *William and Mary Quarterly* 72, no. 2 (April 2015): 243–86, 270–71.

93. Gregory O'Malley, "Beyond the Middle Passage: Slave Migration from the Caribbean to North America, 1619–1807," *William and Mary Quarterly* 66, no. 1 (January 2009): 125–72, 137.

94. Steven Deyle, *Carry Me Back: The Domestic Slave Trade in American Life* (New York: Oxford University Press, 2006), 118.

95. Stephanie Smallwood makes this point about the ways that the visual representation of enslaved people reinforced their commodification. See Smallwood, *Saltwater Slavery: A Middle Passage from Africa to American Diaspora* (Cambridge, MA: Harvard University Press, 2007), 2. Robert E. Desrochers writes that "slavery and the newspaper grew up together" in a "close and synergetic relationship" but highlights the relative significance of private sale as compared with public auction in "Slave-For-Sale Advertisements and Slavery in Massachusetts, 1704–1781," *William and Mary Quarterly* 59, no. 3 (July 2002): 623–64, 623, 629. On the culture of advertisement and its focus on poor people's bodies, see Gwenda Morgan and Peter Rushton, "Visible Bodies: Power, Subordination and Identity in the Eighteenth-Century Atlantic World," *Journal of Social History* 39, no. 1 (Autumn 2005): 42–50.

96. Shaun Armstead, Brenann Sutter, Pamela Walker, and Caitlin Wiesner found a similar pattern of largely private sales of individual enslaved people in late eighteenth- and early nineteenth-century New Brunswick, as opposed to the large vendues of human beings often associated with slave sales. "And I a Poor Slave Yet: The Precarity of Black Life in New Brunswick, 1766–1835," in *Scarlet and Black*, vol. 1, *Slavery and Dispossession in Rutgers History*, ed. Marisa J. Fuentes and Deborah Gray White (New Brunswick, NJ: Rutgers University Press, 2016), 102–4.

97. *Boston Evening-Post*, January 28, 1760.

98. On June 15, 1736, an administrators' sale of John Lloyd's estate listed "a choice parcel of Negroes and other Slaves, household goods, sundry valuable books, sheep, horse & cattle &c." *South Carolina Gazette*, May 22, 1736.

99. Sharon Block, *Colonial Complexions: Race and Bodies in Eighteenth-Century America* (Philadelphia: University of Pennsylvania Press, 2018), 7; David Waldstreicher, "Reading the Runaways: Self-Fashioning, Print Culture, and Confidence in Slavery in the Eighteenth-Century Mid-Atlantic," *William and Mary Quarterly* 56, no. 2 (April 1999): 243–272, 258.

100. Block, *Colonial Complexions*, 40.

101. Simon Middleton, "Runaways, Rewards, and the Social History of Money," *Early American Studies* 15, no. 3 (Summer 2017): 617–47, 620.

102. Middleton, "Runaways, Rewards," 638.

103. "A Supplement to the ACT relating to Servants and Slaves," in *A Compleat Collection of the Laws of Maryland* (Annapolis, MD: William Parks, 1727), 209–10.

104. Priest, "Creating an American Property Law," 387.

105. In *To Her Credit*, chapter 4, Sara Damiano's discussion of witnessing in eighteenth-century civil law cases highlights the enduring influence of witnesses from a wide range of social positions.

CHAPTER 2

1. Benjamin Franklin, *Father Abraham's Speech* (Boston: Benjamin Mecom, 1760), 10. This speech, published in 1758, was reprinted frequently for the next fifty years and was incorporated into Franklin's *The Way to Wealth*.

2. Lawrence, who was also an alderman, rented the vendue stall under the courthouse. "At a Common Council held at Philadelphia, for the City of Philadelphia, the 16th Day of September 1760," in *Minutes of the Common Council of the City of Philadelphia 1704 to 1776* (Philadelphia, PA: Crissy and Markley, 1847), 660.

3. See, for example, T. H. Breen, *The Marketplace of Revolution: How Consumer Politics Shaped American Independence* (New York: Oxford University Press, 2004), 140–43; and Emma Hart, *Building Charleston: Town and Society in the Eighteenth-Century British Atlantic World* (Charlottesville: University of Virginia Press, 2010), 55–56.

4. Sheryllynne Haggerty, *The British-Atlantic Trading Community, 1760–1810: Men, Women, and the Distribution of Goods* (Leiden: Brill, 2006), chapter 6.

5. Serena R. Zabin, *Dangerous Economies: Status and Commerce in Imperial New York* (Philadelphia: University of Pennsylvania Press, 2009), chapter 3. As Zabin points out, "The existence of this market, by providing a new outlet for used goods, energized the formal economy" (66).

6. See discussion of scholars' debates over informational efficiency in the context of the eighteenth century, including Friedrich von Hayek's "economy of knowledge," in David Hancock, *Oceans of Wine: Madeira and the Emergence of American Trade and Taste* (New Haven, CT: Yale University Press, 2009), xix.

7. On customary prices and market ethics in colonial America, see Simon Middleton, "'How it came that the bakers bake no bread': A Struggle for Trade Privileges in Seventeenth-Century New Amsterdam," *William and Mary Quarterly* 58, no. 2 (April 2001): 347–73; and Mark Valeri, *Heavenly Merchandize: How Religion Shaped Commerce in Puritan America* (Princeton, NJ: Princeton University Press, 2010).

8. For some leading examples of scholarship on merchant business practices and decision making, see Haggerty, *British-Atlantic Trading Community*; Toby L. Ditz, "Shipwrecked; or Masculinity Imperiled: Mercantile Representations of Failure and the Gendered Self in Eighteenth-Century Philadelphia," *Journal of American History* 81, no. 1 (June 1994): 51–80; David Hancock, *Citizens of the World: London Merchants and the Integration of the British Atlantic Community, 1735–1785* (New York: Cambridge University Press, 1997); Cathy Matson, *Merchants and Empire: Trading in Colonial New York* (Baltimore: Johns Hopkins University Press, 1998); John J. McCusker and Kenneth Morgan, eds., *The Early Modern Atlantic Economy* (New York: Cambridge University Press, 2000); and Jacob M. Price, *Overseas Trade and Traders: Essays on Some Commercial, Financial, and Political Changes Facing British Atlantic Merchants, 1660–1775* (Aldershot: Ashgate, 1996).

9. Charles W. Smith, *Auctions: The Social Construction of Value* (Berkeley: University of California Press, 1990), 16.

10. For example, see Jeffrey Sklansky, *Sovereign of the Market: The Money Question in Early America* (Chicago: University of Chicago Press, 2017), chapter 2. Rebecca L. Spang

links the ideas of political economists to the "enacted practices" of money in France in *Stuff and Money in the Time of the French Revolution* (Cambridge, MA: Harvard University Press, 2015). For a discussion of the currency debate that sparked reflection on value, see T. H. Breen and Timothy Hall, "Structuring the Provincial Imagination: The Rhetoric and Experience of Social Change in Eighteenth-Century New England," *American Historical Review* 103, no. 5 (December 1998): 1411–39, 1422.

11. Barbara Clark Smith, *The Freedoms We Lost: Consent and Resistance in Revolutionary America* (New York: New Press, 2010), 84–85.

12. Carole Shammas, "The Decline of Textile Prices in England and British America Prior to Industrialization," *Economic History Review*, 2nd ser., 47, no. 3 (1994): 483–507; Jan de Vries, *The Industrious Revolution: Consumer Behavior and the Household Economy, 1650 to the Present* (New York: Cambridge University Press, 2008), chapters 3 and 4.

13. Important examples of this literature include Carole Shammas, *The Pre-Industrial Consumer in England and America* (New York: Oxford University Press, 1990); Stana Nenadic, "Middle-Rank Consumers and Domestic Culture in Edinburgh and Glasgow 1720–1840," *Past and Present*, no. 145 (November 1994): 122–56; and Lorna Weatherill, *Consumer Behavior and Material Culture in Britain, 1660–1760* (New York: Routledge, 1996).

14. Some highlights in this rich literature include Amanda Vickery, *The Gentleman's Daughter: Women's Lives in Georgian England* (New Haven, CT: Yale University Press, 1998); Susan M. Stabile, *Memory's Daughters: The Material Culture of Remembrance in Eighteenth-Century America* (Ithaca, NY: Cornell University Press, 2004); Laurel Thatcher Ulrich, *The Age of Homespun: Objects and Stories in the Creation of an American Myth* (New York: Knopf, 2001); and John Styles and Amanda Vickery, eds., *Gender, Taste, and Material Culture in Britain and North America, 1700–1830* (New Haven, CT: Yale University Press, 2007).

15. This literature, as well, is extensive. See Breen, *Marketplace of Revolution*; Ann Smart Martin, *Buying into the World of Goods: Early Consumers in Backcountry Virginia* (Baltimore: Johns Hopkins University Press, 2008); Linzy A. Brekke, "The 'Scourge of Fashion': Political Economy and the Politics of Consumption in the Early Republic," *Early American Studies* 3, no. 1 (Spring 2005): 111–39; and essays in John Brewer and Roy Porter, eds., *Consumption and the World of Goods* (New York: Routledge, 1994).

16. Zabin, *Dangerous Economies*, chapter 3; Wendy A. Woloson, *In Hock: Pawning in America from Independence Through the Great Depression* (Chicago: University of Chicago Press, 2009), chapter 4.

17. John J. McCusker, "The Demise of Distance: The Business Press and the Origins of the Information Revolution in the Early Modern Atlantic World," *American Historical Review* 110, no. 2 (April 2005): 295–321, 308.

18. McCusker, "Demise of Distance," 311.

19. *American Weekly Mercury*, February 16, 1720.

20. *American Weekly Mercury*, January 26, 1725.

21. Cathy Matson, "'Damned Scoundrels' and 'Libertisme of Trade': Freedom and Regulation in Colonial New York's Fur and Grain Trades," *William and Mary Quarterly* 51, no. 3 (July 1994): 389–418, 408.

22. Matson, "'Damned Scoundrels,'" 412.

23. On market activity and "common good," see Martha Howell, "Whose 'Common Good'? Parisian Market Regulation, c. 1300–1800," in *Market Ethics and Practices, c. 1300–1850*, ed. Simon Middleton and James E. Shaw (New York: Routledge, 2018), 46–62; and Emma Hart, *Trading Spaces: The Colonial Marketplace and the Foundations of American Capitalism* (Chicago: University of Chicago Press, 2019), 8–16, 44–49.

24. Valeri, *Heavenly Merchandize*, 67–68.

25. B. C. Smith, *Freedoms We Lost*, 54.

26. B. C. Smith, *Freedoms We Lost*, 57.

27. Tyler v. Richards, quoted in Morton J. Horowitz, *The Transformation of American Law, 1780–1860* (Cambridge, MA: Harvard University Press, 1977), 172. Legal scholars debated Horowitz's broader claims about contracts. See A. W. B. Simpson, "The Horowitz Thesis and the History of Contracts," in *Legal Theory and Legal History: Essays on the Common Law* (London: Hambledon Press, 1987), 203–72.

28. Michael O'Malley, *Face Value: The Entwined Histories of Money and Race in America* (Chicago: University of Chicago Press, 2012), 5, argues that money always represents "value" in both senses of the word. For a helpful discussion of price signaling in auctions, see Alvin E. Roth, *Who Gets What—and Why: The New Economics of Matchmaking and Market Design* (Boston: Mariner Books, Houghton Mifflin Harcourt, 2016), 180–89.

29. Hugh Vans, *An Inquiry into the Nature and Uses of Money* (Boston: Kneeland and Green, 1740), 7.

30. Vans, *Inquiry into the Nature and Uses of Money*, 2. On prices and perceived scarcity of money, see Bennett T. McCallum, "Money and Prices in Colonial America: A New Test of Competing Theories," *Journal of Political Economy* 100, no. 1 (February 1992): 143–61; and Carl Wennerlind, *Casualties of Credit: The English Financial Revolution, 1620–1720* (Cambridge, MA: Harvard University Press, 2011), chapter 1.

31. Daniel Defoe, *The Compleat English Tradesman*, vol. 2 (London, 1727), 124.

32. Samuel Willard, *A Compleat Body of Divinity* (Boston, 1726), quoted in Valeri, *Heavenly Merchandize*, 156.

33. B. C. Smith, *Freedoms We Lost*, 119.

34. *The examination of Doctor Benjamin Franklin, before an August Assembly, relating to the Repeal of the Stamp-Act, &c* (Philadelphia, PA, 1766), 8.

35. *New-York Journal; or, the General Advertiser*, May 26, 1768.

36. The act clarified, though, that its regulations were "not to be construed to extend to affect any Sale by Executors or Administrators of their Testator or Intestates Effects, or Goods attached, seized, distrained, or taken in Execution." "An Act For keeping the Streets of Charles-Town clean: And establishing such other Regulations for the Security, Health, and Convenience of the Inhabitants of the said Town, as are therein mentioned: And for establishing a New Market in the said Town," *Acts Passed by the General Assembly of the Province of South Carolina* (Charleston: Peter Timothy, 1750), 25.

37. "An Act to Restrain and prevent the too frequent Sales of Goods, Wares, and Merchandize by public Auction or Outcry in Charles-Town: And for the better Regulation of such Sales," *Acts Passed by the General Assembly of South Carolina* (Charleston: Peter Timothy, 1751), 9–10.

38. "Act to Restrain and prevent the too frequent Sales of Goods, 9–10.

39. "An Act to restrain and prevent the too frequent Sales of Goods, Wares and Merchandize by public Auction or Outcry in Charles-Town: and for the better Regulation of such Sales," *Acts of the General Assembly of South Carolina Passed the 7th of April, 1759* (Charleston: Peter Timothy, 1759), 17.

40. *South Carolina Gazette*, September 15, 1777.

41. *Pennsylvania Gazette*, March 18, 1756.

42. Defenders of auctions pointed out that the rate of return on an auction sale was higher than the loan obtainable from a pawnshop; they also argued that the social consequences of pawning and interest charges were more dire than the potential social disorder caused by auctions. See the broadside *A Few Reasons in Favor of Vendues* (Philadelphia, PA: Henry Miller, 1772).

43. *Proceedings and Debates of the General Assembly of Pennsylvania, Taken in Short-Hand by Thomas Lloyd*, vol. 1 (Philadelphia, PA: Daniel Humphries, 1787), 81. Lawmakers in early nineteenth-century Baltimore made a similar point about auctions as tools of the desperate poor. See "The Petition of Samuel Butler and Others," February 21, 1805, Special Collections MSA SC 5511, Location 00/23/14/02, RG16, S1, box 2, folder 1805, Baltimore City Archives Records Collection.

44. Frank Trentmann, "Materiality and the Future of History: Things, Practices, and Politics," *Journal of British Studies* 48, no. 2 (April 2009): 283–307.

45. Samuel Cooper, *A Sermon Preached in Boston . . . before the Society, August 8, 1753* (Boston: n.p., 1753), quoted and discussed in Eric G. Nellis, "Misreading the Signs: Industrial Imitation, Poverty, and the Social Order in Colonial Boston," *New England Quarterly* 59, no. 4 (December 1986): 486–507, 493.

46. Society for Encouraging Industry, *Whereas it is Found by Experience . . .* (Boston: n.p., 1754), 2.

47. *Boston Evening Post*, August 17, 1752.

48. Nian-Sheng Huang, "Financing Poor Relief in Colonial Boston," *Massachusetts Historical Review* 8 (2006): 72–103, 93–94. See also Nellis, "Misreading the Signs," 504–5. Poor relief efforts in Philadelphia fifty years later also experimented with "selling surplus textiles and samples at auction, and putting cotton goods out on consignment." Monique Bourque, "Women and Work in the Philadelphia Almshouse, 1790–1840," *Journal of the Early Republic* 32, no. 3 (Fall 2012): 383–413, 394.

49. On economists' understanding of "private-value" and "pure common-value" and how they intersect in the competitive bidding at an auction, see Paul Klemperer, *Auctions: Theory and Practice* (Princeton, NJ: Princeton University Press, 2004), 13–15.

50. Mary Coates receipts, 1748–1759, Coates and Reynell Family Collection 140, vol. 119, Historical Society of Pennsylvania (hereafter cited as HSP); Mary Coates Receipt Book, 1760–1772, Coates and Reynell Family Collection, HSP.

51. Receipt signed by William Bell, December 20, 1768, Mary Coates Receipt Book, 1760–1772, Coates and Reynell Family Collection, HSP.

52. *Pennsylvania Gazette*, August 2, 1750; Mary Coates receipts, 1748–1759, Coates and Reynell Family Collection 140, vol. 119, HSP; *Pennsylvania Gazette*, October 11, 1750. Isaac

Williams's estate was also "sold for the benefit of his creditors" that same month. See *Pennsylvania Gazette*, August 16, 1750.

53. *Pennsylvania Gazette*, August 16, 1750.

54. *Pennsylvania Gazette*, August 23, 1750. In March 1751, the sheriff sold off two pieces of Foulke's land, taken in execution of a lawsuit. *Pennsylvania Gazette*, March 12, 1751. Foulke later served as a sheriff himself.

55. *New-York Gazette*, January 9, 1764; see also *New York Mercury*, November 17, 1766, for similar imported items sold in his store.

56. The analysis in this paragraph is based on the multiple accounts of auction sales in John Keteltas Papers, 1761–1769, New-York Historical Society, New York City. Between 10 and 30 percent of the bidders at each Keteltas auction were women.

57. On stockings in mid-eighteenth-century urban economies, see Zabin, *Dangerous Economies*, 68–69.

58. My analysis of these lists is informed by Mary Poovey's scholarship on the invention of "the modern fact," an early modern process involving merchants and writers who ultimately privileged numbers as uniquely true and unburdened by political interference. See Mary Poovey, *A History of the Modern Fact: Problems of Knowledge in the Sciences of Wealth and Society* (Chicago: University of Chicago Press, 1998).

59. Holly Izard, "Random or Systematic? An Evaluation of the Probate Process," *Winterthur Portfolio* 32, nos. 2/3 (Summer–Autumn 1997): 147–67, 153–54.

60. On "unwritten rules" in York County, Virginia, probate, see Wendy Lucas and Noel Campbell, "Unwritten Rules and Gendered Frames Amongst Probate Appraisers? Evidence from Eighteenth-Century York County, Virginia," *Essays in Economic and Business History* 36, no. 1 (2018): 47–94.

61. "Inventory and Appraisement of the Estate of Littleton Hill" and "Account of Sales of Sundrys belonging to Mr. John Chalkhill Sold at Auction by William Glen being part of the Estate of Littleton Hill 1752," *Inventories, Charleston County, 1751–1753*, 79:239–43, South Carolina Room, Charleston County Public Library, Charleston, South Carolina.

62. "Inventory and appraisement of the Goods and Chattells of Richard Baker of Charles Town 1752," *Inventories, Charleston County, 1751–1753*, 79:460–64; and "Sales of Sundry Goods and Chattells belonging to the Estate of Captn. Richard Baker Deceased sold by order of Mrs. Sarah Baker Administratrix," *Inventories, Charleston County, 1751–1753*, 79:512–16.

63. My conclusions come from comparing probate cases that had an inventory and a report of auction sales. I used the WPA volumes of Charleston County inventories held in the South Carolina Room of the Charleston Public Library.

64. "An Act to prevent Losses to Executors, and Administrators, by the Sale of Negroes, Goods, and Chattels, taken in Execution . . . ," *A Collection of All the Acts of Assembly, Now in Force, in the Colony of Virginia* (Williamsburg, 1733), 444. A 1748 revision of the law included the executors' and administrators' oaths as well as details about the bonds to be posted and the restrictions on how the executor or administrator used the estate. "An Act directing the Manner of granting Probates of Wills, and Administration of Intestate Estates," *The Acts of Assembly, Now in Force, in the Colony of Virginia* (Williamsburg: W. Rind, A. Purdie, and J. Dixon, 1769), 162–67. Toby Ditz discusses the role of families in probate processes and

charges of improper administration of inventories in *Property and Kinship: Inheritance in Early Connecticut, 1750–1820* (Princeton, NJ: Princeton University Press, 1986), chapter 8.

65. "An Act to prevent Losses to Executors, and Administrators, by the Sale of Negroes, Goods, and Chattels, taken in Execution . . . ," *A Collection of All the Acts of Assembly, Now in Force, in the Colony of Virginia* (Williamsburg, 1733), 444.

66. "An Account of the Goods and Effects of Sarah Saxby Deceased appraised by us the Appraisers whose Names are under written this 8th day of March 1747," and "Sale of Sarah Saxby's Effects this March 13th 1747 by Daniel Crawford Vendue Master," *Inventories, Charleston County, South Carolina, 1746–1748*, 74:416–21, South Carolina Room, Charleston County Public Library, Charleston, South Carolina.

67. "An Inventory and Appraisement of all and Singular the Goods and Chattels Rights & Credits which were of David Villaret late of this Province Baker Decd. At the time of his death," and "An Acct. of the Sales of the Goods & affects of David Villaret Decd. Sold att Publick Vendue the Six day of September 1742," *Inventories, Charleston County, 1739–1743*, 71:229–33.

68. "Inventory and Appraisement . . . of David Villaret," 33.

69. Burwell v. Christie, cited in Samuel Livermore, *A Treatise on the Law Relative to Principals, Agents, Factors, Auctioneers, and Brokers* (Boston: Thomas B. Wait, 1811), 105.

70. "An Act to restrain and prevent the too frequent Sales of Goods, Wares and Merchandize by public Auction or Outcry in Charles-Town: and for the better Regulation of such Sales," *Acts Passed by the General Assembly of South-Carolina* (Charleston: Peter Timothy, 1751), 9.

71. *Proceedings and Debates of the General Assembly of Pennsylvania*, 81.

72. Trevor Burnard, "Collecting and Accounting: Representing Slaves as Commodities in Jamaica, 1674–1784," in *Collecting Across Cultures; Material Exchanges in the Early Modern Atlantic World*, ed. Daniela Bleichmar and Peter C. Mancall (Philadelphia: University of Pennsylvania Press, 2011), 187–88; and *New-York Gazette, or Weekly Post-Boy*, September 26, 1748.

73. "An Inventory of Appraisement made this 19th Day of August 1743 of all the goods and Chattels Belonging to John Ninion Deceast," and "The Account of the Sales, of the Within Appraisment made the 19th of Aug. 1743," *Inventories, Charleston County, 1739–1743*, 71:352–55.

74. Daina Ramey Berry, *The Price for Their Pound of Flesh: The Value of the Enslaved, from Womb to Grave, in the Building of a Nation* (Boston: Beacon Press, 2017), 41. In the introduction, Berry discusses four types of values: soul value, appraised value, market value, and ghost value.

75. Steven Deyle, *Carry Me Back: The Domestic Slave Trade in American Life* (New York: Oxford University Press, 2005), 169.

76. Deyle, *Carry Me Back*, 169.

77. Justene Hill Edwards, *Unfree Markets: The Slaves' Economy and the Rise of Capitalism in South Carolina* (New York: Columbia University Press, 2021), 5.

78. *South-Carolina Gazette*, August 10, 1765.

79. *South-Carolina Gazette*, July 13, 1765.

80. Livermore, *Treatise on the Law*, 106. For brief discussions of widows, auctions, and probate, see Vivian Bruce Conger, *The Widow's Might: Widowhood and Gender in Early British America* (New York: New York University Press, 2009), 140–41; and Izard, "Random or Systematic?," 154–56. Sara Damiano's study of Newport, Rhode Island, found that 40 percent of town administrators in the mid-eighteenth century were women. Sara T. Damiano, "'To Well and Truly Administer': Female Administrators and Estate Settlement in Newport, Rhode Island, 1730–1776," *New England Quarterly* 86, no. 1 (March 2013): 89–124, 92.

81. Cited in Conger, *Widow's Might*, 57.

82. On dower rights in colonial South Carolina, see Marylynn Salmon, *Women and the Law of Property in Early America* (Chapel Hill: University of North Carolina Press, 1986), 156–60.

83. "Sales of Sundry Goods and Chattells belonging to the Estate of Captn. Richard Baker Deceased sold by order of Mrs. Sarah Baker Administratrix," *Inventories, Charleston County, 1751–1753*, 79:512–16.

84. Securing these goods was important. When, in the following year, her deceased husband's creditors came after her, she claimed "that she hath no Goods or Chattels which belonged to the said Richard at the time of his death in her hands to be administered." Freeman, William George, v. Sarah Baker, Admix of Richard Baker, Judgment Roll, 1753, box 34B, item 20A; Motte, Jacob, v. Sarah Baker, Admix of Richard Baker, Judgment Roll, 1753, box 34B, item 33A; Binford, Thomas, and James Osmond v. Sarah Baker, Admix of Richard Baker, Judgment Roll, 1753, box 34B, item 63A; all at the South Carolina Department of Archives and History, Columbia. Several others of her husband's creditors did recover their debts against her; she claimed that those payments used up all the administered money.

85. Mary Beth Sievens, *Stray Wives: Marital Conflict in Early National New England* (New York: New York University Press, 2005), 36; discussion of property rights in their own labor, 54–58.

86. *Georgia Gazette*, September 16, 1767.

87. *Georgia Gazette*, June 29, 1768.

88. There are limitations to using estate auctions as representative of Americans' experience, of course. As scholars have long pointed out, people's estates entered the probate process only if they had done one or more of the following: written a will, owned real estate, left minor children, or had outstanding debts or credits. Many did not meet these criteria, and so evidence from probate records is not representative in one sense. Izard, "Random or Systematic?," 147–67, 148.

89. Mrs. Manigault to G. Manigault, November 28, 1792, box 1, folder 17, Manigault Family Papers, South Caroliniana Library, Columbia, SC. Susan M. Stabile discusses late eighteenth- and early nineteenth-century memory practices in *Memory's Daughters*. She highlights "the collective nature of reminiscence" seen in the interaction between souvenir objects and women's writing about them on 148. See also Mrs. Manigault to G. Manigault, November 28 and 30, 1792, box 1, folder 17, Manigault Family Papers. The will stated that all the plate marked with the family "arms" would go to Daniel, but all but one piece was instead marked with the family crest and therefore sold.

90. *Boston Evening Post*, March 23, 1741; *Boston Evening Post*, September 25, 1758.

91. *Boston Evening Post*, March 20, 1769; *Boston Evening Post*, June 12, 1769; *Massachusetts Spy*, April 25, 1771.

92. In Britain, auctioneers sometimes advertised sales in Latin or French to highlight their exclusivity, and leisured gentlemen attended and competed regularly. Brian Cowan, *The Social Life of Coffee: The Emergence of the British Coffeehouse* (New Haven, CT: Yale University Press, 2005), 135–38.

93. Charles W. Smith calls auctions "social processes for resolving definitional ambiguities" about the price, ownership, and distribution of goods in *Auctions: The Social Construction of Value* (New York: Free Press, 1989), 3.

94. Paula Findlen, *Possessing Nature: Museums, Collecting, and Scientific Culture in Early Modern Italy* (Los Angeles: University of California Press, 1994); Pamela H. Smith and Paula Findlen, eds., *Merchants and Marvels: Commerce, Science, and Art in Early Modern Europe* (New York: Routledge, 2001); Oliver Impey and Arthur MacGregor, eds., *The Origins of Museums: The Cabinet of Curiosities in Sixteenth- and Seventeenth-Century Europe*, 2nd ed. (London: House of Stratus, 2001); Deborah Harkness, "Accounting for Science: How a Merchant Kept His Books in Elizabethan London," in *The Self-Perception of Early Modern Capitalists*, ed. Margaret C. Jacob and Catherine Secretan (New York: Palgrave Macmillan, 2008), 205–28, 211. In *Savages Within the Empire: Representations of American Indians in Eighteenth-Century Britain* (New York: Oxford University Press, 2005), Troy Bickham argues that auctions helped encourage collecting in Britain. He also states that, in Britain, many auctioneers were also undertakers.

95. Daniela Bleichmar, "Seeing the World in a Room: Looking at Exotica in Early Modern Collections," in *Collecting Across Cultures*, ed. Bleichmar and Mancall, 15–30. See also the introduction to the same volume.

96. Troy Bickham, "'A Conviction of the Reality of Things': Material Culture, North American Indians and Empire in Eighteenth-Century Britain," *Eighteenth-Century Studies* 39, no. 1 (Fall 2005): 29–47, 33–34.

97. *Boston News-Letter*, March 17–24, 1710.

98. Shammas, *Pre-Industrial Consumer*, 266; Hart, *Trading Spaces*, chapter 1; Ann Smart Martin, *Buying into the World of Goods: Early Consumers in Backcountry Virginia* (Baltimore: Johns Hopkins University Press, 2008), 146–60. See also Hart, *Building Charleston*, chapter 2. For itinerant sales after the Revolution, see David Jaffee, *A New Nation of Goods: The Material Culture of Early America* (Philadelphia: University of Pennsylvania Press, 2010), chapter 4.

99. Bleichmar, "Seeing the World in a Room," 23–24, 30.

100. Wendy Martin, ed., *Colonial American Travel Narratives* (New York: Penguin Books, 1994), 69.

101. *Boston Gazette or Country Journal*, November 28, 1763.

102. *Boston Post-Boy*, February 12, 1759.

103. *South-Carolina Gazette*, August 30, 1748.

104. "An Act For Keeping the Streets in Charles-Town clean; And establishing such other Regulations for the Security, Health, and Convenience of the Inhabitants of the Said Town . . . ," *Laws Passed by the General Assembly of South-Carolina in June 1749 and May 1750* (Charles-Town, SC: Peter Timothy, 1750), 25.

105. "An Act to repeal an Act entitled 'An Act to prohibit the Sales of Goods, Wares and Merchandizes . . . ,'" *The Statutes at Large of South Carolina*, ed. Thomas Cooper and David J. McCord, 10 vols. (Columbia, SC: A. S. Johnson, 1836–1841), 4:403.

106. "Act to repeal," 403.

107. *Boston Gazette or Country Journal*, November 22, 1762.

108. *Boston Evening-Post*, March 14, 1768.

109. *Boston Gazette or Country Journal*, June 27, 1757.

110. *Boston Gazette or Country Journal*, November 13, 1769.

111. *Pennsylvania Packet, and Daily Advertiser*, January 4, 1790.

112. Thomas David Russell, "Sale Day in Antebellum South Carolina: Slavery, Law, Economy and Court-Supervised Sales" (PhD diss., Stanford University, 1993).

113. B. C. Smith, *Freedoms We Lost*, chapter 1.

114. Archibald Simpson, Journals and Sermons, 1748–1784, 11:301, Charleston Library Society, Charleston, SC.

115. *Boston Post-Boy*, February 12, 1759.

116. For some examples, see the documents in Charles Nicoll, Account Books, 1753–1781, and Jacamiah Akerly Papers, 1786–1816, New-York Historical Society, New York City.

117. Mary Poovey, *Genres of the Credit Economy: Mediating Value in Eighteenth- and Nineteenth-Century Britain* (Chicago: University of Chicago Press, 2008), 4.

118. Testimony of account filed in Jacob Hasey v. Abigail Pinnegar, Newport Court of Common Pleas, 1748 November term, no. 36, Rhode Island Judicial Records Center, Pawtucket.

119. For influential introductions to the idea of a moral economy, see E. P. Thompson, *Customs in Common: Studies in Traditional Popular Culture* (New York: New Press, 1992); and Daniel Vickers, "Competency and Competition: Economic Culture in Early America," *William and Mary Quarterly* 47, no. 1 (January 1990): 3–29.

120. William J. Novak surveys the many facets of the nineteenth-century regulated economy, including auctions, in *The People's Welfare: Law and Regulation in Nineteenth-Century America* (Chapel Hill: University of North Carolina Press, 1996), esp. chapter 3.

121. *Providence (RI) Gazette*, January 18, 1772.

122. C. W. Smith, *Auctions*, 3.

123. Laurel Thatcher Ulrich, *A Midwife's Tale: The Life of Martha Ballard, Based on Her Diary, 1785–1812* (1990; repr., New York: Vintage Books, 1991), 197. Ulrich notes that the midwife Martha Ballard received payments in shillings, but she more often received food, textiles, or household goods.

124. Nancy Folbre, *Greed, Lust, and Gender: A History of Economic Ideas* (New York: Oxford University Press, 2010), 13. Viviana Zelizer provocatively explores the ways that personal relationships shaped capitalism and vice versa. See, for example, *The Purchase of Intimacy* (Princeton, NJ: Princeton University Press, 2005).

125. Charles W. Smith argues that although all economic activity takes place in a social context, auctions are "explicitly concerned" with creating both communities and values (*Auctions*, 14).

CHAPTER 3

1. The records of the Loyalist Claims Commission are preserved at the National Archives (United Kingdom). The Audit Office (AO) records are available on microfilm at libraries in the United States, identified either as AO 12 (film 263) or AO 13 (film 264), followed by volume and page or folio number. I accessed them at the David Library of the American Revolution. Letter by James Scovil, August 23, 1786, AO 13/76–100/415.

2. Court Clerk's certified testimony, AO 13/76–100/403.

3. AO 13/76–100/400–412; quotation AO 12/1–9/49.

4. Sworn testimony of Thomas Osborn, January 16,1784, AO 13/76–100/404–5; Sworn testimony of Ezekiel Welton, November 15, 1788, AO 13/76–100/417–18.

5. Sworn testimony of Ezekiel Welton, November 15, 1788, AO 13/76–100/417–18.

6. AO 12/1–9/50/25.

7. Memorial of Joseph Munn, May 2, 1780, Collection of the Connecticut State Library, State Archives, Hartford, CT. The Mattatuck Museum places Munn's story in broader context: http://www.fortunestory.org/waterburysafricanamericans/josephmunn.asp.

8. Works that emphasize the use of loyalist auctions to punish political opponents include Maya Jasanoff, *Liberty's Exiles: American Loyalists in the Revolutionary World* (New York: Vintage Books, 2011), 34–35, 68; and Jim Piecuch, *Three Peoples, One King: Loyalists, Indians, and Slaves in the Revolutionary South, 1775–1782* (Columbia: University of South Carolina Press, 2008), 98–101. Rebecca Brannon, in *From Revolution to Reunion: The Reintegration of South Carolina Loyalists* (Columbia: University of South Carolina Press, 2016), suggests that in South Carolina the goal was to threaten and coerce men in the political middle. Works that focus on their role in financing the Revolution include Robert S. Lambert, "The Confiscation of Loyalist Property in Georgia, 1782–1786," *William and Mary Quarterly* 20, no. 1 (January 1963): 80–94; Peter M. Mitchell, "Loyalist Property and the Revolution in Virginia" (PhD diss., University of Colorado, 1965); and Stephen Mihm, "Funding the Revolution: Monetary Policy and Fiscal Policy in Eighteenth-Century America," in *The Oxford Handbook of the American Revolution*, ed. Edward G. Gray and Jane Kamensky (New York: Oxford University Press, 2012), 327–52, 333–34. Matthew Spooner frames confiscation as a tool to legitimize patriot plunder in "Origins of the Old South: Revolution, Slavery, and Changes in Southern Society, 1776–1800" (PhD diss., Columbia University, 2015).

9. [Thomas Paine], *The American Crisis, Number I* (Philadelphia, 1777?), 6.

10. Nicole Eustace, *Passion Is the Gale: Emotion, Power, and the Coming of the American Revolution* (Chapel Hill: University of North Carolina Press, 2008), 448.

11. New Jersey General Assembly, *The Acts of the General Assembly of the province of New-Jersey, from the time of the surrender of the government in the second year of the reign . . .* (Philadelphia, 1752), 46, 358, 306, 88.

12. Elizabeth V. Spelman discusses "suffering and the economy of attention" in the introduction to *Fruits of Sorrow: Framing Our Attention to Suffering* (Boston: Beacon Press, 1997).

13. T. H. Breen, *The Marketplace of Revolution: How Consumer Politics Shaped American Independence* (New York: Oxford University Press, 2004) and Alfred F. Young, *The*

Shoemaker and the Tea Party: Memory and the American Revolution (Boston: Beacon Press, 1999) explore the various forms of consumer protest in the American Revolution.

14. For dynastic uses of goods, see Amanda Vickery, *The Gentleman's Daughter: Women's Lives in Georgian England* (New Haven, CT: Yale University Press, 1998), chapter 4; and Laurel Thatcher Ulrich, "Hannah Barnard's Cupboard: Female Property and Identity in Eighteenth-Century New England," in *Through a Glass Darkly: Defining Self in Early America*, ed. Ronald Hoffman and Mechal Sobel (Chapel Hill: University of North Carolina Press for the Institute of Early American History and Culture, 1997), 238–73.

15. Comptroller Records—RG8, Receipts, 1776–1788, box 11, folder 7-1, "A.C.P. Moses Seymour's Receipts, 1780–1781," Connecticut State Library. Note that the price was in Connecticut money.

16. *Journals of the Provincial Congress, Provincial Convention, Committee of Safety and Council of Safety of the State of New York*, Volume 1 (Albany: Thurlow Weed, 1842), 858–59.

17. *Journals of the Provincial Congress* [New York], 1:859.

18. *Journals of the Provincial Congress* [New York], 1:810.

19. Wayne E. Lee, *Crowds and Soldiers in Revolutionary North Carolina: The Culture of Violence in Riot and War* (Gainesville: University Press of Florida, 2001), 177.

20. Wayne Lee discusses the spectrum of purchase, impressment, and plunder as well as the breakdown of these distinctions toward the end of the war in North Carolina in *Crowds and Soldiers in Revolutionary North Carolina*, 180–85. For McCorkle's sermon, see 181.

21. *Journals of the Provincial Congress* [New York], 1: 811.

22. *Journals of the Provincial Congress* [New York], 1:826.

23. Anne M. Ousterhout, "Pennsylvania Land Confiscations During the Revolution," *Pennsylvania Magazine of History and Biography* 102, no. 3 (July 1978): 328–43, 331.

24. Daniel J. Hulsebosch, "A Discrete and Cosmopolitan Minority: The Loyalists, the Atlantic World, and the Origins of Judicial Review," *Chicago-Kent Law Review* 81, no. 3 (2006): 825–66. In regions occupied by the British, in turn, commissioners sequestered patriot estates and attempted to make them profitable for the war effort by hiring out enslaved laborers and selling farm produce. Jasanoff, *Liberty's Exiles*, 74; Lauren Duval, "Mastering Charleston: Property and Patriarchy in British-Occupied Charleston, 1780–82," *William and Mary Quarterly* 75, no. 4 (October 2018): 589–622.

25. *Journals of the Continental Congress* (Washington, DC: Government Printing Office, 1912), 7:285.

26. Hulsebosch, "Discrete and Cosmopolitan Minority," 835.

27. For example, *Statutes at Large of Pennsylvania from 1682 to 1801*, vol. 9, *1776–1779* (Harrisburg, PA: Wm. Stanley Ray, State Printer of Pennsylvania, 1903), 209.

28. Richard D. Brown, "The Confiscation and Disposition of Loyalists' Estates in Suffolk County, Massachusetts," *William and Mary Quarterly* 21, no. 4 (October 1964): 534–50, 535.

29. Brown, "Confiscation and Disposition of Loyalists' Estates," 537.

30. Brannon, *From Revolution to Reunion*, 54.

31. *Newport (RI) Mercury*, April 27, 1782.

32. Mary Greene Nye, ed., *State Papers of Vermont*, vol. 6, *Sequestration, Confiscation and Sale of Estates* (Montpelier, VT: Office of Secretary of State, 1941), 213.

33. Grace Growden Galloway and Raymond C. Werner, "Diary of Grace Growden Galloway," *Pennsylvania Magazine of History and Biography* 55, no. 1 (1931): 32–94, 40–41.

34. Galloway and Werner, "Diary of Grace Growden Galloway," 45.

35. Galloway and Werner, "Diary of Grace Growden Galloway," 52.

36. Elizabeth Evans, *Weathering the Storm: Women of the American Revolution* (New York: Paragon House, 1989), 244.

37. *State Papers of Vermont*, 6:215; Lewis Cass Aldrich and Frank R. Holmes, eds., *History of Windsor County Vermont* (Syracuse, NY: D. Mason, 1891), 286.

38. *State Papers of Vermont*, 6:249–55.

39. AO 12/107/15.

40. Kimberly M. Nath, "The British Are Coming, Again: Loyalists, Property Confiscation, and Reintegration in the Mid-Atlantic, 1777–1800" (PhD diss., University of Delaware, 2016), 95.

41. Thomas Lynch Montgomery, ed. *Pennsylvania Archives*, 6th ser., vol. 12, *Fortified Estates, Inventories, and Sales* (Harrisburg: Harrisburg Publishing, 1907), 102.

42. Barbara Clark Smith, "Food Rioters and the American Revolution," *William and Mary Quarterly* 51, no. 1 (January 1994): 3–38; 4, 6–8.

43. Peter Oliver's outraged account of the attack on Thomas Hutchinson's house is found in Douglass Adair and John A. Schutz, eds., *Peter Oliver's Origin and Progress of the American Rebellion: A Tory View* (Stanford, CA: Stanford University Press, 1967), 53. Crowd action in the American Revolution is explored in Benjamin L. Carp, *Rebels Rising: Cities and the American Revolution* (New York: Oxford University Press, 2007); and Smith, "Food Rioters and the American Revolution," 3–38.

44. Montgomery, *Pennsylvania Archives*, 6th ser., 12:102. Commissioners did find, and appraise, some sheaves of grain, along with a mare and colt that had been sold out of town.

45. Montgomery, *Pennsylvania Archives*, 6th ser., 12:5.

46. Montgomery, *Pennsylvania Archives*, 6th ser., 12.13.

47. "An Act for the Attainder of Divers Traitors if they render not themselves by a certain day, and for vesting their estates in this commonwealth, and for more effectually discovering the same and for ascertaining and satisfying the lawful debts and claims thereupon," *Statutes at Large of Pennsylvania*, 9:210–15. For the process of selling estates in the mid-Atlantic, see Nath, "British Are Coming, Again," chapter 3.

48. Brown, "Confiscation and Disposition of Loyalists' Estates," 535.

49. Simon Gratz, ed., "Some Material for a Biography of Mrs. Elizabeth Fergusson, *née* Græme," *Pennsylvania Magazine of History and Biography* 39, no. 3 (1915): 257–321, 298–99.

50. Andrew McFarland Davis, *The Confiscation of John Chandler's Estate* (Boston: Houghton, Mifflin, 1903), 76.

51. *State Papers of Vermont*, 6:350.

52. *Pennsylvania Packet*, October 6, 1778. The announcement, which was dated September 2, also appeared in the newspaper on October 10.

53. Gratz, "Material for a Biography of Mrs. Elizabeth Fergusson," 295.

54. Gratz, "Material for a Biography of Mrs. Elizabeth Fergusson," 296.

55. *Journals of Congress Containing the Proceedings from January 1st, 1777, to January 1st, 1778* (Philadelphia, PA: John Dunlap, 1778), 3:431. They rejected this proposal and voted instead to link the obligation to the value of privately owned land, buildings, and improvements in each state.

56. *Journals of the Provincial Congress* [New York], 1:846.

57. *Journals of the Provincial Congress* [New York], 1:869.

58. *Journals of the Provincial Congress* [New York], 1:872. The commissioners later took testimony from Catharine's mother and another woman that Cornelius gave the enslaved people to his daughter (942).

59. Thomas Cooper and David J. McCord, eds., *Statutes at Large of South Carolina*, 10 vols. (Columbia, SC: A. S. Johnston, 1836–1841), 4:556, March 16, 1783.

60. Matthew Spooner, "The Problem of Order and the Transfer of Slave Property in the Revolutionary South," in *The American Revolution Reborn*, ed. Patrick Spero and Michael Zuckerman (Philadelphia: University of Pennsylvania Press, 2016), 231–47, 242.

61. Lee, *Crowds and Soldiers in Revolutionary North Carolina*, 166–67.

62. Brown, "Confiscation and Disposition of Loyalists' Estates," 545.

63. The newspaper notices circulated among the population and nearby British forces. Numerous British officers testified to having seen notices of attainder linked with Major Daniel McAlpin's name in newspapers as being guilty of "outlawry," to have his property confiscated and sold. AO 12/21–51/62, 65.

64. Thomas Lewis to Henry Livingston, December 16, 1777; letter from Isaac Sheldon, November 13, 1777, Dutchess County, NY, May 20, 1773–June 1887, Dutchess County Committee of Sequestration, New-York Historical Society.

65. For example, Israel Smith paid John Wright 5 shillings for spirits at a 1779 vendue in Vermont. *State Papers of Vermont*, 6:231.

66. Montgomery, *Pennsylvania Archives*, 6th ser., 12:42–47.

67. *State Papers of Vermont*, 6:306.

68. *State Papers of Vermont*, 6:314.

69. Brannon, *From Revolution to Reunion*, 49. See also Spooner, "Origins of the Old South."

70. Commissioners of Forfeited Estates, Accounts/Sales Book, S126211, pp. 8–10, South Carolina Department of Archives and History, Columbia. Document uses "Jackson'sburgh."

71. Benjamin Whipple, tasked with writing up the advertisements for a sale in the spring of 1779, had to revise and arrange for the reprinting of an advertisement "on Acct of 2 More Estates being given in." *State Papers of Vermont*, 6:337.

72. Connecticut Archives, Miscellaneous Papers, Second Series, 1686–1820, 1:68, 69, 71, 72, 88, 89, 93–96. Connecticut State Library.

73. Breen, *Marketplace of Revolution*, 257.

74. Montgomery, *Pennsylvania Archives*, 6th ser., 12:53–56.

75. Montgomery, *Pennsylvania Archives*, 6th ser., 12:56–60.

76. Account Book for George Palmer, Revolutionary War Miscellaneous Manuscripts, box 2, New-York Historical Society.

77. See, for example, Account Book for George Palmer, Revolutionary War Miscellaneous Manuscripts, box 2. Rebecca Brannon states that it would be impossible to sell confiscated estates if families were still living on them, which may have motivated lawmakers to make provisions for wives and children. See *From Revolution to Reunion*, 55.

78. Howard Pashman, "The People's Property Law: A Step Toward Building a New Legal Order in Revolutionary New York," *Law and History Review* 31, no. 3 (August 2013): 587–626, 603.

79. Cooper and McCord, *Statutes at Large of South Carolina*, 4:555, February 26, 1782.

80. *Freeman's Journal; or, the North-American Intelligencer* (Philadelphia, PA), July 11, 1781.

81. *Massachusetts Resolves of the General Assembly of the State of Massachusetts Bay, September 10–October 25, 1777*, 35. The assembly later abandoned such a methodical practice. See Thomas N. Ingersoll, *The Loyalist Problem in Revolutionary New England* (New York: Cambridge University Press, 2016), 268n49.

82. Montgomery, *Pennsylvania Archives*, 6th ser., 12:29.

83. Quoted in Kacy Dowd Tillman, "Women Left Behind: Female Loyalism, Coverture, and Grace Growden Galloway's Empire of Self," in *Women's Narratives of the Early Americas and the Formation of Empire*, ed. Mary McAleer Balkun and Susan C. Imbarrato (New York: Palgrave Macmillan, 2016), 141–55, 151.

84. See, for example, Comptroller Records—RG8, Receipts, 1776–1778, box 12—receipts, 1782, 1784–1788, folder 8-1, Connecticut State Library.

85. *Massachusetts Spy, published as Thomas's Massachusetts Spy or, the Worchester Gazette*, January 3, 1782.

86. Reprinted letter from the *St. James's Chronicle*, in the *Connecticut Journal*, January 10, 1782.

87. Thomas Paine, *Common Sense; Addressed to the Inhabitants of America* (Philadelphia, PA: W. and T. Bradford, 1776), 87.

88. Barbara Clark Smith, *The Freedoms We Lost: Consent and Resistance in Revolutionary America* (New York: New Press, 2010), 143–44.

89. Smith, *Freedoms We Lost*, 149.

90. An Act for Regulating Prices of sundry Articles therein enumerated (State of New Hampshire, 1777), in Trumbull Papers, 1631–1784, vol. 23, part 1, item 71a–71c, Connecticut State Library.

91. *Journals of the Continental Congress* (Washington, DC: Government Printing Office, 1912), 15:1175.

92. *Statutes at Large of Pennsylvania*, 9:136–37. South Carolina passed a similar act in 1777: An Act to Prohibit the sale of Goods, Wares, and Merchandizes at Public Vendue, in this State. Cooper and McCord, *Statutes at Large of South Carolina*, 4:396.

93. *Statutes at Large of Pennsylvania*, 10:18. The same bill that banned most auctions also forbade white men "capable of bearing arms" from peddling or hawking goods to support themselves in wartime. Two years later, the revised law allowed any commissioned officer in the militia or constable to seize goods from such a man, fine him, and take half of the profits, though only for the duration of the war. *Statutes at Large of Pennsylvania*, 10:21.

94. Spooner, "Origins of the Old South," 110–11.

95. *New Jersey Gazette*, April 20, 1784.

96. *New Jersey Gazette*, July 19, 1784.

97. AO 12/107/15.

98. Brown, "Confiscation and Disposition of Loyalists' Estates," 542.

99. *Pennsylvania Packet or General Advertiser*, March 21, 1780.

100. *Statutes at Large of Pennsylvania*, 9:331.

101. Edwin J. Perkins, *American Public Finance and Financial Services, 1700–1815* (Columbus: Ohio State University Press, 1994), 138.

102. Robin Einhorn, *American Taxation, American Slavery* (Chicago: University of Chicago Press, 2008), 72–74.

103. John E. Selby, *The Revolution in Virginia, 1775–1783* (Charlottesville: University of Virginia Press, 2007), 152–53.

104. Einhorn, *American Taxation, American Slavery*, 46–49.

105. Einhorn, *American Taxation, American Slavery*, 48.

106. Woody Holton, *Unruly Americans and the Origins of the Constitution* (New York: Hill and Wang, 2007), chapter 1.

107. See, for example, *Thomas's Massachusetts Spy, or, Worcester Gazette*, November 6, 1783; *Pennsylvania Packet, or, General Advertiser*, September 30, 1783. Claims adjusters in the new United States reported back to London on the state-by-state sales and property condemnations that continued after the draft treaty was circulated, and even after it was ratified. Report to the Loyalist Claims Commissions, AO 12/107/178–208.

108. Petition of Rachel Wells, May 18, 1786, *Papers of the Continental Congress*, (M-247), roll 56, item 42: VIII, 354–55; New Jersey Women's History, accessed March 2, 2019, http://www.njwomenshistory.org/discover/topics/art/petition-rachel-lovell-wells/.

109. Quoted in Jasanoff, *Liberty's Exiles*, 135. Jasanoff notes that just over half of Black petitioners received payment; women, too, were less likely to receive payments.

110. AO 13/72/210.

111. AO 13/129/604.

112. AO 12/109/2.

113. L. F. S. Upton, "The Claims: The Mission of John Anstey," in *Red, White, and True Blue: The Loyalists in the Revolution*, ed. Esmond Wright (New York: AMS Press, 1976), 135–47, 138–39.

114. "The Memorial of Richd. Swanwick late of Chester County in the Province of Pennsylvania," AO 12/42/29–36.

115. AO 12/113/14.

116. AO 12/113/16.

117. AO 12/113/33.

118. Claim on John Hamilton of South Carolina, AO 13/138/417.

119. AO 12/109/3.

120. Quoted in Upton, "Claims," 143.

121. AO 12/109/3.

122. Jasanoff, *Liberty's Exiles*, 138.

123. Henrik Ronsbo and Steffen Jensen, "Histories of Victimhood: Assemblages, Transactions, and Figures," in *Histories of Victimhood*, ed. Steffen Jensen and Henrik Ronsbo (Philadelphia: University of Pennsylvania Press, 2014), 2–3.

124. For example, laws that had associated the privilege of voting with the possession of a certain valued property were replaced with laws that lowered and eventually replaced that value bar.

125. Ousterhout, "Pennsylvania Land Confiscations During the Revolution," 334–35.

126. Commissioner of Forfeited Estates, Accounts/Sales Book S126211, p. 16, South Carolina Department of Archives and History, Columbia.

127. *State Papers of Vermont*, 6:314.

128. Pepperell's letter, and more appeals from the Loyalists as a lobbying group, appear in John Eardley-Wilmot, *Historical View of the Commission for Enquiring into the Losses, Services, and Claims of the American Loyalists, at the close of the war between Great Britain and her colonies in 1783 with an account of the compensation granted to them by Parliament in 1785 and 1788* (London: J. Nichols, Son, and Bentley, 1815), 78.

CHAPTER 4

1. Quoted in Rachel N. Klein, *Unification of a Slave State: The Rise of the Planter Class in the South Carolina Back Country, 1760–1808* (Chapel Hill: University of North Carolina Press, 1990), 127.

2. A series of laws responded to such debtor-relief measures by focusing on the auction sale, including "An Act to Prevent Debtors from Purchasing Repeatedly their Own property at Sheriff's Sales, to the Delay of their Creditors, and for the Better Regulation of Sheriff's and Other Sales at Public Auction," in *Statutes at Large of South Carolina*, ed. Thomas Cooper and David J. McCord, 10 vols. (Columbia, SC: A. S. Johnston, 1836–1841), 5:282–84; "An Ordinance for Regulating the Public Vendues in this State, and for Repealing Part of an Ordinance entitled, 'An Ordinance for regulating all Vendues in this State, and for Raising Supplies to the Government,'" Cooper and McCord, *Statutes at Large*, 4:670–73; "An Act to Regulate the Recovery and Payments of Debts; and For Prohibiting the Importation of Negroes for the time Herein Mentioned," Cooper and McCord, *Statutes at Large*, 5:36–38. For attacks on Courts of Common Pleas and sheriffs, see Robert A. Becker, "Salus Populi Suprema Lex: Public Peace and South Carolina Debtor Relief Laws, 1783–1788," *South Carolina Historical Magazine* 80, no. 1 (January 1979): 65–75, Ramsey quotation on 68.

3. Common Sense—Continued, "For the Columbian," *Columbian* (New York, NY), February 27, 1817.

4. Patrick Griffin, *American Leviathan: Empire, Nation, and Revolutionary Frontier* (New York: Hill and Wang, 2007), 257.

5. Thomas D. Russell, "South Carolina's Largest Slave Auctioneering Firm—Symposium on the Law of Slavery: Criminal and Civil Law of Slavery," *Chicago-Kent Law Review* 68, no. 3 (June 1993): 1241–82, 1241.

6. Paul A. Gilje, *Free Trade and Sailors' Rights in the War of 1812* (New York: Cambridge University Press, 2013), 13.

7. T. H. Breen's *The Marketplace of Revolution: How Consumer Politics Shaped American Independence* (New York: Oxford University Press, 2004) has been highly influential in interpreting the abundance of goods presented in advertisements as "inventories of desire" that stoked consumer choice. Joanna Cohen connects politics to consumer desire in the nineteenth century in *Luxurious Citizens: The Politics of Consumption in Nineteenth-Century America* (Philadelphia: University of Pennsylvania Press, 2017).

8. Joseph M. Adelman, *Revolutionary Networks: The Business and Politics of Printing the News, 1763–1789* (Baltimore: Johns Hopkins University Press, 2019).

9. See David Steigerwald, "All Hail the Republic of Choice: Consumer History as Contemporary Thought," *Journal of American History* 93, no. 2 (September 2006): 385–403. In the same issue of the *Journal of American History*, T. H. Breen agrees that it is crucial to understand individual acts of consumption "within a complex economic system." Breen, "Will American Consumers Buy a Second American Revolution?," *Journal of American History* 93, no. 2 (September 2006): 404–8.

10. On the "divided self," see Toby L. Ditz, "Secret Selves, Credible Personas: The Problematics of Trust and Public Display in the Writing of Eighteenth-Century Philadelphia Merchants," in *Possible Pasts: Becoming Colonial in Early America*, ed. Robert Blair St. George (Ithaca, NY: Cornell University Press, 2000), 219–42, 221, 233. Sarah A. Kidd, "The Search for Moral Order: The Panic of 1819 and the Culture of the Early American Republic" (PhD diss., University of Missouri–Columbia, 2002); Karen Halttunen, *Confidence Men and Painted Women: A Study of Middle-Class Culture in America, 1830–1870* (New Haven, CT: Yale University Press, 1982); Jane Kamensky, *The Exchange Artist: A Tale of High-Flying Speculation and America's First Banking Collapse* (New York: Viking, 2008); Stephen Mihm, *A Nation of Counterfeiters: Capitalists, Con Men, and the Making of the United States* (Cambridge, MA: Harvard University Press, 2007); Scott A. Sandage, *Born Losers: A History of Failure in America* (Cambridge, MA: Harvard University Press, 2006).

11. Toby L. Ditz explores "standards of manhood and their associated practices" in early America in her afterword, "Contending Masculinities in Early America," to Thomas A. Foster, *New Men: Manliness in Early America* (New York: New York University Press, 2011), 256–67, 256.

12. Anyone could sell goods at auction—Pennsylvania law by midcentury referred to people who "take upon him, her or themselves to sell or expose to sale by Way of Vendue or Auction—but only a subset were auctioneers. "An Act for Regulating Pedlars, Vendues, &c," *A Collection of all the laws of the province of Pennsylvania: now in force* (Philadelphia, PA: B. Franklin, 1742), 406.

13. William J. Novak portrays auctioneers, innkeepers, and public carriers as enduring examples of economic operations that were regulated through a licensing system. *The People's Welfare: Law and Regulation in Nineteenth-Century America* (Chapel Hill: University of North Carolina Press, 1996), 90–95.

14. Ann Fabian, introduction to *Card Sharps and Bucket Shops: Gambling in Nineteenth-Century America* (New York: Routledge, 1999). In *Capitalism Takes Command*, Michael

Zakim and Gary Kornblith argue that in the nineteenth century "the exchange relationship emerged as a dominant form of social intercourse as well as an equally dominant form of social thought." Michael Zakim and Gary J. Kornblith, eds., *Capitalism Takes Command: The Social Transformation of Nineteenth-Century America* (Chicago: University of Chicago Press, 2012), 1.

15. As the scholar Cynthia Wall writes, "The auction is the site for the disassembling of one instance of the existing world and the promise of the reconstruction of a new one." Cynthia Wall, "The English Auction: Narratives of Dismantlings," *Eighteenth-Century Studies* 31, no. 1 (Fall 1997): 1–25, 3.

16. "Gone to a Book Auction," *Ariel: A Semimonthly Literary and Miscellaneous Gazette* 4, no. 6 (July 10, 1830): 45.

17. "Gone to a Book Auction," 45.

18. *City Gazette* (Charleston, SC), January 22, 1794.

19. *Inventory of the Furniture and Goods of the Hon. John Penn, Senr.* (Philadelphia, PA: Dunlap and Claypoole, 1788).

20. Trevor Burnard, "Collecting and Accounting: Representing Slaves as Commodities in Jamaica, 1674–1784," in *Collecting Across Cultures: Material Exchanges in the Early Modern Atlantic World*, ed. Daniela Bleichmar and Peter Mancall (Philadelphia: University of Pennsylvania Press, 2011), 177–91, 188. As discussed in Chapter 2, further adjustments were made to the grouping of objects and people between the inventory and estate sale.

21. The widow Dorothy Whetherhead planned to auction household goods from her own house. For three days prior to the sale, people could come to view the goods and pick up a free catalog at the same time. *Boston Weekly News-Letter*, March 8–15, 1733.

22. For examples of "conditions of sale" printed in an auction catalog, see Giles Mandelbrote, "The Organization of Book Auctions in Late Seventeenth-Century London," in *Under the Hammer: Book Auctions Since the Seventeenth Century*, ed. Robin Myers, Michael Harris, and Giles Mandelbrote (New Castle, DE: Oak Knoll Press, 2001), 15–50, 21, 29.

23. "Catalogue of DRY GOODS, to be sold, At the Auction Store, No. 20, south Front-st. On Saturday morning, 12th September, 1818"; "Catalogue of Silk, Nankeens, &c. TO BE SOLD, On Saturday morning, the 19th September, 1818, At 10 o'clock precisely"; "Catalogue of DRY GOODS, TO BE SOLD, On Saturday morning, 26th September, 1818, At 10 o'clock precisely"; all in Auction Accounts of Weir, Willing, Lewis, Smith & Lisle, Auctioneers, August 1818–March 1819, Mrs. Howard W. Lewis Collection of Early Philadelphia Businesses Papers, Historical Society of Pennsylvania (hereafter cited as Lewis Collection).

24. On one auctioneer's copy of the dry goods catalog, someone added handwritten notes about potential or reserve prices and directions as to how to manage the sale. For the case of 1,155 yards of blue-and-white linen striped fabric, the writer noted "If [they sell at a price of] 17 Cts sell 4 more. Account of Messr. Lisle Weir & Co with the Democratic Press Office, September/October 1818; "Catalogue of DRY GOODS, to be sold, At the Auction Store, No. 20, south Front-st. On Saturday, morning 12th September, 1818," p. 4. Auction Accounts of Weir, Willing, Lewis, Smith & Lisle, Auctioneers, August 1818–March 1819, Lewis Collection.

25. *City Gazette*, March 15, 1790.

26. *City Gazette*, March 15, 1790.

27. Walter Johnson, *Soul by Soul: Life Inside the Antebellum Slave Market* (Cambridge, MA: Harvard University Press, 1999), 129.

28. *City Gazette*, March 15, 1790.

29. Johnson, *Soul by Soul*, chapter 6.

30. Solomon Northup, *Twelve Years a Slave*, ed. David Wilson (Minneapolis, MN: Lerner Publishing Group, 2014), 41–44.

31. Johnson, *Soul by Soul*, 130.

32. For enslaved people's memories of the experience of an auction, see Daina Ramey Berry, *The Price for Their Pound of Flesh: The Value of the Enslaved, from Womb to Grave, in the Building of a Nation* (New York: Beacon Press, 2017), 42–46.

33. Bexwell v. Christie, Cowper 395 (1776), cited in Samuel Livermore, *A Treatise on the Law Relative to Principals, Agents, Factors, Auctioneers, and Brokers* (Boston: Thomas B. Wait, 1811), 105.

34. *The Cries of Philadelphia: Ornamented with Elegant Wood Cuts* (Philadelphia, PA: Johnson and Warner, 1810), 15, 20.

35. *The Rural Visiter, and Saratoga Advertiser*, June 23, 1812. For analysis of what he calls Proto English Auction Speech, see Koenraad Kuiper, "The Oral Tradition in Auction Speech," *American Speech* 67, no. 3 (Autumn 1992): 279–89; for discussion of occupational verbal styles, see Amanda Dargan and Steven Zeitlin, "American Talkers: Expressive Styles and Occupational Choice," *Journal of American Folklore* 96, no. 379 (January–March 1983): 3–33. Cynthia Wall considers evidence for the famed British auctioneer James Christie's "oral technique" in "he English Auction: Narratives of Dismantlings," 7–10.

36. Lord Ellenborough in Jones v. Edney, 3 Camp. 285 (1812), quoted in Samuel Livermore, *A Treatise on the Law of Principal and Agent, and of Sales by Auction*, 2 vols. (Baltimore: printed for the author, by Joseph Robinson, 1818), 2:328.

37. *Boston Weekly Advertiser*, August 14, 1758.

38. *Massachusetts Gazette and Boston Newsletter*, July 25, 1765.

39. *Boston Evening Post*, February 19, 1770. Gerrish described the evening vendue as being "upon a very urgent Occasion."

40. Livermore, *Treatise on the Law Relative to Principals, Agents, Factors, Auctioneers, and Brokers*, 1–2.

41. Sara T. Damiano, "Agents at Home: Wives, Lawyers, and Financial Competence in Eighteenth-Century New England Port Cities," *Early American Studies* 13, no. 4 (Fall 2015): 808–35, 816–17.

42. Frequent communication was essential to trust and ensuring good service. Sara T. Damiano, "Writing Women's History Through the Revolution: Family Finances, Letter Writing, and Conceptions of Marriage," *William and Mary Quarterly* 74, no. 4 (October 2017): 697–728, 717–18. David Hancock discusses the deployment of agents across the Atlantic in the Madeira trade in *Oceans of Wine: Madeira and the Emergence of American Trade and Taste* (New Haven, CT: Yale University Press, 2009), xx–xxiv, 163–66. For a sociologist's take on contemporary agency theory in multiple disciplines, see Susan P. Shapiro, "Agency Theory," *Annual Review of Sociology* 31 (2005): 263–84.

43. On the increase in court-ordered vendues after the American Revolution, see Emma Hart, *Trading Spaces: The Colonial Marketplace and the Foundations of American Capitalism* (Chicago: University of Chicago Press, 2019), 182.

44. *Enquirer* (Richmond, VA), December 27, 1810.

45. Livermore, *Treatise on the Law Relative to Principals, Agents, Factors, Auctioneers, and Brokers*, 2.

46. On this body of law, see Morris L. Cohen, *Bibliography of Early American Law*, vol. 1 (Buffalo, NY: William S. Hein, 1998).

47. Livermore, *Treatise on the Law Relative to Principals, Agents, Factors, Auctioneers, and Brokers*, 97.

48. Crary and Babcock to Silas Weir, March 22, 1817, Correspondence of Weir, Willing, Lewis, Smith & Lisle, Auctioneers, January–June 1817, box 14, Lewis Collection; Bayard & Co. [Baynard & Dickinson] to Messrs. Lisle, Weir, & Co., March 6, 1819, Correspondence of Weir, Willing, Lewis, Smith & Lisle, Auctioneers, January–June 1819, box 18, Lewis Collection.

49. Novak, *People's Welfare*, 90. See Emma Hart's description of "The Resurgence of Early Modern Market Values" in *Trading Spaces*, chapter 4.

50. This 1742 law was printed in *The Charters of the Province of Pennsylvania* (Philadelphia, PA: Franklin, 1742), 406.

51. "An Act to Regulate the Sale of Goods at Public Vendue, and to Limit the Number of Auctioneers," *Acts and Resolves Passed by the General Court of Massachusetts, 1772–1773*, chapter 44, p. 248. The original law, passed in February, was amended to allow for more auctioneers, but Bowman was still excluded. See "An Act in Addition to an Act, Made and passed in the present year of his majesty's reign, intitled 'An Act to regulate the sale of goods at public vendue, and to limit the number of auctioneers," *Acts and Resolves, 1773–1774*, chapter 10, pp. 300–301.

52. *Boston Evening Post*, March 29, 1773.

53. *Boston News-Letter*, May 27, 1773.

54. *Boston News-Letter*, July 29, 1773.

55. For example, Moses Deshon was selected when Bowman was not. *Boston Gazette or Country Journal*, August 16, 1773.

56. Handwritten note added to Summons to appear as a juror at the Court of Common Pleas, February 8, 1817, Correspondence of Weir, Willing, Lewis, Smith & Lisle, Auctioneers, January–June 1817, box 14, Lewis Collection. On public economy, Novak, *People's Welfare*, 83–113.

57. *City Gazette*, May 10, 1804.

58. "An Ordinance for Regulating the Public Vendue in this State," Cooper and McCord, *Statutes at Large*, 4:670–71; "An Ordinance for Repealing so much of the ordinance passed March 16, 1783 and March 17, 1785," Cooper and McCord, *Statutes at Large*, 5:81–82.

59. "An ACT laying Duties on Property sold at Auction," *Third Congress of the United States: At the First Session, Begun and Held at the City of Philadelphia, in the state of Pennsylvania, on Monday, the second of December, one thousand seven hundred and ninety-three* (Philadelphia, PA: Francis Childs and John Swaine [?], 1794), 1. The law was to continue for two years and then to the end of the next session of Congress.

60. A0824-78 Entry documentation for state agency expenses, 1784–1909 New York (State), Comptroller's Office, New-York Historical Society.

61. A1443-78 Auctioneers' statements of sales, [ca. 1838–1844] New York (State), Comptroller's Office, New-York Historical Society.

62. See the many returns gathered in seven boxes of A0824-78 Entry documentation for state agency expenses, 1784–1909 New York (State), Comptroller's Office, New-York Historical Society.

63. *Mercantile Advertiser* (New York), December 11, 1801.

64. Michael A. Blaakman, *Speculation Nation: Land Mania in the Revolutionary American Republic* (Philadelphia: University of Pennsylvania Press, 2023), 60.

65. Claire Priest discusses the ways that laws limit and publicize types of property in the interest of reducing information costs and promoting exchange. Priest, *Credit Nation: Property Laws and Institutions in Early America* (Princeton, NJ: Princeton University Press, 2021), 154–56.

66. Petition of John Thwaites & others relating to auctions, February 24th, 1803, Baltimore City Archives Records Collection, Special Collections MSA SC 5511, 1802–1803, box 3, City Council Records, WPA nos. 316–30. This folder contains multiple ordinances and supplements as well as several petitions.

67. "An Ordinance for Regulating all Vendues within this State: and for Raising Supplies to Government, therein mentioned," Cooper and McCord, *Statutes at Large*, 4:562.

68. *Debates of the General Assembly of Pennsylvania* (Philadelphia, 1788), 4:87.

69. *Debates of the General Assembly of Pennsylvania*, 4:87.

70. *Debates of the General Assembly of Pennsylvania*, 4:85–86.

71. Robert J. Gamble, "The Promiscuous Economy: Cultural and Commercial Geographies of Secondhand in the Antebellum City," in *Capitalism by Gaslight: Illuminating the Economy of Nineteenth-Century America*, ed. Brian P. Luskey and Wendy A. Woloson (Philadelphia: University of Pennsylvania Press, 2015), 31–52, 39.

72. The number of auctioneers in American cities increased substantially in the early nineteenth century. See Jacob Milligan, *The Charleston Directory* (Charleston, SC, 1794); David C. Franks, *The New-York Directory* ... (New York: Samuel and John Loudon, 1787); John Macpherson, *Macpherson's Directory, for the City and Suburbs of Philadelphia* ... (Philadelphia, PA: Francis Bailey, 1785); David Longworth, *Longworth's American Almanac, New York Register, and City Directory* ... (New York, 1801); and Eleazer Elizer, *A Directory for 1803* ... (Charleston, SC: W. P. Young, 1803). See also James Robinson, *The Philadelphia Directory* ... (Philadelphia, PA: William W. Woodward, 1802), which lists three auctioneers and two vendue criers in Philadelphia.

73. *Village Record* (West Chester, PA), March 15, 1820; William Findlay to John Binns and response, reprinted in *Spirit of the Times & Carlisle Gazette* (PA), April 13, 1819. On Pennsylvania auctioneers, see A Citizen of Pennsylvania, *Strictures on Monopolies, respectfully submitted to the consideration of the constituted authorities, and people of Pennsylvania* (n.p., 1819?), 9. On patronage, coercion, and gendered power, see Richard R. Beeman, "Deference, Republicanism, and the Emergence of Popular Politics in Eighteenth-Century America," *William and Mary Quarterly* 49, no. 3 (July 1992): 401–30; for coercion specifically, 411–12; and Toby L.

Ditz, "The New Men's History and the Peculiar Absence of Gendered Power: Some Remedies from Early American Gender History," *Gender and History* 16, no. 1 (April 2004): 1–35.

74. Ann Fabian explores the cultural work of antigambling campaigns in the development of nineteenth-century capitalism in *Card Sharps and Bucket Shops: Gambling in Nineteenth-Century America* (New York: Routledge, 1995). See also Marieke de Goede, *Virtue, Fortune, and Faith: A Genealogy of Finance* (Minneapolis: University of Minnesota Press, 2005), chapter 3; and Jonathan Levy, *Freaks of Fortune: The Emerging World of Capitalism and Risk in America* (Cambridge, MA: Harvard University Press, 2012), chapter 7.

75. Colonial American governors jealously held their patronage powers under frequent attack from English aristocrats who sent their own favorites with letters of introduction and suggestions for appropriate positions. See Alison Gilbert Olson, *Making the Empire Work: London and American Interest Groups, 1690–1790* (Cambridge, MA: Harvard University Press, 1992); and Bernard Bailyn, *The Origins of American Politics* (New York: Alfred A. Knopf, 1968). Michael C. Batinski discusses Jonathan Belcher's patronage policies in *Jonathan Belcher, Colonial Governor* (Lexington: University Press of Kentucky, 1996).

76. Investigation of patronage for understanding power relations has been fruitful in Renaissance and early modern European studies. For an introduction to trends in the literature and the discussion of patronage language, see Sharon Kettering, "Patronage in Early Modern France," *French Historical Studies* 17, no. 4 (Autumn 1992): 839–62, esp. 844; and Mario Biagioli, *Galileo, Courtier: The Practice of Science in the Culture of Absolutism* (Chicago: University of Chicago Press, 1993), chapter 1. On typologies, see Edward Andrew, "The Senecan Moment: Patronage and Philosophy in the Eighteenth Century," *Journal of the History of Ideas* 65, no. 2 (April 2004): 277–99, 285–87. The literature on republicanism, liberalism, and political economy is extensive. Influential works include Joyce Appleby, *Capitalism and a New Social Order: The Republican Vision of the 1790s* (New York: New York University Press, 1984); Drew McCoy, *The Elusive Republic: Political Economy in Jeffersonian America* (Chapel Hill: University of North Carolina Press, 1980); Charles Sellers, *The Market Revolution: Jacksonian America, 1815–1846* (New York: Oxford University Press, 1994); and Gordon Wood, *The Radicalism of the American Revolution*, 2nd ed. (New York: Random House, 1993). Since Marcel Mauss's *The Gift: Forms and Functions of Exchange in Archaic Societies* (London: Cohen and West, 1966), the anthropological literature on favors has influenced scholarship on eighteenth- and nineteenth-century Anglo-American material culture and consumerism. See, for example, Ann Smart Martin, *Buying into the World of Goods: Early Consumers in Backcountry Virginia* (Baltimore: Johns Hopkins University Press, 2008); John Styles and Amanda Vickery, eds., *Gender, Taste, and Material Culture in Britain and North America, 1700–1830* (New Haven, CT: Yale University Press, 2007); and Laurel Thatcher Ulrich, *The Age of Homespun: Objects and Stories in the Creation of an American Myth* (New York: Alfred A. Knopf, 2001). Anthropological insights on the alliances formed through gifts and favors have influenced studies of European colonial encounters with Native Americans, from Richard White's *The Middle Ground: Indians, Empires, and Republics in the Great Lakes Region, 1650–1815* (New York: Cambridge University Press, 1991) to Juliana Barr, *Peace Came in the Form of a Woman: Indians and Spaniards in the Texas Borderlands* (Chapel Hill: University of North Carolina Press, 2007) and Joseph M. Hall Jr., *Zamumo's Gifts: Indian-European Exchange in*

the Colonial Southeast (Philadelphia: University of Pennsylvania Press, 2009). On patronage language as an analytical tool, see *An Exposition of Some of the Evils Arising from the Auction System* (Philadelphia, PA: Van Felt and Spear, 1822), 6.

77. Joyce Appleby, *Inheriting the Revolution: The First Generation of Americans* (Cambridge, MA: Harvard University Press, 2000), 21; Eve Tavor Bannet, *Empire of Letters: Letter Manuals and Transatlantic Correspondence, 1688–1820* (New York: Cambridge University Press, 2005), 202; Paul A. Gilje, "The Rise of Capitalism in the Early Republic," *Journal of the Early Republic* 16, no. 2 (Summer 1996): 159–81.

78. *New-York Journal, or Weekly Register*, September 8, 1785; *Rochester Telegraph*, December 22, 1818. A keyword search of the database Archive of Americana (Readex) revealed the trends discussed here. The *Oxford English Dictionary* notes the late eighteenth-century emergence of a definition of "patronage" meaning "custom given to a business, shop, restaurant, theatre, etc." See *OED Online*, s.v. "patronage, n.," accessed January 18, 2011, http://www.oed.com.

79. *New-York Journal, or Weekly Register*, September 8, 1785; John Brewer, *The Pleasures of the Imagination: English Culture in the Eighteenth Century* (London: HarperCollins, 1997), 162.

80. One book about the New York Minturn family of auctioneers states: "The Minturns like the other merchants lived from day to day sifting a few facts from the blowing chaff of rumors along the waterfront." James Hendrickson, *One Hundred and Fifty Years of Auctioneering in America (1798–1948): The Story of the Brown & Seccomb-Fruit Auction Co., Inc.* (New York: The Company, 1948), 17.

81. J. Schmidt & Co. to Messrs. Lisle Weir & Co., March 1, 1819, Correspondence of Weir, Willing, Lewis, Smith & Lisle, Auctioneers, January–June 1819, box 18, Lewis Collection; Francis W. Meriam & Co. to Lisle Weir & Co., August 5, 1819, Correspondence of Weir, Willing, Lewis, Smith & Lisle, Auctioneers, July–December 1819, box 19, Lewis Collection. On the development of business newspapers and prices current, see John J. McCusker, "The Demise of Distance: The Business Press and the Origins of the Information Revolution in the Early Modern Atlantic World," *American Historical Review* 110, no. 2 (April 2005): 295–321.

82. *Carlisle Republican* (PA), February 29, 1820; Amos Ellmaker to Lisle, Weir, & Co., May 23, 1818, Correspondence of Weir, Willing, Lewis, Smith & Lisle, Auctioneers, January–July 1818, box 16, Lewis Collection.

83. *Carlisle Republican* (PA), August 15, 1820; *Village Record* (West Chester, PA), August 30, 1820.

84. Citizen of Pennsylvania, *Strictures on Monopolies*, 5–6.

85. Citizen of Pennsylvania, *Strictures on Monopolies*, 6–7.

86. Pennsylvania General Assembly, *Report of the Committee, Appointed by the House of Representatives, to Inquire into the Conduct of the Governor of the Commonwealth of Pennsylvania* (Harrisburg, 1820), 17, 86. See also *Carlisle Republican* (PA), April 4, 1820.

87. Commission Book, M.R. 1, 1818–1826, Philadelphia City Archive, Philadelphia, PA.

88. Citizen of Pennsylvania, *Strictures on Monopolies*, 10. For the Maryland system, see Clement Dorsey, *The General Public Statutory Law and Public Local Law of the State of Maryland: From the year 1692 to 1839 inclusive, with annotations thereto and a copious index* (Baltimore: J. D. Troy, 1840), 141:1434, accessed July 6, 2011, Archives of Maryland Online,

http://aomol.msa.maryland.gov/megafile/msa/speccol/sc2900/sc2908/000001/000141/html/index.html.

89. "AUCTIONS. From the Providence Journal," *Niles' Weekly Register* (Baltimore) 34, no. 878 (July 12, 1828): 315.

90. Frederic Trautmann, "Pennsylvania Through a German's Eyes: The Travels of Ludwig Gall, 1819–1820," *Pennsylvania Magazine of History and Biography* 105, no. 1 (January 1981): 35–65, 54–55.

91. Andrew Yeakle, *Village Record* (West Chester, PA), September 6, 1820. For a literary interpretation of the links between the figure of the prostitute and anxieties about market relationships, see Laura J. Rosenthal, *Infamous Commerce: Prostitution in Eighteenth-Century British Literature and Culture* (Ithaca, NY: Cornell University Press, 2006).

92. Bruce Mann, *Republic of Debtors: Bankruptcy in the Age of American Independence* (Cambridge, MA: Harvard University Press, 2002), 260.

93. Bruce Mann describes this transition over the late eighteenth and early nineteenth centuries in *Republic of Debtors*.

94. "An Act Supplemental to the Vendue Act, passed on the Seventeenth Day of March, in the Year of our Lord one thousand seven hundred and eighty-five, giving the owners of property disposed of by Vendue Masters or Auctioneers, summary redress against them for the amount of the sales thereof," Cooper and McCord, *Statutes at Large*, 6:3–4.

95. *City Gazette and Commercial Daily Advertiser* (Charleston, SC), October 1, 1822.

96. *City Gazette and Commercial Daily Advertiser*, October 1, 1822.

97. "Message . . . No. 1," *City Gazette and Commercial Daily Advertiser*, November 30, 1822.

98. *City Gazette*, January 5, 1824; *City Gazette*, February 12, 1824.

99. H. H. Brackenridge, *Modern Chivalry: Containing the Adventures of a Captain and Teague O'Regan, His Servant* (Philadelphia, PA: Johnson and Warner, 1815), 130.

100. Mann, *Republic of Debtors*, 261, explores the connections of debt, honor, and masculinity in the early republic.

101. Corey Goettsch, "'The World Is But One Vast Mock Auction': Fraud and Capitalism in Nineteenth-Century America," in Luskey and Woloson, *Capitalism by Gaslight*, 109–26.

102. "Law Intelligence," *Niles' Weekly Register*, supplement to vol. 16 (1819): 8.

103. Goettsch, "'World Is But One Vast Mock Auction,'" 121–24.

104. "The following letter is from a Committee of the Auctioneers of the city of New York to their Delegation in Congress, protesting against a Bill reported by the Committee of Ways and Means, increasing the duties on sales at Auction," *American Mercury* (Hartford, CT), February 17, 1829.

105. Wendy A. Woloson, *In Hock: Pawning in America from Independence Through the Great Depression* (Chicago: University of Chicago Press, 2009), 33–53; Adam D. Mendelsohn, *The Rag Race: How Jews Sewed Their Way to Success in America and the British Empire* (New York: New York University Press, 2015), 10.

106. Goettsch, "'World Is But One Vast Mock Auction,'" 119–20.

107. Bonds of Vendue Masters, 1799–1817, S218119, folder 1808 February–April and folder 1808 June–December, South Carolina Department of Archives and History, Columbia.

108. Steven Deyle, *Carry Me Back: The Domestic Slave Trade in American Life* (New York: Oxford University Press, 2005); Michael Zakim, *Ready-Made Democracy: A History of Men's Dress in the American Republic, 1760–1860* (Chicago: University of Chicago Press, 2003), chapter 6; Brian P. Luskey, *On the Make: Clerks and the Quest for Capital in Nineteenth-Century America* (New York: New York University Press, 2010).

109. Am 1821 N.Y. Auc. New York (N.Y.) Auctioneers, *Memorial from the Auctioneers, of the city of New-York* ([New York?]: n.p., [1821?]), 17, Library Company of Philadelphia, 110479.o.

110. Adelman, *Revolutionary Networks*.

111. "AN ORDINANCE for imposing a tax of two and a half per centum on Goods, Wares, and Merchandises, exposed to public sale, and for regulating Public Auctions," Cooper and McCord, *Statutes at Large*, 4:498.

CHAPTER 5

1. "Auctions," *National Advocate* (New York, NY), July 3, 1816.

2. "Communication," *New-York Commercial Advertiser*, July 18, 1816.

3. "The Memorial of the Subscribers, Merchants and Traders, Respectfully Sheweth," *New-York Courier*, January 11, 1817. Although the debate over taxing auctions has been studied, none of these treatments have examined the founding role of the Ladies' Retail Auction Room in triggering published memorials that supported auction legislation in New York, for example, before spreading.

4. In the eighteenth century, Benjamin Franklin's fictional "Father Abraham" despaired of convincing a frenzied auction crowd to listen to his frugal homilies. See Chapter 2. In 1770 the shopkeepers of Philadelphia complained about competition from auctioneers. *We, the Shopkeepers of Philadelphia . . .* (Philadelphia, PA: Henry Miller, 1770).

5. For "postcolonial" behavior on the part of the United States, especially in terms of material culture, see Kariann Akemi Yokota, *Unbecoming British: How Revolutionary America Became a Postcolonial Nation* (New York: Oxford University Press, 2011).

6. Joanna Cohen, "'The Right to Purchase Is as Free as the Right to Sell': Defining Consumers as Citizens in the Auction-House Conflicts of the Early Republic," *Journal of the Early Republic* 30, no. 1 (Spring 2010): 25–62.

7. Daniel Walker Howe, *What Hath God Wrought: The Transformation of America, 1815–1848* (New York: Oxford University Press, 2007), 373–95; Stephen Mihm, *A Nation of Counterfeiters: Capitalists, Con Men, and the Making of the United States* (Cambridge, MA: Harvard University Press, 2009), chapter 3.

8. Daniel Carpenter, *Democracy By Petition: Popular Politics in Transformation, 1790–1870* (Cambridge, MA: Harvard University Press, 2021), 247–50.

9. Joanna Cohen, *Luxurious Citizens: The Politics of Consumption in Nineteenth-Century America* (Philadelphia: University of Pennsylvania Press, 2017), 89; Cathy Matson, "Mathew Carey's Learning Experience: Commerce, Manufacturing, and the Panic of 1819," *Early American Studies* 11, no. 3 (Fall 2013): 455–85, 472.

10. Michael O'Malley makes this argument for race in *Face Value: The Entwined Histories of Money and Race in America* (Chicago: University of Chicago Press, 2012), 41–43. See also Susan Yohn's point about a "tension" between "liberal ideals, which espoused the importance of self-making, and essentialist ideas about what constituted a man and a woman." Susan M. Yohn, "Crippled Capitalists: The Inscription of Economic Dependence and the Challenge of Female Entrepreneurship in Nineteenth-Century America," *Feminist Economics* 12, no. 1–2 (January/April 2006): 85–109, 88. David Anthony finds anxiety over masculinity in the new paper money economy in Washington Irving's fiction in "'Gone Distracted': 'Sleepy Hollow,' Gothic Masculinity, and the Panic of 1819," *Early American Literature* 40, no. 1 (2005): 111–44.

11. "A Copy of a Letter from a Gentleman in Albany, to his Friend in the Country," *Albany Sentinel*, February 15, 1799. Alan Taylor succinctly lays out conflicting interpretations of the origins of private property in *Liberty Men and Great Proprietors: The Revolutionary Settlement on the Maine Frontier, 1760–1820* (Chapel Hill: University of North Carolina Press, 1990), 24–29.

12. For discussions of enslaved women and reproductive value, see Daina Ramey Berry, *The Price for Their Pound of Flesh: The Value of the Enslaved, from Womb to Grave, in the Building of a Nation* (Boston: Beacon Press, 2017), introduction and chapter 1; Sasha Turner, *Contested Bodies: Pregnancy, Childrearing, and Slavery in Jamaica* (Philadelphia: University of Pennsylvania Press, 2017), chapters 1 and 2.

13. For a summary of the "separate spheres and hostile worlds" framework, see Viviana A. Zelizer, *The Purchase of Intimacy* (Princeton, NJ: Princeton University Press, 2005), 20–29. Historians of women's history have identified and critiqued the nineteenth-century idea of "separate spheres" and its enduring influence on the conceptualization of white women's social and emotional lives; see Linda Kerber "Separate Spheres, Female Worlds, Woman's Place: The Rhetoric of Women's History," *Journal of American History* 75, no. 1 (June 1988): 9–39. Scholarship on women of color, poor women, and economic life has underscored the prescriptive nature of separate spheres.

14. Joanna Cohen describes the rise of postwar auction establishments in New York and Philadelphia along with the subsequent "auction war" in "'Right to Purchase,'" 36–60.

15. "National Industry and Economy," *American Watchman* (Wilmington, DE), December 4, 1819.

16. "Auctions and Manufactures," *Columbian* (New York), January 30, 1817.

17. Common Sense, "Auctions and Manufactures Communication," *Columbian* (New York, NY), January 30, 1817.

18. Hezekiah Niles, ed., *Niles' Weekly Register*, July 12, 1817 (Baltimore: Franklin Press, 1817), 12:312.

19. J. Cohen, "Right to Purchase," 38–39.

20. Philo Ghost, "Communication, Auctions," *Columbian* (New York, NY), February 18, 1817.

21. For secondary economies, see Wendy A. Woloson, *In Hock: Pawning in America from Independence Through the Great Depression* (Chicago: University of Chicago Press, 2009); Serena R. Zabin, *Dangerous Economies: Status and Commerce in Imperial New York* (Philadelphia:

University of Pennsylvania Press, 2009); and Ann Fabian, *Card Sharps and Bucket Shops: Gambling in Nineteenth-Century America* (New York: Routledge, 1999). For the gender of failure, see Bruce H. Mann, *Republic of Debtors: Bankruptcy in the Age of American Independence* (Cambridge, MA: Harvard University Press, 2002); Scott A. Sandage, *Born Losers: A History of Failure in America* (Cambridge, MA: Harvard University Press, 2006); Brian P. Luskey, *On the Make: Clerks and the Quest for Capital in Nineteenth-Century America* (New York: New York University Press, 2010); and Edward J. Balleisen, *Navigating Failure: Bankruptcy and Commercial Society in Antebellum America* (Chapel Hill: University of North Carolina Press, 2001).

22. "The Memorial of the Subscribers, Merchants and Traders, Respectfully Sheweth," *New-York Courier*, January 11, 1817.

23. *Niles' Weekly Register*, July 5, 1828, 34:297.

24. For the shift in courts' adjudication of responsibility for prices in the early nineteenth century, see Morton J. Horowitz, *Transformation of American Law, 1780–1860* (Cambridge, MA: Harvard University Press, 1976), 180–81.

25. Joshua R. Greenberg, *Bank Notes and Shinplasters: The Rage for Paper Money in the Early Republic* (Philadelphia: University of Pennsylvania Press, 2020), 25–44.

26. For a description of the early nineteenth-century banking system, see Sharon Ann Murphy, *Other People's Money: How Banking Worked in the Early Republic* (Baltimore: Johns Hopkins University Press, 2017).

27. Matson, "Mathew Carey's Learning Experience," 465–73. James Thompson, in *Models of Virtue: Eighteenth-Century Political Economy and the Novel* (Durham, NC: Duke University Press, 1996), offers a way to think about the bifurcation of value achieved by the development of political economy on the one hand and the romance-focused novel on the other.

28. "The Memorial of the Subscribers, Merchants, and Traders, Respectfully Sheweth . . . ," *New-York Courier*, January 11, 1817. The New York Legislature, on February 4, 1817, passed "An ACT to regulate the sales by public auction" that put in place a series of taxes, licensing, and business practice requirements for auctioneers. See *Columbian* (New York, NY), February 14, 1817.

29. *Niles' Weekly Register*, July 12, 1817, 12:312; *The Following Important Letter was Addressed to the Hon. Henry Baldwin, in 1819 . . .* (New York: American Antiquarian Society in Worcester, MA, 1820).

30. "Shopkeepers Prices," *New-England Galaxy and Masonic Magazine*, September 1, 1820.

31. "Merchants, Manufacturers, and Auctioneers," *Poulson's American Daily Advertiser* (Philadelphia, PA), December 4, 1820.

32. "To the Ladies," *New-York Herald*, August 19, 1809.

33. *Boston Evening-Post*, December 25, 1758.

34. *Daily Advertiser; Political, Historical, and Commercial* (New York, NY), May 17, 1786.

35. *Poulson's American Daily Advertiser* (Philadelphia, PA), February 4, 1817.

36. "Ladies Auction," *Baltimore Patriot and Mercantile Advertiser*, June 27, 1817.

37. *National Advocate* (New York, NY), February 28, March 20, May 14, August 21, 1817.

38. See, for example, *The Federal Gazette, and Philadelphia Evening Post*, January 1, 1791; and *New-York Daily Gazette*, April 26, 1791.

39. Amanda Vickery, *Behind Closed Doors: At Home in Georgian England* (New Haven, CT: Yale University Press, 2009), 279–90.

40. John Pintard to Eliza Davidson in New Orleans, April 3, 1816, in *Letters from John Pintard to His Daughter Eliza Noel Pintard Davidson, 1816–1833*, ed. Dorothy C. Barck (New York: New-York Historical Society, 1941), 1:5.

41. *Columbian* (New York, NY), July 19, 1816.

42. Shane White, "'We Dwell in Safety and Pursue Our Honest Callings': Free Blacks in New York City, 1783–1810," *Journal of American History* 75, no. 2 (September 1988): 445–70, 448.

43. On the economic significance of New York auction houses, see Ira Cohen, "The Auction System in the Port of New York, 1817–1837," *Business History Review* 45, no. 4 (Winter 1971): 488–510. For "gentlemen who wear corsets," *New England Galaxy and Masonic Magazine* (Boston, MA), November 26, 1819.

44. *Columbian* (New York, NY), March 1, 1817.

45. *South-Carolina Weekly Gazette*, March 8, 1783.

46. Whitfield J. Bell Jr. et al., "Addenda to Watson's Annals of Philadelphia: Notes by Jacob Mordecai, 1836," *Pennsylvania Magazine of History and Biography* 98, no. 2 (April 1974): 131–70; J. F. Watson, *Annals of Philadelphia and Pennsylvania* (Philadelphia, PA: Elijah Thomas, 1857), 138.

47. *City Gazette, and Daily Advertiser* (Charleston, SC), February 12, 1790.

48. Laura F. Edwards makes this point about married women and textiles, in the context of legal ownership and legal control, in "Textiles: Popular Culture and the Law," *Buffalo Law Review* 64, no. 1 (January 2016): 193–214, 199–200.

49. Quoted in Mary Beth Sievens, *Stray Wives: Marital Conflict in Early National New England* (New York: New York University Press, 2005), 54.

50. Laura F. Edwards, *Only the Clothes on Her Back: Clothing and the Hidden History of Power in the 19th-Century United States* (New York: Oxford University Press, 2022), 14.

51. *New-England Galaxy and Masonic Magazine*, November 12, 1819.

52. *City of Washington Gazette*, November 9, 1818. The charge that women who attended auctions in search of bargains were in fact wasting time and exposing themselves to public tumult continued into the nineteenth century. See, for examples, "Ladies at Auction," *Home Journal*, April 3, 1847, 3; and "Ladies at Auctions," *Godey's Lady's Book and Magazine*, February 1867, 146–47.

53. "Ladies' Auction," *New-England Galaxy and Masonic Magazine*, November 26, 1819.

54. *New-England Galaxy*, November 19, 1819.

55. C. D. Rishel, ed., *The Life and Adventures of David Lewis, the Robber and Counterfeiter: The Terror of the Cumberland Valley* (Newville, PA: C. D. Rishel, 1890), 49–50. Perhaps not coincidentally, Lewis may have been right about Elijah Mix, one of the auctioneers who presided at the 58 Broadway location Lewis attended. Mix was discharged as an insolvent debtor in 1817 and later tried as a forger.

56. Old Kaleidoscope, *City of Washington Gazette*, November 9, 1818. For the classic study of the shifting ideology surrounding women's housework, see Jeanne Boydston, *Home and Work: Housework, Wages, and the Ideology of Labor in the Early Republic* (New York: Oxford University Press, 1990).

57. The theft was allegedly by John Miller, "a negro." *New-York Columbian*, March 26, 1818.

58. Woloson, *In Hock*, 58–59.

59. Balleisen, *Navigating Failure*, 160.

60. Boydston, *Home and Work*, chapter 6.

61. For example, Wendy Gamber, *The Boardinghouse in Nineteenth-Century America* (Baltimore: Johns Hopkins University Press, 2007); Katie M. Hemphill, "Selling Sex and Intimacy in the City: The Changing Business of Prostitution in Nineteenth-Century Baltimore," in *Capitalism by Gaslight: Illuminating the Economy of Nineteenth-Century America*, ed. Brian Luskey and Wendy A. Woloson (Philadelphia: University of Pennsylvania Press, 2015), 168–89.

62. Michael Zakim, *Ready-Made Democracy: A History of Men's Dress in the American Republic, 1760–1860* (Chicago: University of Chicago Press, 2003), 162.

63. Edwards, *Only the Clothes on Her Back*, 1–2, 53–54, 252–53.

64. Jenny Bourne Wahl, *The Bondsman's Burden: An Economic Analysis of the Common Law of Southern Slavery* (New York: Cambridge University Press, 1998), 37. Wahl cites the 1829 Louisiana case of *Pilie v. Lalande* in which just such a promise about skilled female labor proved false.

65. For more information on the relationship between various kinds of gendered skills and price, see Daina Ramey Berry, "'In Pressing Need of Cash': Gender, Skill, and Family Persistence in the Domestic Slave Trade," *Journal of African American History* 92, no. 1 (Winter 2007): 22–36.

66. The term "chattel principle," coined by J. W. C. Pennington, an enslaved man who escaped to freedom, is explored in Walter Johnson, *Soul by Soul: Life Inside the Antebellum Slave Market* (Cambridge, MA: Harvard University Press, 2000), chapter 1; and Walter Johnson, ed., *The Chattel Principle: Internal Slave Trades in the Americas* (New Haven, CT: Yale University Press, 2005).

67. Alexandra J. Finley, *An Intimate Economy: Enslaved Women, Work, and America's Domestic Slave Trade* (Chapel Hill: University of North Carolina Press, 2020), 26, 6.

68. "American Grass Bonnets," *Boston Recorder*, July 28, 1821, 123. For the manufacture of Leghorn bonnets, see Jacob Johnson, *The Book of Trades or Library of Useful Arts, Part I* (Whitehall, PA: Jacob Johnson, 1807), 109–12, which depicts the work as needing little capital and yielding potentially significant earnings.

69. See, for example, *New England Farmer* 2, no. 13 (October 25, 1823): 100.

70. Some exhibitions ended with auctions of prized goods on the spot. See, for example, the reprinted newspaper announcements gathered in the *Ladies' Literary Cabinet, Being a Repository of Miscellaneous Literary Productions . . .* 4, no. 24 (October 20, 1821): 192. Others were sold by lottery tickets.

71. "American Grass Bonnets," 123. The British society imported and distributed the seeds of the Connecticut grass among English farmers; they also established a competition,

with premiums, for those who could produce similar bonnets from native English grasses. See "Hats or Bonnets of British Manufacture in Imitation of Leghorn," *Transactions of the Society, Instituted at London, for the Encouragement of Arts, Manufactures, and Commerce . . .* 42 (January 1824): 74–79.

72. "American Grass Bonnets," 123.

73. *The Ruinous Tendency of Auctioneering, and the Necessity of Restraining It for the Benefit of Trade, Demonstrated in a Letter to the Right Hon. Lord Bathurst, President of the Board of Trade* (New York: Eastburn, Kirk, 1813), 35.

74. Royall Tyler, *The Contrast,* in *The Contrast: Manners, Morals, and Authority in the Early American Republic,* ed. Cylthia A. Kierner (New York: NYU Press, 2007), 35–100, 48.

75. Laura J. Rosenthal, *Infamous Commerce: Prostitution in Eighteenth-Century British Literature and Culture* (Ithaca, NY: Cornell University Press, 2006), 2.

76. Sharon Ann Murphy, *Investing in Life: Insurance in Antebellum America* (Baltimore: Johns Hopkins University Press, 2010), 125–42.

77. Murphy, *Investing in Life,* 132.

78. Patricia Cline Cohen, "Public and Print Cultures of Sex in the Long Nineteenth Century," in *The Oxford Handbook of American Women's and Gender History,* ed. Ellen Hartigan-O'Connor and Lisa G. Materson (New York: Oxford University Press, 2018), 195–215, 199.

79. *Boston Courier,* July 29, 1795.

80. *Alexandria (VA) Advertiser,* March 5, 1798.

81. See Viviana A. Zelizer's discussion of "hostile worlds practices" and their role in reasserting the boundaries of intimate relationships. Zelizer, *Purchase of Intimacy,* 20–29. For an earlier expression of a free woman using newspaper announcements to declare "If I am your Wife, I am not your Slave," see Sarah M. S. Pearsall, "Women, Power, and Families in Early Modern North America," in *The Oxford Handbook of American Women's and Gender History,* ed. Ellen Hartigan-O'Connor and Lisa G. Materson (New York: Oxford University Press, 2018), 147.

82. *New-York Courier,* August 7, 1816.

83. "Tax Upon Beauty—and the Beauty of Ugliness," *Washington City Weekly Gazette,* December 23, 1815.

84. The "gentlemen" versions appeared in *Springer's Weekly Oracle* (New London, CT), December 9, 1797; *Impartial Herald* (Suffield, CT), January 24, 1798; *Companion and Commercial Centinel* (Newport, RI), May 23, 1798; *Spirit of the Press,* February 1, 1812; *Lady's Miscellany, or Weekly Visitor* 15, no. 5 (May 23, 1812): 71–72; the "ladies" version in *Rural Visiter, and Saratoga Advertiser* (Ballston Spa, NY), June 23, 1812.

85. *Niles' Weekly Register,* 1821–22, 21:146.

86. Stephanie E. Jones-Rogers, *They Were Her Property: White Women as Slave Owners in the American South* (New Haven, CT: Yale University Press, 2019), 113.

87. Later in the nineteenth century, Elizabeth Cady Stanton would link a woman's ownership of her body with John Locke's ideas about self-ownership. In championing "voluntary motherhood," she argued that even a married woman should determine whether and when to have children, which, given the state of birth control at the time, meant that a woman had a right to decide when her husband could have sex with her. This idea was counter to

the understanding of Anglo-American law, in which a husband had unlimited "access" to his wife's body. See Nancy Folbre, *Greed, Lust, and Gender: A History of Economic Ideas* (New York: Oxford University Press, 2009), 215–16.

88. Lightner v. Martin, 2 McC. 214 (S.C. 1822), cited in Wahl, *Bondsman's Burden*, 35.

89. Another example of enslaved women as specifically gendered products is the "fancy maid" sales of the nineteenth century. See Edward E. Baptist, "'Cuffy,' 'Fancy Maids,' and 'One-Eyed Men': Rape, Commodification, and the Domestic Slave Trade in the United States," *American Historical Review* 106, no. 5 (December 2001): 1619–50.

90. Wahl, *Bondsman's Burden*, 38. The case of Hannah, a forty-one-year-old sold as a twenty-nine-year-old, entered the Tennessee courts in 1808.

91. Philip Morgan, "Slave Sales in Colonial Charleston," *English Historical Review* 113, no. 435 (September 1998): 905–27, 918. Jennifer Morgan has an extended discussion of the iconography and meanings of high-breasted and low-breasted women in the creation of the Atlantic slave system in Jennifer Morgan, *Laboring Women: Reproduction and Gender in New World Slavery* (Philadelphia: University of Pennsylvania Press, 2004), chapter 1.

92. Berry, *Price for the Pound of Flesh*, 72–85.

93. Morgan, *Laboring Women*, 80–92. On "breeder" language, see Berry, *Price for Their Pound of Flesh*, 11–26.

94. Lawrence v. Speed, 2 Bibb 401, 404 (KY, 1811), quoted in Wahl, *Bondsman's Burden*, 45.

95. Lawrence, &c. v. Speed, &c. 5 Bibb 404 (KY, 1811), Caselaw Access Project, last modified September 24, 2019, https://cite.case.law/ky-bibb/5/401/.

96. Finley, *Intimate Economy*, 44.

97. Between Thomas Hinde, plaintiff, and Edmund Pendleton and Peter Lyons, administrators of John Robinson, with his testament Annexed, defendants. 1788 Va. Ch Dec. 354, March 1, 1799, Caselaw Access Project, last modified, September 24, 2019, 354, 355.

98. Hinde v. Pendleton, Wythe 354, March 1791, in Helen Tunnicliff Catterall, ed., *Judicial Cases Concerning American Slavery and the Negro*, vol. 1, *Cases from the Courts of England, Virginia, West Virginia, and Kentucky* (Washington, DC: Carnegie Institution of Washington, 1926), 96.

99. Hinde, Caselaw Access Project, 355. See Cynthia Lynn Lyerly, *Methodism and the Southern Mind, 1770–1810* (New York: Oxford University Press, 1998), 3–4.

100. Hinde, Caselaw Access Project, 357. Ultimately, a body of commissioners determined the value of the woman and her children at the time of sale. *Decisions of Cases in Virginia by the High Court of Chancery . . .* (Richmond: J. W. Randolph, 1852), 357.

101. Baptist, "'Cuffy,' 'Fancy Maids,' and 'One-Eyed Men,'" 1641–49.

102. Baptist, "'Cuffy,' 'Fancy Maids,' and 'One-Eyed Men,'" 1648.

103. Finley, *Intimate Economy*, 22–23.

104. Luskey, *On the Make*, chapter 3 explores the sexualized satire of clerks; for milliners, see, for example, the satirical print *A Morning Ramble, or: The Milliner's Shop* (London: Carington Bowles, 1782), the British Museum, 1935,0522.1.31.

105. Luskey, *On the Make*, 94–97.

106. Zelizer, *Purchase of Intimacy*, 23.

107. Luskey, *On the Make*, 100. See also Harry E. Resseguie, "Alexander Turney Stewart and the Development of the Department Store, 1823–1876," *Business History Review* 39, no. 3 (Autumn 1965): 301–22, 309–10.

108. *American Telegraph*, August 20, 1817.

109. William Van Hook's Deposition, "Contract for stone at the Rip Raps and Old Point Comfort, Communicated to the House of Representatives, May 7, 1822," *American State Papers* 017, *Military Affairs*, 17th Congress, 1st Session, 2:449. Mix had been indicted for forgery, but the prosecution ceased when he enlisted in the military during the War of 1812.

110. *New-York Evening Post*, August 27, 1818.

111. In truth, there had been signs of trouble from the beginning. If his enterprise was a success, P. B. Van Beuren should have reported and paid a 1½ percent duty to the state on most of the goods he had for sale. He, along with a number of other New York auctioneers, paid none in 1816. This does not necessarily mean that the business was a failure. As was noted in the newspapers, the reported amounts were what had been paid, "not the sums due from the actual sales." *Columbian* (New York, NY), February 21, 1817. See Jones-Rogers, *They Were Her Property*, 140–42, for additional ladies' auctions in the South later in the nineteenth century.

112. Richard Peters, ed., *The Public Statutes at Large of the United States of America* (Boston: Charles S. Little and James Brown, 1845), 3:44–47, 159–61, 401–3, Law Library of Congress Digitized Collection. States continued to tax auction sales, as they had for decades, and use the revenue for public projects. See, for example, *The Laws of the State of New York, passed at the thirty-ninth session of the legislature begun and held at the city of Albany, the thirtieth day of January, 1816* (Albany: J. Buel, 1816), 326–32.

113. *Niles' Weekly Register*, August 25, 1828 (Baltimore: Franklin Press, 1828), 34:419. The process of "unbecoming British" and the role of material culture in that process is discussed in Yokota's *Unbecoming British*.

114. Matson, "Mathew Carey's Learning Experience," 472–73.

115. Daniel Carpenter, *Democracy by Petition: Popular Politics in Transformation, 1790–1870* (Cambridge, MA: Harvard University Press, 2021), 248.

116. "The Anti-Auction Party in New-York," *New-Bedford (MA) Mercury*, November 21, 1828; "To the Editor of the National Journal," *Daily National Journal*, January 1, 1829.

117. "Washington Correspondence," *Richmond Enquirer*, January 3, 1829.

118. Carpenter, *Democracy by Petition*, 248.

119. "Interesting to Ladies and Subscribers to Newspapers," *Literary Register; A Weekly Paper* 2, no. 12 (March 7, 1829): 90.

CHAPTER 6

1. Harriet Jacobs, *Incidents in the Life of a Slave Girl*, in *The Classic Slave Narratives*, ed. Henry Lewis Gates (New York: Penguin Books, 1987), 347. "Aunt Martha" was in reality Molly Horniblow. See Janet Yellin, ed., *Incidents in the Life of a Slave Girl, Written by Herself*, 3rd ed. (Cambridge, MA: Harvard University Press, 1987), xvii.

2. Janet Neary, *Fugitive Testimony: On the Visual Logic of Slave Narratives* (New York: Fordham University Press, 2016), 157. Saidiya Hartman analyzed the spectacle of the slave market in her field-defining *Scenes of Subjection: Terror, Slavery, and Self-Making in Nineteenth-Century America* (New York: Oxford University Press, 1997).

3. Jacobs, *Incidents in the Life of a Slave Girl*, 347.

4. Historians have greatly expanded our understanding of the relationship between the history of slavery and the development of capitalism as the dominant political and economic system in the United States in the nineteenth century. See Edward Baptist, *The Half Has Never Been Told: Slavery and the Making of American Capitalism* (New York: Basic Books, 2014); Sven Beckert, *Empire of Cotton: A Global History* (New York: Vintage Books, 2014); Sven Beckert and Seth Rockman, eds., *Slavery's Capitalism: A New History of American Economic Development* (Philadelphia: University of Pennsylvania Press, 2016); Daina Ramey Berry, *The Price for Their Pound of Flesh: The Value of the Enslaved, from Womb to Grave, in the Building of a Nation* (Boston: Beacon Press, 2017); Justene Hill Edwards, *Unfree Markets: The Slaves' Economy and the Rise of Capitalism in South Carolina* (New York: Columbia University Press, 2021); Walter Johnson, *River of Dark Dreams: Slavery and Empire in the Cotton Kingdom* (Cambridge, MA: Harvard University Press), 2–13; Sharon Ann Murphy, *Investing in Life: Insurance in Antebellum America* (Baltimore: Johns Hopkins University Press, 2010); Seth Rockman, *Scraping By: Wage Labor, Slavery, and Survival in Early Baltimore* (Baltimore: Johns Hopkins University Press, 2009); and Caitlin Rosenthal, *Accounting for Slavery: Masters and Management* (Cambridge, MA: Harvard University Press, 2018).

5. Jean-Christophe Agnew, *Worlds Apart: The Market and the Theater in Anglo-American Thought, 1550–1750* (New York: Cambridge University Press, 1986).

6. For an extensive analysis of white women as purchasers and owners of enslaved people, including their role in attending auctions, see Stephanie E. Jones-Rogers, *They Were Her Property: White Women as Slave Owners in the American South* (New Haven, CT: Yale University Press, 2019). For scholarship on masculine command and its failures in the nineteenth-century American economy, see Scott Sandage, *Born Losers: A History of Failure in America* (Cambridge, MA: Harvard University Press, 2006); and Brian Luskey, *On the Make: Clerks and the Quest for Capital in Nineteenth-Century America* (New York: New York University Press, 2010).

7. See, for example, *City Gazette and Commercial Daily Advertiser* (Charleston, SC), January 17, 1820.

8. Joanna Cohen, *Luxurious Citizens: The Politics of Consumption in Nineteenth-Century America* (Philadelphia: University of Pennsylvania Press, 2017), 164, 154–55.

9. Robert J. Gamble, "The Promiscuous Economy: Cultural and Commercial Geographies of Secondhand in the Antebellum City," in *Capitalism by Gaslight: Illuminating the Economy of Nineteenth-Century America*, ed. Brian P. Luskey and Wendy A. Woloson (Philadelphia: University of Pennsylvania Press, 2015), 31–52, 33.

10. Tamara Plakins Thornton finds a "capitalist aesthetics" in early nineteenth-century visual and textual representations of the London and Liverpool docks in "Capitalist Aesthetics: Americans Look at the London and Liverpool Docks," in *Capitalism Takes Command:*

The Social Transformation of Nineteenth-Century America, ed. Michael Zakim and Gary J. Kornblith (Chicago: University of Chicago Press, 2012), 169–98.

11. Luskey, *On The Make*, chapter 3.

12. Teresa A. Goddu, *Selling Antislavery: Abolition and Mass Media in Antebellum America* (Philadelphia: University of Pennsylvania Press, 2020), 31; Neary, *Fugitive Testimony*, 156.

13. Daina Ramey Berry describes this print culture associated with the sale of enslaved people as "propaganda," highlighting its purpose and its carefully selected words, in *Price for Their Pound of Flesh*, 136–37.

14. Ellen Gruber Garvey, "Nineteenth-Century Abolitionists and the Databases They Created," *Legacy* 27, no. 2 (2010): 357–66, 359.

15. *American Slavery as It Is: Testimony of a Thousand Witnesses* (New York: American Anti-Slavery Society, 1839), 83.

16. *American Slavery as It Is*, 167.

17. Lori Merish explores this dynamic in *Sentimental Materialism: Gender, Commodity Culture, and Nineteenth-Century American Literature* (Durham, NC: Duke University Press, 2000).

18. Joanna Cohen, "'The Right to Purchase Is as Free as the Right to Sell': Defining Consumers as Citizens in the Auction-House Conflicts of the Early Republic," *Journal of the Early Republic* 30, no. 1 (Spring 2010): 25–62.

19. Joanna Cohen uses the language of "economies of capital" and "economies of meaning" in "Reckoning with the Riots: Property, Belongings, and the Challenge to Value in Civil War America," *Journal of American History* 109, no. 1 (June 2022): 68–98, 71.

20. Nora Doyle, *Maternal Bodies: Redefining Motherhood in Early America* (Chapel Hill: University of North Carolina Press, 2018), 185–86.

21. Erin Austin Dwyer, *Mastering Emotions: Feelings, Power, and Slavery in the United States* (Philadelphia: University of Pennsylvania Press, 2021), 160.

22. Dwyer, introduction to *Mastering Emotions*.

23. Henry Watson, *Narrative of Henry Watson, a Fugitive Slave* (Boston: Bela Marsh, 1849), 8. The image had appeared two decades earlier in George Bourne's *Picture of Slavery in the United States of America*. See Maurie McInnis, *Slaves Waiting for Sale: Abolitionist Art and the American Slave Trade* (Chicago: University of Chicago Press, 2011), 45–46. In fact, as Watson explains in the text, unlike the depiction in the image, he was at the time a boy, who burst into tears during his sale.

24. Christine Leigh Heyrman, *Southern Cross: The Beginnings of the Bible Belt* (Chapel Hill: University of North Carolina Press, 1998), 236, and chapter 5 for a discussion of mastery and the clergy.

25. Watson, *Narrative*, 29.

26. Jon Butler, *Awash in a Sea of Faith: Christianizing the American People* (Cambridge, MA: Harvard University Press, 1992), chapter 9.

27. "Slaveholding Sanctity—Horrible," *Colored American II*, no. 5, April 3, 1841. Tappan himself held an auction of antislavery books on May 12, 1841, to raise money for the American Antislavery Society, as advertised in the *Colored American II*, no. 9, May 1, 1841.

28. "Our Vice President," *Colored American I*, no. 20, July 18, 1840. McInnis explores the use of auction-block imagery among abolitionists in *Slaves Waiting for Sale*, 23–24. Amy Dru Stanley and Kathleen Brown both discuss abolitionists' focus on how enslaved people's bodies—suffering and packaged for sale—mobilized empathy and also supported their insistence on the right of self-proprietorship and self-sovereignty. Amy Dru Stanley, *From Bondage to Contract: Wage Labor, Marriage, and the Market in the Age of Slave Emancipation* (New York: Cambridge University Press, 1998), 22–23; Kathleen M. Brown, *Undoing Slavery: Bodies, Race, and Rights in the Age of Abolition* (Philadelphia: University of Pennsylvania Press, 2023).

29. McInnis, *Slaves Waiting for Sale*, chapter 2.

30. Frederick Douglass, "The Internal Slave Trade," printed in *My Bondage and My Freedom*, introduction and notes by David W. Blight (1855; New Haven, CT: Yale University Press, 2014), 374–78, 377. Douglass reprinted this section of his famous speech "What to the Slave Is the Fourth of July?" as an appendix to his biography.

31. Jones-Rogers discusses visual depictions of slave auctions in *They Were Her Property*, 138–40.

32. On slave auctions as ritualized performances of race and class, see Jason Stupp, "Slavery and the Theater of History: Ritual Performance on the Auction Block," *Theater Journal* 63, no.1 (March 2011): 61–84, 66–67.

33. "A Slave Auction" *Christian Reflector*, October 3, 1844, 160.

34. "A Slave Auction," 160.

35. Matthew Fox-Amato demonstrates that "slavery produced a key element of modern political culture" in the development of photographic practices in the mid-nineteenth century. See *Exposing Slavery: Photography, Human Bondage, and the Birth of Modern Visual Politics in America* (New York: Oxford University Press, 2019), 13.

36. R. V. Tiffey in King Geo to R. H. Dickinson & Bro., February 7, 2847, box 1, folder 2, Correspondence of Auctioneers, 1806–1868, Slavery in the US Collection, American Antiquarian Society.

37. Jennifer Morgan discusses enslaved women as "economic thinkers" in *Reckoning with Slavery: Gender, Kinship, and Capitalism in the Early Black Atlantic* (Durham, NC: Duke University Press, 2021), 3.

38. R. V. Tiffey in King Geo to R. H. Dickinson & Bro., February 7, 1847.

39. Quoted in Hartman, *Scenes of Subjection*, 37. See her broader discussion of "innocent amusements" in chapter 1.

40. Thomas David Russell, "Sale Day in Antebellum South Carolina: Slavery, Law, Economy and Court-Supervised Sales" (PhD diss., Stanford University, 1993), 120.

41. Haddix's Heirs vs. Haddix's Adm'rs, &c. 15 Ky. (Litt.) 201, May 28, 1824, Caselaw Access Project https://cite.case.law/ky/15/201/. The appellate decision is also printed in William Littell, *Reports of Cases at Common Law and in Chancery Decided by the Court of Appeals of the Commonwealth of Kentucky*, 2nd ed., vol. 5 (Cincinnati, OH: Henry W. Derby, 1848), 150–53.

42. Littell, *Reports of Cases at Common Law*, 152.

43. Goddu, *Selling Antislavery*, 91 and chapter 4.

44. Goddu, *Selling Antislavery*, 93.

45. Carol Faulkner, "The Root of the Evil: Free Produce and Radical Antislavery, 1820–1860," *Journal of the Early Republic* 27, no. 3 (Fall 2007): 377–405, 387.

46. Quoted in Lawrence B. Glickman, "'Buy for the Sake of the Slave': Abolitionism and the Origins of American Consumer Activism," *American Quarterly* 56, no. 4 (December 2004): 889–912, 892.

47. Glickman, "Buy for the Sake of the Slave," 894–99.

48. Cohen, *Luxurious Citizens*, 150.

49. Bronwen Everill, *Not Made by Slaves: Ethical Capitalism in the Age of Abolition* (Cambridge, MA: Harvard University Press, 2020), 52.

50. Martha S. Jones, *Vanguard: How Black Women Broke Barriers, Won the Vote, and Insisted on Equality for All* (New York: Basic Books, 2020), 54.

51. One famous case was that of the extended Fossett family, whose members were part of the group of enslaved people sold off upon the death of Thomas Jefferson to cover his debts. See Joshua D. Rothman, *Notorious in the Neighborhood: Sex and Families Across the Color Line in Virginia, 1787–1861* (Chapel Hill: University of North Carolina Press, 2003), 53.

52. Margaret M. R. Kellow, "Conflicting Imperatives: Black and White American Abolitionists Debate Slave Redemption," in *Buying Freedom: The Ethics and Economics of Slave Redemption*, ed. Kwame Anthony Appiah and Martin Bunzi (Princeton, NJ: Princeton University Press, 2007), 200–12.

53. Kellow, "Conflicting Imperatives," 205.

54. "Benevolence of an African," *African Repository and Colonial Journal*, January 1826, 352.

55. "Colored People of Cincinnati," *Colored American I*, no. 33, October 17, 1840.

56. "Colored People of Cincinnati."

57. "Free Colored People at the North," *Colored American II*, no. 35, November 13, 1841, 137.

58. "Free Colored People at the North," 137.

59. Bryan Edwards, *The History of the British Colonies in the West Indies*, vol. 2 (Philadelphia, PA: James Humphreys, 1806), 367–68.

60. Edwards, *History of the British Colonies*, 367.

61. Edwards, *History of the British Colonies*, 367.

62. "Miscellany: A Christian Land," reprinted in *New-England Galaxy* 3, no. 138 (June 2, 1820): 136.

63. Nehemiah Adams, *A South-Side View of Slavery, or Three Months in the South in 1854* (Boston: T. R. Marvin and B. B. Mussey, 1854), 70.

64. Alexandra J. Finley explores the tropes of the auction scene used by abolitionists in the sale of so-called Fancies in *An Intimate Economy: Enslaved Women, Work, and America's Domestic Slave Trade* (Chapel Hill: University of North Carolina Press, 2020), 25–26.

65. The quotation is from Steven Deyle, *Carry Me Back: The Domestic Slave Trade in American Life* (New York: Oxford University Press, 2006), 142. Chapter 5 of Deyle's book details the everyday texture of slave sales. Joshua D. Rothman discusses the business of

domestic slave traders across the South in *The Ledger and the Chain: How Domestic Slave Traders Shaped America* (New York: Basic Books, 2021).

66. Jonathan Levy discusses the intersection of new ideas about risk, financial instruments, and the market as an abstraction in *Freaks of Fortune: The Emerging World of Capitalism and Risk in America* (Cambridge, MA: Harvard University Press, 2012), chapter 1. He takes for granted that "the market economy was, after all, a field of competition between men, a test of skill" (16).

67. "An Act Directing the Sale of Certain Lands Granted for the Use of an Academy or Public School, in Beavertown," *The Statutes at Large of Pennsylvania from 1806 to 1809* (Harrisburg, PA: Wm. Stanley Ray, 1915), 214.

68. Wayne Shaw, "The Plymouth Pulpit: Henry Ward Beecher's Slave Auction Block," *American Transcendental Quarterly* 14, no. 4 (December 2000): 335–43; William C. Beecher, Samuel Scoville, and Mrs. Henry Ward Beecher, *A Biography of Rev. Henry Ward Beecher* (New York: Charles L. Webster, 1888), chapter 15.

69. Shaw, "Plymouth Pulpit," 340.

70. Stupp, "Slavery and the Theater," 72–80.

71. Stephanie E. Yuhl, "Hidden in Plain Sight: Centering the Domestic Slave Trade in American Public History," *Journal of Southern History* 79, no. 3 (August 2013): 593–624, 595.

72. Rockman, *Scraping By*, 235; Walter Johnson, "Introduction: The Future Store," in *The Chattel Principle: Internal Slave Trades in the Americas*, ed. Walter Johnson (New Haven, CT: Yale University Press, 2005), 1–31.

73. For vivid explorations of enslaved people's attempts to avoid sale, see Calvin Schermerhorn, *Money over Mastery, Family over Freedom: Slavery in the Antebellum Upper South* (Baltimore: Johns Hopkins University Press, 2011); and Walter Johnson, *Soul by Soul: Life Inside the Antebellum Slave Market* (Cambridge, MA: Harvard University Press, 1999). On "soul value," see Berry, *Price for Their Pound of Flesh*, chapter 3.

74. "Narrative of Stephen Dickenson, Jr.," *Colored American I*, no. 40, December 5, 1840.

75. Adams, *South-Side View*, 73.

76. Sean Kelly, "Scrambling for Slaves: Captive Sales in Colonial South Carolina," *Slavery and Abolition* 34, no. 1 (2013): 1–21, 12.

77. Yuhl, "Hidden in Plain Sight," 597. This ordinance was one in a sequence of laws that sought to centralize and contain the public and private sales of human property in mid-nineteenth-century Charleston. "An Ordinance to reorganize the Work House department, to establish a Mart for the public sale of slaves, and for other purposes," ratified on November 20, 1839, in City Council of Charleston, *Ordinances of the City of Charleston, from the 24th May, 1837, to the 18th March, 1840. Together with such of the Acts and Parts of the Acts of the Legislature of South Carolina as Relate to Charleston, from December 1837, to December 1839—Inclusive* (Charleston, SC: B. R. Getsinger, 1840), 190–208. For additional details and quotations from the ordinance, see Edmund Drago and Ralph Melnick, "The Old Slave Mart Museum, Charleston, South Carolina: Rediscovering the Past," *Civil War History* 27, no. 2 (June 1981): 138–54. For a narrative description of this history, see Nic Butler, "Street Auctions and Slave Marts in Antebellum Charleston," Charleston County Public Library,

accessed September 9, 2021, https://www.ccpl.org/charleston-time-machine/street-auctions -and-slave-marts-antebellum-charleston#_edn11.

78. Judiciary Committee, "Report on the Petition of the City Council of Charleston for a Law Directing all Slave auctions in the City be held at the proposed slave mart, including sales by the sheriff and master in equity." Series S165005, item 02550, (c.1839), South Carolina Department of Archives and History, Columbia.

79. Judiciary Committee, "Report on the Petition."

80. Thomas D. Russell, "South Carolina's Largest Slave Auctioneering Firm—Symposium on the Law of Slavery: Criminal and Civil Law of Slavery," *Chicago-Kent Law Review* 68, no. 3 (1993): 1241–82, 1241.

81. Russell, "South Carolina's Largest Slave Auctioneering Firm," 1278.

82. See Tiya Miles, introduction to Harriet Jacobs, *Incidents in the Life of a Slave Girl, Written by Herself* (New York: Modern Library, 2021), ix.

83. Yellin, *Incidents in the Life of a Slave Girl*, xx.

84. John S. Jacobs, "A True Tale of Slavery," in Yellin, *Incidents in the Life of a Slave Girl*, 207–28, 209.

85. Jacobs, "True Tale of Slavery," 209.

CONCLUSION

1. For a thoughtful approach to centering human relationships and social reproduction in analyzing the economy, rather than exchange, see Susana Narotzky and Niko Besnier, "Crisis, Value, and Hope: Rethinking the Economy: An Introduction to Supplement 9," *Current Anthropology* 55, no. S9 (August 2014): S4–S16.

2. Oneida Seaton, *It Is All for the Best, or, Clarke the Baker* (Boston: William D. Ticknor, 1845), 26.

3. Andrew H. Browning, "The Moralization of Poverty in the Panic of 1819," *Journal of the Early Republic* 40, no. 4 (Winter 2020): 715–20; Scott Sandage, *Born Losers: A History of Failure in America* (Cambridge, MA: Harvard University Press, 2006).

4. For a timeline, see the "Slave Auction Block" timeline, with documents, at the City of Fredericksburg website, accessed September 12, 2021, https://www.fredericksburgva.gov /1287/Slave-Auction-Block.

5. D. Brad Hatch, Kerri S. Barile, Danae Peckler, and Kerry González, "Archaeological Testing of the George Street Tunnel and Intersection of William and Charles Street, City of Fredericksburg, Virginia," VDOT Project No. EN17-111-302, C501, P101 (January 2019, filed December 27, 2019, Fredericksburg Circuit Court), 53, accessed September 12, 2021, https://www.fredericksburgva.gov/DocumentCenter/View/16637/Ex-12-2019-01-Dovetail -Archaeology-excerpt-filed-PDF. See also Michael Rosenwald, "After a Long Debate, Fredericksburg, Va., Finally Removes a Slave Auction Block from Downtown," *Washington Post*, June 6, 2020, accessed September 12, 2021, https://www.washingtonpost.com/history/2020 /06/06/slave-auction-block-fredericksburg/.

6. The results of some of the community responses in surveys and focus groups conducted by the International Coalition of Sites of Conscience capture the perspectives on how to acknowledge that history, particularly in light of the importance of historic memory to the town. See Dina Bailey and Braden Paynter, "City of Fredericksburg: Phase One Report" (New York: International Sites of Conscience, July 31, 2018), accessed September 12, 2021, https://www.fredericksburgva.gov/DocumentCenter/View/11198/City-of-Fredericksburg---Phase-One-Report---Final?bidId=.

7. Anne C. Bailey and Dannielle Bowman, "For hundreds of years, enslaved people were bought and sold in America. Today most of the sites of this trade are forgotten," *New York Times Magazine*, accessed September 16, 2021, https://www.nytimes.com/interactive/2020/02/12/magazine/1619-project-slave-auction-sites.html.

ACKNOWLEDGMENTS

I am very grateful to the many people and institutions who shared ideas, sources, and support as I worked on this book. The research took me across the country and over a decade as the fascinating topic of auctions opened up a wider world of questions about value and values.

I first want to thank the many archivists and librarians at the American Antiquarian Society, Baltimore City Archives, Charleston County Public Library, Connecticut State Library, David Library of the America Revolution, Gilder Lehrman Institute for American History, Historical Society of Pennsylvania, Library Company of Philadelphia, New York Historical Society, New York State Archives, Philadelphia City Archives, and the South Carolina Department of Archives and History who all helped with sources, leads, and valuable suggestions.

Financial support to conduct research and to offer precious time to think and write came from a faculty fellowship from the National Endowment for the Humanities as well as grants from the University of California Davis Humanities Institute, Academic Senate Research Committee, and University of California Davis Institute of Governmental Affairs.

Several scholars have graciously given their time over and over with sparkling conversation and feedback on multiple drafts and earlier versions of the work. My deepest thanks for this heavy lifting to Brian Luskey, Lisa Materson, and Lorena Oropeza as well as to Rebecca Brannon, Toby Ditz, Catherine Kelly, and Cathy Matson. I feel lucky to know so many brilliant and humane historians who also have a keen eye for an ill-advised comma.

The people who invited me onto panels, asked questions, made suggestions, and in every way helped me clarify my ideas and make new intellectual connections carried the project forward. Colleagues at conferences and meetings—of the Omohundro Institute for Early American History and Culture, the Society for Historians of the Early Republic, the Organization of American Historians, the Western Association of Women Historians, the Business History

Conference, and especially the Program in Early American Economy and Society—offered a wealth of ideas about markets in my attempts to tell a story that crossed centuries. I have been fortunate to enjoy many conversations about value and capitalism with incredibly generous scholars, only some of whom I can include by name: Linzy Brekke-Aloise, Joanna Cohen, Sara Damiano, Nina Dayton, Tracey Deutsch, Alejandra Dubcovsky, Laura Edwards, Alexandra Finley, Sheryllynne Haggerty, David Hancock, Emma Hart, April Haynes, Stephanie Jones-Rogers, Susan Juster, Carl Robert Keyes, Jen Manion, Michelle McDonald, Stephen Mihm, Mary Beth Norton, Sarah Pearsall, Seth Rockman, Carole Shammas, Edie Sparks, Kathryn Tomasek, Mark Valeri, Georg Vogeler, Wendy Woloson, Judy Tzu-Chun Wu, and Serena Zabin.

My colleagues at the University of California, Davis, have provided advice and encouragement in countless ways. It is a pleasure to thank them publicly, especially Beverly Bossler, Joan Cadden, Corrie Decker, Jean-Pierre Delplanque, Edward Dickenson, Stacy Fahrenthold, Ari Kelman, Kyu Hyun Kim, Susette Min, A. Katie Harris, James Housefield, Rachel Jean-Baptiste, Susan Mann, Sudipta Sen, Jocelyn Sharlet, Marian Schlotterbeck, John Smolenski, Alan Taylor, Cecilia Tsu, and Clarence Walker. UC Davis graduate students helped chase down quotations and images and taught me plenty along the way. Thanks especially to Jessica Blake, Emma Chapman, Sean Gallagher, Tom O'Donnell, and Kelly Sharp. Even more research support came across the country from Daniel Morales and Emilie Connolly. Elena Abbott provided a vital writing intervention.

Portions of this book appeared in earlier form in Ellen Hartigan-O'Connor, "Gender's Value in the History of Capitalism," *Journal of the Early Republic* 36, no. 4 (Winter 2016): 613–35; "'Auctioneer of Offices': Patronage, Value, and Trust in the Early Republic Marketplace," *Journal of the Early Republic* 33, no. 3 (Fall 2013): 463–88; and "Public Sales and Public Values in Eighteenth-Century North America," *Early American Studies* 13, no. 4 (Fall 2015): 749–73. I thank the University of Pennsylvania Press for permission to reprint the revised work.

The University of Pennsylvania Press has, as always, been the scholarly ideal for an author. Bob Lockhart is a delight to work with, offering great insights and incredible patience. Reviewers for the press, including Simon Middleton, Kathleen Brown, and an anonymous reviewer, gave generously of their expertise to improve the manuscript. Book production was handled skillfully by Noreen O'Connor-Abel and copyediting by Karen Carroll; I am grateful for their talents.

My family and friends have patiently awaited the completion of this book and cheered its author all along the way. For walks, meals, and texts I thank Anne Conley, Elana Gordis, Maria Elena Kim, Eve Korshak, Bhrett Lash, Amy

Locke, Brian Mickey, Julie Goldsmith Reiser, Nathalie van Linder, and Meredith Woocher. My love and deep gratitude go to Margaret, John, and Meg O'Connor as well as to Lorraine Hartigan and all my extended family, who helped in ways large and small through both challenging and exciting times. I owe the most to those who lived with the book every day—Dennis, Eamon, Finn, and Desmond. Their value to me is beyond measure.